MW00784941

FRANK MCGUIRE

THE LIFE AND TIMES OF A BASKETBALL LEGEND

FRANK McGUIRE

THE LIFE AND TIMES OF A
BASKETBALL LEGEND

By

Don Barton

&

Bob Fulton

With a Foreword by Coach Dean Smith

Summerhouse Press
Columbia, South Carolina

FIRST EDITION

ISBN 1-887714-04-9 (Hardcover)
ISBN 1-887714-05-7 (Paperback)

Photo Credits
McGuire Family: *Photo #1, #2, #3, #5, #6, #7, #8, #9, #10, #11, #12, #14, #15, #16, #22 #55, #56, #57, #58, #59, #60, #61.*
Sherwood Studio: *Photo #32.*
UPI/Bettman Newsphotos: *Photo #4, #19, #20.*
University of South Carolina Department of Athletics: *Photo #23, #24, #25, #26, #27, #28, #29, #33, #34, #35, #36, #37, #38, #39, #40, #41, #43, #45, #46, #48, #49, #50, #51, #52 #62, cover photos*
University of North Carolina Communications Center: *Photo # 17, #18.*

CONTENTS

FOREWORD

It is my hope that the reader of this book will discover the one truly unique individual who was Frank J. McGuire. Not only will reading about him be interesting and entertaining, but also, one can learn from the many experiences that were his.

Coach McGuire has one of the greatest coaching records, not only in basketball, but in any sport. He was highly successful in his chosen vocation, because of his natural leadership qualities, his charming charisma, and his ability to be comfortable with all kinds of people be they "kings" or "commoners." However, in my opinion, those same qualities would have enabled him to be equally successful in any vocation he would have chosen.

I did not really know Coach McGuire until the 1957 NCAA Coaches' Convention in Kansas City, even though the Kansas University Basketball team, of which I was a member, played Coach McGuire's St. John's University basketball team in the 1952 NCAA Championship game. As was their custom, Coach McGuire, Coach Ben Carnevale of Navy, Coach Bob Spear of the Air Force Academy, and Coach Hoyt Brawner of Denver University roomed together in a two bedroom suite during the convention...undoubtedly, the suite was Frank's idea! As a lieutenant in the Air Force and assistant to Bob Spear at the Air Force Academy, I also stayed in the suite.

Ben had been close to Frank when the two of them were in the Navy's V-5 program at Chapel Hill during World War II. After the war, Ben became the basketball coach at the University of North Carolina in Chapel Hill. He later became the basketball coach at the Naval Academy where Bob Spear had served as his assistant.

I appreciated staying with these coaches who had been friends a long time even though my alma mater, Kansas, was playing in the Final Four with Coach McGuire's North Carolina team. The Sunday morning after North Carolina's championship victory over Kansas, the five of us were having breakfast. I was still upset that Kansas had lost. In spite of that, Coach McGuire asked me if I would be interested in being his assistant coach when his great assistant, Buck Freeman, retired later in 1957 or 1958. Apparently, Bob, Ben and Hoyt had been highly recommending me to Frank. I did express an interest in the position, with urging from Bob. However, I did not hear from Coach McGuire until the five of us were together again at the NCAA Convention of 1958 in Louisville. At that time, he told me that Buck was retiring and that he would like me to be his assistant. I accepted and began my life with Frank McGuire!

From August of 1958 through August of 1961, we spent more hours together than we did with our families! We became not only co-workers, but also, close friends. We were a two man staff until Ken Rosemond joined us in the third year as an assistant. During those years together, Frank told me stories of his New York life, some of which are in this book. He talked about Bill O'Brien, New York Police Commissioner; of Bob Fitzsimmons, the legal council; of his best friend, Jack LaRocca, as well as close friends Danny Patrissy, Joe Powell and Harry Gotkin.

Certainly, South Carolina players, as well as any of the players Frank coached, will remember the stories of his teammates at St. Johns--Java Gotkin and Rip Kaplinsky. Coach would yell at his players to "play smart like Kaplinsky!" His stories were entertaining and his friends became my friends too. But even more importantly, hearing the stories, meeting his friends, and learning about his life in New York, helped me learn more about the man who was my boss, my mentor and my friend. He later gave me confidence in my coaching ability by going to New York to recruit and leaving me to coach the team in practice sessions. He let me do the practice plans, but he was totally in charge.

Frank, his wife, Pat, and I were at Kutchers Hotel in Monticello, New York, the summer of 1961. Frank had just heard from Eddie Gottlieb of the Philadelphia Warriors inviting him to coach the pro team. Pat and I stayed up with Frank until 2 a.m. talking him out of accepting that offer. We finally went to bed thinking that we were set to continue at North Carolina. However, one week later, Frank told me he had decided to accept the offer and become the Warriors' coach.

He asked me to accompany him to Philadelphia or if I preferred, he would recommend that I be the head coach at North Carolina. I told him that I honestly felt that I would enjoy coaching at the college level much more. So, he recommended me to Chancellor William Aycock to replace him at North Carolina. I had come to know the Chancellor during my time as assistant coach and had great respect for him and for his outstanding leadership at North Carolina. Therefore, I was very honored that he chose to offer me the position of head basketball coach. I accepted his generous offer and began my head coaching experience at North Carolina in the 1961-62 basketball season.

In 1964, when Frank left Philadelphia to coach the basketball team at the University of South Carolina, he added excitement to the Atlantic Coast Conference. The ACC, because of his success at South Carolina, became a conference of more than just the "Big Four." His being at South Carolina also placed me in the position of being a rival coach with my old boss. We remained friends, but for forty minutes were fierce opponents. Our teams had some great games against each other.

When Frank retired from coaching we continued to have a close relationship. Through all the years of our association, our families were also friends and shared a common interest in each other's welfare. I feel privileged to have known both of Frank's wives. He was blessed with two fine marriages--first to Pat, who died of cancer, and later, to Jane who remains a close friend.

Frank often talked about the value of a true friend. He told me that if over a lifetime one had five "true friends" he could count on, he was indeed fortunate. I am pleased to be able to count Frank McGuire as one who has been a "true and special" friend to me during my lifetime.

Coach Dean E. Smith
Head Basketball Coach
University of North Carolina
9/20/95

COACH FRANK MCGUIRE
BY ALEX ENGLISH

You were the big city coach;
I was a skinny, country kid.
You asked me to play,
And that's what I did
You said, "Come, trailbraze a path
For others of your race."
We were civil rights comrades
In a non civil rights place.
Your compassionate side
Was most impressive to me.
It turned out to be
The most important lesson to see.
For when you believed you were standing up
For the right and the truth
Your Irish stubborness would not
Let anything else through.
I consider myself lucky
To have played for the man.
And like hundreds of your players
I will always be your fan.
You were the big city coach
Who showed me you were just a man.

Alex English played under Frank McGuire at South Carolina from 1972-73 to 1975-76, setting the school's all-time scoring record of 1,972 points. He started every game during his four-season college career. After being graduated from Carolina he played in the NBA for 15 seasons, including 11 with the Denver Nuggets and a final year with Dallas. As of 1995 English ranked eighth among the NBA's all-time scoring leaders with 25,343 points.

In 1993 he became an executive with the NBA Players Association in New York City but maintained his residence in Columbia.

One of English's hobbies is poetry, and he has had several books of poems printed. He wrote "Coach Frank McGuire" for a special ceremony honoring the memory of McGuire following a basketball game between the Gamecocks and Georgia on January 28, 1995 in the Frank McGuire Arena.

PREFACE

In the latter years of his life on this Earth, Frank McGuire was a wealthy man. Although his financial means were adequate, his real treasure was not measurable in tangible assets. However, he was a rich man in terms of friends and memories.

His physical means had been depleted by a massive stroke, but that did not take away his ability to reminisce over the events that took place during his legendary career as a basketball coach and to recall the hundreds of people who participated with him in this human drama.

During his forty-two years as a coach, he was eminently successful at St. Xavier High School in New York City, St. John's University, the University of North Carolina, the Philadelphia Warriors of the NBA and the University of South Carolina. His overall record was 725 victories against 304 defeats--a winning percentage of 70.5%.

As of 1995, McGuire was the only coach to win 100 or more games at three different colleges, and the only coach to win Atlantic Coast Conference championships at two schools-North Carolina and South Carolina. In 1957 his North Carolina team won the NCAA championship, completing an undefeated (32-0) campaign.

In 1977, three years before ending his coaching career at South Carolina, McGuire was installed in the Naismith National Collegiate Basketball Hall of Fame.

Before McGuire came to the University of South Carolina in 1964, the school had experienced little success in basketball, and high schools in the state were in the poverty class, insofar as basketball talent was concerned. McGuire spread basketball fever throughout the state, and basketball goals began sprouting in backyards from the mountains to the ocean.

Thanks to McGuire and the excitement and interest created by his teams, South Carolina has become a leading producer of college and professional basketball talent. For example, in 1995 the recruiting class of South Carolina Coach

Eddie Fogler was ranked among the top ten in the United States. All six of his signees were from South Carolina high schools.

In sixteen years at South Carolina, McGuire's teams won 66.6 percent of their games, competing in the tough Atlantic Coast Conference and against major teams from across the United States. His 283 victories against 142 losses make him a runaway leader among Gamecock coaches.

In his sixteen seasons at South Carolina, McGuire's teams competed in the NCAA playoffs four times, and that was in an era when the field was composed of less than half the number of the 64 teams that compete in the format of the 1990's. His Gamecocks also competed in the National Invitation Tournament three times and were champions of a number of holiday tournaments.

Six of McGuire's South Carolina players were named to All-America teams, and 12 played in the major professional leagues. Six of his Gamecock teams won 20 or more games and were ranked in the nation's top 20 at the end of those seasons. Of four Gamecocks who have been honored by the retirement of their jerseys, three played for McGuire. They are John Roche, Kevin Joyce and Alex English.

McGuire's playing and coaching careers spanned five decades and brought him into relationships with legends of the game and with many notables outside the field of sports. His world of basketball saw the sport emerge from the shadows of college football into a game that rivals baseball as our national pastime.

This book follows McGuire from his childhood in New York City, through his playing days at St. John's and into his storied coaching career. It also reveals his associations with people outside of the world of basketball, including the famous and the not so famous.

McGuire's memories were taken over many hours of audio-taped conversations with the coach during the final year (1993-1994) of his life. Therefore, in a sense, he is the co-author of this book.

McGuire could look out of the window of his sixth floor condominium beside the Congaree River near downtown Columbia and see Carolina Coliseum, scene of many of his coaching triumphs, standing almost dead center amidst commercial and University of South Carolina structures. Since 1992 he had been confined to a wheel chair as a result of a massive stroke. His speech lacked the distinct qualities that were so familiar to sports audiences during his coaching years.

Yet the memories that brightened his latter years were still there. Memories of a distinguished coaching career and of friends and family that were so much a part of his life. Fading were recollections of a boyhood that began so inauspiciously in Lower Manhattan, yet he harked back to those days with an appreciation for the many good things that took place in his life, rather than dwell on the tougher breaks that came his way.

Other material was compiled through research and interviews with former players, associates and family members. This book is intended to provide a comprehensive view of McGuire's life, his coaching career, his personality and his character.

To include all of the examples of how he touched the lives of others, and how others touched his life, would be impossible. The ones in this book should be enough to confirm the observation by one of his famous disciples, former Marquette Coach Al McGuire, that "there will never be another Frank McGuire."

Yet there will always be a "Frank McGuire" in the hearts and memories of those who played for him and those who followed his teams.

They can still hear the crisp New York accent that was so distinctive, especially in the predominance of Southern drawls of the Carolinas.

The image of his dramatic entrance to Carolina Coliseum prior to a home game, as the band played, "When Irish Eyes Are Smiling," is still visible to Gamecock fans. And, enroute to the court, the Irishman detours to embrace his son, Frankie, who sat behind the Carolina bench.

They remember his presence on the bench, impeccably dressed and ostensibly calm, even in the most perilous game situations. And who can forget the manner in which he straightened his tie, as he discussed a call with an official. McGuire even had a style about the way he called a time-out and gathered his players to discuss the strategy of the moment.

He had a charisma that few sports figures achieve, because it reflects who you are, and it cannot be contrived.

It is hoped that this book will enable Frank McGuire's legions of admirers to re-live many of the magic moments of his career and to preserve memories of a man who came from the streets of New York City to lead North Carolina and South Carolina into the basketball promised land.

PART ONE

MCGUIRE AS COACH

CHAPTER ONE

REFLECTIONS ON YOUTH

One of the historic events of the fall of 1913 was the Army-Notre Dame football game at South Bend, Indiana, in which an obscure quarterback named Gus Dorais shocked a great Army team, 35-13, by completing a number of forward passes to Knute Rockne, a skinny end, thereby establishing the pass as a serious weapon in the game.

Baseball immortal Christy Mathewson had earlier pitched the Philadelphia Athletics over the New York Giants in the World Series, and Detroit's Ty Cobb had won the American League Batting championship again.

Basketball wasn't being taken seriously as an intercollegiate sport, although St. John's coach Claude Allen was embarking on an 18-game schedule dominated by opponents in the New York area.

Over in Greenwich Village, a 13th child was born on November 13 to Anna and Robert McGuire. They named their new son Francis Joseph, which would inevitably be shortened to "Frank." There was nothing in the family background to suggest that this newborn would some day become one of the most famous personalities in sports.

The McGuire home at 282 West 11th Street--between Bleeker and Fourth Streets--was in what was recognized as the Italian-Irish district. It was a brown, two-story house with a stoop out front--nothing to make it stand out from other homes in the neighborhood.

Robert McGuire was a New York City policemen--a big man who had done some amateur boxing, which provided a hint of athleticism in young Frank's heredity.

Sadly, Frank never really got to know his father. Robert was bitten by a bulldog, and it was found that the dog had rabies. An infected needle was used in injecting the rabies serum, and Robert McGuire contracted yellow jaundice, a malady of the blood that was often fatal in that era. The illness proved fatal for the two-year-old McGuire's father, and Anna was left with the responsibility of a large family.

MCGUIRE: "My father was Irish, but my mother wasn't. In fact, she didn't particularly like Irishmen. I was really a 'narrowback,' the term they used for an Irishman born in the United States. You had to be born in Ireland to be a true Irishman.

"My mother didn't have a job--she had to stay home and take care of her children. She had a pension of $25 a month, and all of my brothers and sisters who were old enough worked somewhere and contributed to the support of the household. When I was old enough I worked down at the waterfront, which wasn't very far from our home, and I started out at twenty-five cents an hour, as far as I can recall.

"My mother and I were very close, and we did a lot of things together. Even when I was a very small boy I used to hold a candle for her to chop wood for the two woodstoves that heated our home. Our bathroom was outside of the main house, and I have a vivid memory of going out there late one night in the midst of a big snowstorm!

"My mother liked to shop, and I would go out with her practically every day to places like Macy's and Gimbel's. I don't think she bought much, but she liked to walk through the stores and look at the merchandise, and I would tag along.

"I attended Saint Veronica elementary school--an all-white Catholic school that went through the eighth grade. After that I went to St. Xavier, a Jesuit high school that was just a few blocks from our house. It was an all-boys military school and very tough academically.

"Ours was a pretty tough neighborhood, particularly around Sixteenth Street, which I had to cross on the way to school. However, some of the cops along the way had known my father, and they always looked out for me.

"Some days after school a few of the big boys would make the smaller ones go steal sweet potatoes from the store on the corner, or they wouldn't let them stand by the fire that they built on the street to stay warm. Then they would put the sweet potatoes on sticks and roast them by the fire. For the rest of my life, I never had sweet potatoes at a meal that I didn't think about those days around a fire on the street!

"We were hired by the day down at the waterfront, but the wages were extremely low. Things improved, however, one summer when they went on strike, wages were raised all the way up to a dollar and a half an hour.

"The longshoremen wouldn't let black people come near the waterfront, because they didn't want them competing for their jobs. Italians also found it difficult competing for jobs down there, but there wasn't much trouble between the Irish and Italian kids.

"Ironically, it was a black man who got me interested in sports--particularly basketball. His name was Ted Carroll, who was a cartoonist for the *Amsterdam News* , a small suburban paper. Carroll became director of Greenwich House, the community settlement house, which was a ten-story building. And Ted Carroll was the only black in this predominantly Irish and Italian neighborhood.

"I spent a lot of time there. In fact, the first shower bath I ever had was at Greenwich House. Carroll sort of took me under his wing, and we'd do things such as go to a ball game.

"Carroll made me workout on a punching bag, and told me, 'You can use this some day.' Later I got into a fight during a basketball game, and he pulled me out and lectured me, 'That's not for basketball games, it's for protection!'

"Back then boys hung around street corners at night, and there were a lot of fights. That's what Ted Carroll was talking about!

"Baseball was the big sport in New York, and basketball didn't get much publicity in the newspapers. The Yankees were in the era of Babe Ruth and Lou Gehrig, but I was more of a Giants fan. Carroll took us to see some of the Giants' games in the Polo Grounds, and this was when they had a pitcher named Carl Hubbell, who had an unusual pitch they called a 'screwball.'

"Ted also took us to some boxing matches, which were very big, because Gene Tunney, who grew up near where I lived, and Jack Dempsey were fighting it out for the heavyweight championship. Ted was also a friend of Joe Louis, who came along in the early thirties, and he once brought Louis into the neighborhood so we could meet him.

"Even with the excitement that surrounded baseball and boxing, I still liked basketball best. I played baseball and football in their seasons, but basketball was always number one with me.

"I went through the eighth grade at St. Veronica, which was a parochial school, and I received a very good background for high school. When it was time for me to go to high school my mother wanted me to attend St. Xavier, which was a private school run by the Jesuit priests. It was a military school and very strict, which didn't appeal to me. I wanted to go to public school, but my mother insisted that I go to St. Xavier, and that was the best thing that ever happened to me.

"The school wasn't far from where we lived and you had to pay a tuition to go there. It had about a thousand students--all boys. We wore uniforms, drilled every afternoon and had two hours of Latin everyday."

MRS. FRANK (JANE) MCGUIRE: "Because of that military school background, Frank has always had good posture. He had the same type of arthritis that Dick Riley (former South Carolina governor who served as Secretary of Education in President Clinton's cabinet) has. People who have that type of arthritis are usually bent over, but Frank was still straight-up, and I believe that it's because of that military training."

MCGUIRE: "One of the big things we learned was that we should respect everybody, and I have tried to carry that philosophy with me throughout my life.

"I participated in three sports at St. Xavier. I was a guard in basketball, right end in football and a pitcher on the baseball team.

"Rules of basketball were completely different from those that are in effect today. Back then, following every field goal or free throw, officials would take the ball back to the center of the court and have a jump ball. It was very important to have a tall center, because that gave you a big advantage in controlling the game. There was no contact allowed in basketball then, so you didn't see the tight defenses you see now. Anytime a player was fouled he got a free throw. Everybody shot free throws underhanded then.

"Except for layups, most of the shots were two-hand set shots, and there was little shooting on the run. The high school players of that day couldn't compare to the ones we have now. They didn't start playing on organized teams as early, didn't have the coaching or the conditioning programs players have now.

"Possession was the big thing that coaches stressed. Hold on to the ball. So there wasn't a lot of scoring. Scores in the twenties and thirties were not unusual. If an individual averaged in double figures, that was something else.

"My coach at St. Xavier was Marty O'Malley, who became a father figure to me and a wonderful inspiration. He was the epitome of an Irish gentleman, very warm but still very demanding. He insisted on discipline and proper behavior, which gave me a invaluable foundation on which to build my life and profession.

"Perhaps it was Coach O'Malley who first sowed the seeds of my desire to become a coach, because he, to me, was a model for what a man should be.

"O'Malley was a rawbone Irishman who had grown up in Boston and attended Holy Cross, one of the finest Catholic institutions in the country.

"He is still (1994) one of my mentors and I continue to be in touch with him. When they had a dinner to celebrate my induction into the Hall of Fame, it was most appropriate that Coach O'Malley be present, and I will forever be grateful for that.

"I developed, athletically and personally, under him, and his guidance led to my becoming captain of the football, basketball and baseball teams when I was a senior.

"I felt that I was a good athlete--not a great player in any one sport--but one who could compete in any of them. In basketball I considered myself better at defense than as a shooter. I've always felt that defense was the backbone of a team in any sport, and I made it a priority as a coach.

"You can reach your own conclusion as to why, but I was given the nickname, 'Elbows' by my teammates!

MCGUIRE -THE COLLEGE ATHLETE

"When I finished St. Xavier and was ready for college, I had an offer of a football scholarship to Georgetown, and that's where I had wanted to go at first. However, the priest at St. John's contacted me about coming to school there to play basketball, and that had a greater appeal. I had seen St. John's play, and the coach, Buck Freeman, was the most famous basketball coach of that day. While I was at St. Xavier, Freeman had his famous 'Wonder Five' that was beating all the New York area teams but didn't get the national recognition they deserved, because they weren't playing intersectional opponents.

"Buck had played for St. John's in the mid twenties and coached at Iona Prep before taking the job as head coach in 1927. He was a devout Catholic and that appealed to my mother, so everything added up to taking the scholarship at St. John's.

"My scholarship consisted of tuition, books and meals, but no side money. The school itself was a good one. It had been founded in 1870 by the Vincentian Fathers over on Lewis Avenue in Brooklyn but later they built a campus in Jamaica and another on Staten Island.

"The students went to Mass every morning, and we wore jackets and ties. St. John's had a football team but did away with it, because it was a losing proposition. They made money on basketball, because the expenses were relatively low. We did very little travel, which is one of the big expenses in basketball programs today.

"Besides playing basketball, I was also a pitcher on the baseball team. I was no great pitcher, but I think I was as good as other pitchers on college teams in the area. I definitely was not a strikeout pitcher. Buck even had some of the Brooklyn Dodger pitchers come over and help me. I remember Dazzy Vance, one of the top pitchers in the majors at the time, was one of the Dodgers who came.

"As far as my teammates on the basketball team are concerned, the only one that became a national sports figure was Gerard Bush. Gerry played pro ball with the Akron Firestones and was head coach at the University of Nebraska for ten years, beginning in 1955. None of the teams I coached ever played Gerry. Nebraska was strictly a football school while he was there, and they never did much in basketball.

"I was fortunate to have Buck Freeman for a coach, because he was ahead of his time and was a great teacher. He introduced multiple defenses, screens, switching on defense and give and go, things that are so prevalent in the modern game of basketball. That's why he had such an outstanding record. In nine years at St. John's his teams won 85 per cent of their games, and that's an all-time high for college coaches. Higher than the percentage of wins by John Wooden or Adolph Rupp.

"He was a tough coach and very strict on fundamentals. Long after his career as a head coach and when he was my assistant at North Carolina and at South Carolina, he was very valuable, particularly in helping our players with their shooting. He was very good at teaching how to get the proper rotation on the ball, and so forth.

"Buck was always a confirmed bachelor, but he was married to the game of basketball. It was hard for him to understand why anyone would put something ahead of that. It bothered him for our players to have distractions like girl friends.

"I didn't do very much dating when I was playing for Buck, but some of the other players did. It was hard to get caught in New York City, so it was not much of a problem. St. John's was an all-male school, so we didn't have any of what Buck considered distractions on the campus.!

"His demise as a head coach had nothing to do with his ability or record. At the peak of his career he developed a drinking problem that ended that part of his basketball life. However, he did score a victory over that, which was to his everlasting credit, and he was an able coach and good influence over young men at Long Island, North Carolina and South Carolina."

Freshmen were not eligible to play on the varsity, so McGuire and his teammates patiently waited for their varsity years. His sophomore year was a good one, as McGuire played in all 19 games, 16 of which were won by the Redmen. McGuire considered himself primarily a defensive player, but as a sophomore he averaged 3.2 points, which was not bad, considering that John McGuiness led the team with a 6.9 average.

As a junior McGuire became part of basketball history by participating in the first regular season doubleheader in Madison Square Garden. That game on December 19, 1934 was won by Westminster over the Redmen, 37-33. Most of St. John's games continued to be played in DeGray gym, but the Redmen did play three more games in the Garden during the 1934-35 season, losing to CCNY and Long Island, but defeating Manhattan. The Redmen experienced their worst won-lost record of Freeman's tenure, 13-8, and it was the only Freeman-coached team that didn't win at least 80 per cent of its games.

McGuire's point production was up to 5.7 per game as a sophomore, not far below Joe Marchese's team leading 7.3.

There was no National Invitation Tournament or NCAA play-off during McGuire's playing years at St. John's, or surely the Redmen would have been involved in the playoffs, based on their won-lost records.

Five of the Redmen's games were played in Madison Square Garden in

McGuire's senior season, 1935-36. They compiled an 18-4 record, bringing McGuire's three-year record as a player to 47 wins against only 15 losses for a percentage of 75.8.

McGuire, Java Gotkin and Rueben Kaplinsky were in a three-way tie for the individual scoring honors with identical 7.0 averages.

As it turned out this was be Freeman's final season as head coach of the Redmen, and he was succeeded by Joe Lapchick. Freeman's teams had won 177 games against only 31 losses, an amazing accomplishment for someone in his only college head coaching position.

However, the McGuire-Freeman connection was far from over.

CHAPTER TWO

A COACHING CAREER IS BORN

When McGuire received his diploma from St. John's in 1937, professional sports, except for baseball and boxing, had gained little of the prominence achieved in the post World War II years. Like most college athletes, McGuire had little ambition to make a career out of playing basketball or baseball.

Guided by his mentor, Buck Freeman, McGuire had been a good student and was prepared to make a career out of something other than athletics. McGuire made emphasis on academics a continual part of his coaching philosophy during his ensuing years at St. John's, North Carolina and South Carolina.

McGuire obviously made impressions on the administrations at both St. Xavier High School and St. John's University, as he was later offered positions at both institutions.

St. Xavier was first, following McGuire's college graduation, employing him to teach English and help with coaching the athletic teams. Later he even taught some classes in Latin, four years of which were requirements for entrance into St. John's.

To supplement his salary of around $4,000 a year, McGuire did some officiating and played basketball in the old American Basketball League, forerunner of the more organized ABA. Later the ABA merged with the National Basketball Association.

McGuire soon became head basketball coach and baseball coach at St. Xavier, where he established a record of 126 victories against only 39 losses over 11 seasons for a winning percentage of 76.4.

MCGUIRE: "St. Xavier played mostly Catholic schools in the area, and we didn't have players with ability that would make them major college prospects. First, you had to pay a tuition to go to Xavier, and, of course, you had to drill every day and wear a uniform, because it was a military school. But it was a wonderful school and gave you, not only a good academic back-

ground, but instilled in you the discipline and other qualities that are just as important in life as what you learn out of books."

In April of 1940 McGuire was married to Patricia Johnson, whom he had met several years earlier at a dance that followed a basketball game. Pat, as she was known, was the daughter of Charles and Margaret Johnson, and was a featured member of the original "Our Gang" comedies cast, which included Spanky McFarland and Jackie Cooper. The series was later entitled, "The Little Rascals."

SERVICE TO HIS COUNTRY

When the Japanese bombed Pearl Harbor, on December 7, 1941, Frank McGuire responded immediately. He and boyhood friend, Jim Fitzpatrick, who had finished at the Naval Academy, volunteered for service in the Naval Air Force on the day after the attack. Several months later, in April of 1942, Pat and Frank celebrated the birth of their first child, Patricia Jean.

McGuire's ROTC training, along with his coaching experience led to his commission as an Ensign and assignment to North Carolina Pre-Flight School at Chapel Hill. It never entered his mind that years later this would be the base for his greatest coaching accomplishment.

MCGUIRE: "When I was commissioned, the Navy gave me three possible stations to choose from, and I can't remember the other two, but I do recall that Chapel Hill was my last choice. I learned that this is not unusual with the military. I'm thankful that the Navy ignored my other choices, because I met people in Chapel Hill who would become lifelong friends. One was Ben Carnevale, who coached basketball at North Carolina for two seasons before serving as coach of the Naval Academy for 20 years.

"My job at North Carolina Pre-Flight was to work with Navy flyers on physical fitness. Among the people there were Bear Bryant, the immortal Alabama football coach; Ted Williams, the Boston Red Sox outfielder and probably the best hitter in the history of baseball; and Otto Graham, the great NFL quarterback, who played collegiately at Northwestern.

"It was also the first time I met Rex Enright (head football coach and athletics director at the University of South Carolina for many years). When I went to North Carolina, Enright was on the Atlantic Coast Conference basketball committee, so I developed more of an acquaintanceship with him then. In fact, it was Rex that introduced me to Jim Tatum for the first time, and this was several years before Jim came to North Carolina from Maryland as football coach.

COACHING AT ST. JOHN'S--THE 1947-48 SEASON

MCGUIRE: "When the war ended, and I was finally discharged from the Navy, I headed on back to New York to continue my career as a high school coach. And it was something that I loved to do. Even after coaching on the college level and in the NBA, there is still no doubt in my mind that coaching a high school team is the most enjoyable and satisfying job I could have.

"However, circumstances have a way of changing the course of your life. After my first season back at St. Xavier, Joe Lapchick, who replaced Buck Freeman as coach of St. John's, was hired to coach the New York Knickerbockers in the NBA."

Lapchick had succeeded Buck Freeman as coach of the Redmen in 1936, the same year that McGuire graduated from that institution. When Lapchick was offered the job, he was rather frightened over going into the college ranks–he hadn't even finished grammar school.

Joe had been born a basketball player, joining the pro ranks in 1919 and then becoming a member of the original Celtics team as one of the taller players in the game at 6'6". Lapchick obviously didn't need a college degree to coach, as he guided the Redmen to 11 straight winning seasons. During that period Lapchick's teams had played in seven National Invitational Tournaments, winning the championship twice.

With America moving into the post war era, interest in sports was on the rise, and in 1946 the National Basketball League, forerunner of the NBA, was formed. One of the key members of this new professional league was the New York Knickerbockers, coached by Neil Cohalan.

The Knicks, looking for a coach to take them into the future, found the most prominent in New York basketball circles--Lapchick. He had a fine reputation as a pro player and as a college coach, so the Knicks lured him away from St. John's.

The Redmen didn't have to look far for a replacement, as one of their own-Frank McGuire-was back in town, and there was no more successful high school coach in the area than he.

MCGUIRE: "Getting an opportunity to go directly from high school into the position of head coach at, not only a major college, but one of the leading basketball programs in the country, was more than I could have hoped for. When they gave me the job they told me that the salary was $7,000, then the next day, they raised it to $7,500. That, incidentally, made me the highest paid college basketball coach in the country. It wasn't because I asked for it, because I was just happy to get the job. I have never made career decisions based on money.

"I would like to have had my college coach--Buck Freeman--as an assistant, but the administration wouldn't let me do that. So I chose Al Destefano, who had played at St. John's in 1939-40.

"Unfortunately, the best players from Lapchick's previous team had graduated, and I was faced with somewhat of a rebuilding job. I knew high school basketball in New York as well or better than anybody, so I had a pretty good line on who the top players were. This would be the first time I had ever had to recruit talent, but I was confident that I could handle that.

"I'll never forget my experience in recruiting Bob Zawoluk, who turned out to be one of the all-time great players in the history of St. John's. Zawoluk was a gangling, 6'6", and all the area colleges were interested in him. I've always recruited parents as much as I have their sons, because I like players who have strong family ties. It says something about them as a person, and it's important that they be good people, as well as good basketball players.

"So I went to visit his mother one morning while he was at school. Her name was Gussie, a tall blonde German woman, whose husband had been hit by a truck and killed a few months earlier, leaving her with the responsibility of raising their young son, Bob. They lived in a stone house that was nothing pretentious, but certainly comfortable enough.

"I explained to Mrs. Zawoluk who I was and that I would like for her son to enroll at St. John's on a basketball scholarship. This was nothing new to her, because a lot of schools would have liked for her son to play basketball for them. Not only New York schools, but also colleges in other states.

"She told me that she might prefer that her son go off to college, so she wouldn't have to be bothered with him coming home at night and having to look after him all the time.

"While we were talking, she looked at me and said, 'Do you dance?' That was completely unexpected--certainly on my first recruiting visit. I managed a weak response, and that's all she needed. I was not a great dancer, by any means, but I had learned to do the waltz with some degree of acceptability.

"So, she walks over to this big hand-cranked Victrola, puts on a record and cranked it up. Then we began to waltz around the room, and I wondered if my dancing was good enough to convince her that her son should play basketball for me.

"When the Victrola ran down, she asked me if I would like some tea, and I accepted immediately. It would provide a welcome rest from the dancing. I presume that my dancing and tea drinking had been good enough for her, because, as I prepared to leave, she said, 'Can you come back tomorrow?'

"This went on for a few mornings, and I felt that I had danced my way into the inside track on recruiting Bob Zawoluk. Several mornings later, the St. John's treasurer, Father Collins, who was a big supporter of the basketball team, asked me, 'How are we doing?' He was referring to Zawoluk.

"I answered, 'Can you dance?' I might could use some help in that department! Whether it was my dancing, my personality, my salesman-ship, or whatever, Mrs. Zawoluk decided that her son would go to college in New York City, after all, and that it would be at St. John's. That was the first block in building a winning basketball program."

When McGuire greeted his first St. John's squad to prepare for the 1947-48 season, the leading players from Lapchick's team had departed. That included Harry Boykoff, who had become the Redmen's first 1,000 point scorer with 1,129 and a 16.6 average during his three varsity seasons.

On the plus side was Dick McGuire, who had played for St. John's in 1943-44, served in the military during W.W.II and returned for the 1946-47 season. Other carryovers included Gerry Calabrese and Ed Redding, but the depth of talent that had been typical of Redmen teams of the past six seasons was missing.

Therefore, landing Zawoluk was a big step forward for McGuire, but this prize recruit would have to play on the freshman team for a season before he could help the varsity. After defeating the St. John's Alumni in the first game, the Redmen lost to Denver, Loyola (Illinois) and in overtime to Georgetown, before giving McGuire his first collegiate victory over Iona, 66-46.

After 14 games McGuire had the prospect of a losing season facing him, as St. John's had won only six. However, they finished strong, winning six of the final nine, including a season-ending overtime win over Iona. That gave McGuire a 12-11 record in his inaugural year as a college coach.

McGuire's biggest win came against Nat Holman's CCNY team, 38-34 in Madison Square Garden. It was the lowest scoring game in which McGuire was involved as a coach at St. John's. Dick McGuire, who captained the Redmen during McGuire's first two seasons, led the scoring for 1947-48 with a 10.4 average.

THE 1948-49 SEASON

McGuire had the Redmen back on track in the 1948-49 season, leading them to a 15-9 record and an invitation to the NIT, which involved only 12 teams and was considered by many to be more prestigious than the NCAA tournament.

With Dick McGuire again leading the way, averaging 12.8 points per game, the Redmen scored victories over city rivals Manhattan, NYU, Fordham and Brooklyn College but lost in overtime to CCNY in the Garden. In the NIT St. John's was eliminated by Bowling Green in the first round.

Dick McGuire, whose brother Al had joined him as a sophomore on the varsity, received the Haggerty Award as the Most Valuable player in the Metropolitan area, and he was picked by the New York Knicks in the first round of the NBA draft.

Although Dick McGuire would be gone the next season, McGuire could look forward to promising new talent, including Zawoluk, Jack McMahon and Ron Macgilvray. These three would lead the Redmen through three of their greatest seasons ever.

MCGUIRE: "It didn't take me long to learn that coaching a college team was much more involved than high school. You not only have to recruit players, but also be their father. There were the dealings with faculty and administration at the college, and handling the press. I say press, because the newspaper was the only media that really covered basketball in that period.

"As far as press relations were concerned, I was lucky enough to receive some great guidance and advice on how to get along. Tom Paprocki was a writer for the Associated Press, and I had taught his son at St. Xavier, so I had a head start on knowing him. He told me that as long as I was in the game that I needed the press and to get along with them.

"This might be someone else's quote, but what he meant was that if you get into a fight with the press, 'You will run out of blood before they run out of ink!'

"Pap also told me, 'I'm your friend, but don't ever tell me anything you wouldn't want printed in the paper. That is my business and it comes first.'

"One day Pap was riding with me to a game with CCNY, and a taxi cab cut me off in traffic. I was pretty mad and got out of the car to settle things with the cab driver.

"Pap said, 'Frank, get back in this car. I don't care what happened--you were wrong. In the morning, when people read the paper--they won't remember what the cab driver's name was, but they'll sure as hell remember yours!"

"I worked on cultivating the faculty and getting their support, and also assuring them that I was just as concerned about a player's academics as I was his athletics. That was important.

"During Jack McMahon's freshman year he had a hard time adjusting to college and was in danger of flunking out. I needed Jack in the worst sort of way. So, I went to one of his instructors, Father O'Riley, obviously a good Irish Catholic, and cried on his shoulder.

"Father O'Riley didn't appear to be sympathetic at first. A freshman having trouble with his studies was nothing new to him. And he observed that he didn't know if McMahon had what it took to make it academically. Then he asked me what kind of a player Jack was.

"I told him that Jack would be a great player--the very heart of our team.

"Father O'Riley thought for a moment and said, 'Come to think of it, that young man does have some smarts. Send him to see me tomorrow morning.' McMahon became a much better student after that!

Prior to 1961, when Alumni Hall was opened, St. John's played its home games in little Degray Gym, which was adequate for the pre-war basketball era. However, there was little opportunity to create revenue from the sport, which was becoming more and more important and increasingly expensive, with more scholarship players, bigger staffs and a desire to play opponents from other areas of the country.

Therefore, Madison Square Garden became the Redmen's home away from home. In five years as head coach at St. John's, McGuire's teams played 72 of their total of 138 games in the Garden.

Madison Square Garden began its claim as the capital of college basketball in 1934. That's when Ned Irish, a 29-year-old sports writer for the New York World-Telegram became weary of going into out of the way places and finding himself in poor facilities to cover college games. He felt that college basketball should be more accessible to the public, so he made arrangements to rent the Garden and scheduled the first college doubleheader for December 29, 1934. St. John's played Westminster in one game, and NYU met Notre Dame in the other. One of the players on the St. John's team was Frank McGuire.

That inaugural event was so successful that Irish quit his job with the newspaper and went into the promotion business full time.

MCGUIRE: "In that first game we played Westminster, and there were 18,000 people in the stands. We had been accustomed to playing before 400 or 500. I couldn't believe it! On top of that we lost the game (37-33), but it was still exciting to play an event that made basketball history.

"Ned Irish was a quiet man but a good promoter. He had the advantage of knowing the New York sports writers personally, and they gave his doubleheaders great coverage. Irish later became president of the Garden, and he had it made. He would pay the Garden practically nothing in rent, and he didn't have to pay the teams much to play there.

"The college teams wanted to play in the Garden, because it gave them exposure to the New York press, which meant national publicity. There weren't any large college arenas at that time, so the colleges weren't losing any big gates at home by accepting the nominal fees they received for coming to New York.

"This really moved college basketball into the big time. Prior to that it couldn't hold a candle to football in spectator interest. Irish was a great promoter, and he even booked games in other cities, such as Boston and Philadelphia.

"Playing in Madison Square Garden became a real prestige accomplishment, so Irish could be very selective in the teams he matched up. For instance, in 1936 Stanford was invited to play Long Island in the Garden, purely because they had Hank Luisetti, who had introduced the one-hand shot to basketball.

"Teams in the East had never seen anyone like that, so Stanford was able to beat Long Island because of Luisetti's unusual shooting style. Prior to that Long Island had won 43 straight games.

"As a player, it was always exciting to play in the Garden, and I think it inspired players to try harder, because of the big crowds and the coverage the games received from the newspapers. I played in nine games in the Garden, and it was always something special."

THE 1949-50 SEASON

McGuire's third year as coach of the Redmen was the most exciting and successful in the school's history. The 25 victories were the most ever in a single season for St. John's, which also attained its first season-end national ranking--9th in the Associated Press poll.

The most significant victory was over Kentucky, which ranked third in the AP poll. The Redmen downed Adolph Rupp's Wildcats, 69-58, in Madison Square Garden, bringing the Redmen's record to 8-0 at that point in the season. They won 12 straight before losing to City College by two points in the Garden. During the regular season St. John's lost by six points to DePaul, in overtime to Fordham and by one point to Brooklyn College in the 69th Regiment Armory.

In their final regular season game, St. John's set several records in beating St. Peter's, 105-61, an individual team scoring mark. Zawoluk had an amazing 65 points on 25 for 46 field goal shooting in setting a record that still stood in 1994.

Zawoluk finished his sophomore season with 588 points, almost 200 more than any Redman had scored in a year up until then. His 20.3 average was also easily the best ever by a St. John's player.

St. John's was invited to play in the NIT and defeated Western Kentucky in the quarterfinals, but lost to Bradley in the semis. In a consolation game St. John's downed Duquesne to earn third place among the 12 teams that competed. Six of the teams in the NIT were ranked in the AP final top ten, including St. John's, Bradley (No. 1), Kentucky, Duquesne, Western Kentucky and LaSalle.

McGuire's third St. John's team firmly entrenched him as a legitimate member of the New York City's fraternity of outstanding coaches. There was Clair Bee at Long Island University, Nat Holman at CCNY, Howard Cann at NYU, Ken Norton at Manhattan and Pete Carlissimo at Fordham. City College and NYU were St. John's biggest rivals, and although Long Island was under Bee, one of the game's great coaches and one of McGuire's close friends, they didn't face each other in a regularly-scheduled game. However, they did meet under a more casual circumstance.

MCGUIRE: "One year we wanted to look at our teams under game conditions before the season started, so we arranged to scrimmage each other one Saturday morning in the Garden. I told my players that Coach Bee was very close to me and that I didn't want anything to happen in that scrimmage that would affect our friendship.

"Al McGuire was on the team at the time, and he was a completely different personality from his brother Dick. Dick was a great basketball player, but very easy going. I never saw him get into an argument. I don't think he would know what to say! Al was the fiery type who might not go out of his way to start a fight, but be certainly wouldn't back away either.

"We didn't have any referees, because this was just going to be a friendly game--serious and all-out basketball but not a matter of life or death. Well, someone threw the ball up, and the next thing I know there are two guys on the floor--Al McGuire and a long Island player named Ralph Bigos. Al had Bigos down and was choking him.

"I told Al to let him up. I was screaming at Al, and Bigos was turning blue in the face. Al said, 'Not until he says I give up.'

"I said, 'The guy can't talk as long as you're chokin' him.' So, Al let him up, and we managed to play the game without having a free-for-all. But I learned that Al had a temper that he needed to control."

The 1949-50 season also featured another landmark for the McGuires, as Pat gave birth to another daughter, Carol Ann, on December 30.

THE 1950-51 SEASON

Looking ahead to the 1950-51 season, George Kalabrese, a second round pick by Syracuse in the NBA draft, would not be back. However, Zawoluk and McMahon, who averaged 11.9 points per game, would give McGuire a solid nucleus around which to build.

The 1950-51 season was the one in which St. John's firmly established itself as a national basketball power. In their previous season they had increased the number of intersectional and non-New York area opponents, and this enhanced the Redmen's image nationally. They were now scheduling the likes of Kentucky, Louisiana State, Virginia Tech, San Francisco, Utah, DePaul, Kansas, Washington State, Southern Methodist and others.

MCGUIRE: "Because of the small number of seats in our gym, we were playing more and more games in Madison Square Garden; it became our home floor. In the 1950-51 season we played only four games on the campus, compared to 13 in the Garden, and that doesn't include post-season games. At one stretch we played 11 straight games in the Garden, and the only two we lost were to Kentucky, which won the NCAA championship that season, and Phog Allen's Kansas team, which beat us by one point.

"In certain respects Ned Irish had more to do with my schedule than I did. He made up the schedules for most of the New York teams, as far as the Garden was concerned. And that's where the money games were. Not much money, but more than we could make playing on the campus.

"We had the right to say 'no' to a game, but we weren't involved in picking the teams that would come into New York for the big double-headers. We really didn't have a basketball budget. The school treasurer, Father Collins, would pay the bills. All money would go into the school account, and student fees were the major part of the support for basketball.

"Father Collins and I had become good friends and saw a lot of each other. He liked basketball, and that was a big help to me. Back then we could give the players $15 a month-what they called laundry money, but we didn't play outside of New York very much, so we didn't need much of a travel budget."

The Redmen opened their 1950-51 season by winning six of their first eight games, losing the one-pointer to Kansas and by six to top-ranked Kentucky. St. John's then embarked on a 12-game winning streak, including a 68-59 verdict over Bradley, which was ranked No. 1 the previous year, advancing to the finals of the NCAA playoffs and the NIT. This victory caught the attention of the New York Press and resulted in St. John's moving into the national rankings.

The win streak ended in a 77-75 loss to Niagara in the Garden, but St. John's finished the regular season with four straight victories to run their record to 22 win against only three defeats. The Redmen were ranked in the final AP poll, which did not include post season games in that era.

The Redmen received bids to both the NIT and NCAA playoffs, which included 16 teams for the first time, instead of eight as in the past. There were still only two regionals-eight teams in the East and eight in the West.

The NIT and the East Regional were to be played in Madison Square Garden, which was good news to McGuire, whose teams always played well in the Garden. In the NIT St. John's received a bye to the quarterfinals and defeated St. Bonaventure, which had eliminated Cincinnati in the first round.

Dayton overcame the Redmen in two overtimes, leaving them with a consolation game against Seton Hall, a game won easily by St. John's, 62-43, to give McGuire a third place finish among a field of 12. Brigham Young won the championship over Dayton, by the same score of the consolation final.

The NCAA regional followed, and St. John's defeated Connecticut, 63-52, in the first round but lost to Kentucky, 59-43, in the semi-finals. In the consolation game, the Redmen faced North Carolina State and defeated the Wolfpack, 71-59. This planted the first seed in a coaching rivalry between McGuire and State's Everett Case that would reach full bloom later in the decade.

Zawoluk had another banner season, scoring 654 points and averaging 21.9 per game, while McMahon had 401 points and an average of 12.9 per game. Al McGuire, who served as co-captain with Frank Mulzoff, was a sixth-round pick by the Knicks in the NBA draft, joining brother Dick, who had made the team two years before.

The 26-5 final won-lost record and ranking of ninth in the final AP poll made this easily the best season ever for St. John's.

THE 1951-52 SEASON

There was nothing like 26 wins, bids to both post-season tournaments, and three returning stars to boost the confidence of the Redmen and the anticipation of the 1951-52 season. Zawoluk, McMahon and Ron Macgilvray, whom McGuire had recruited during his first season as St. John's coach, were back for their senior seasons. They were the major players in the previous season, and they were to be bolstered by some promising newcomers.

Solly Walker, Jim Davis, Dick Duckett and Jim Walsh joined the three returning stars, and there was good reason for optimism at St. John's. Walker was the first black player ever recruited at St. John's and would be the only one of his race on the squad for his sophomore season.

The Redmen opened the season with relatively easy victories over Arnold, Brigham Young, Washington and Jefferson, Wagner and Rhode Island. However, a major challenge lay ahead, as they prepared to entrain for Lexington to meet Kentucky, which was defending national champion. The Wildcats had defeated Kansas State in the NCAA finals for their third title in four years.

Kentucky, led by seven-foot Bill Spivey, Cliff Hagan and Frank Ramsey was heavily favored to repeat as national champion. The Redmen had lost to the Wildcats in the Garden twice during the previous season, once in the regular season and again in the semi-finals of the East regional. The Wildcats were practically unbeatable on their home court.

Kentucky coach Adolph Rupp, a basketball tyrant who gave no mercy and accepted nothing short of absolute domination of an opponent, had played for Phog Allen at Kansas, who had been coached by James Naismith, inventor of the game. His philosophy was summarized when he made the statement, "I'd rather be the most hated winning coach in the country than the most popular losing one."

Another example of his merciless approach to a game came in 1948, when the Wildcats were 36-3 and NCAA champions. Although Kentucky was leading an opponent 38-4 at the half, Rupp berated his team for allowing one player to score all four of the opponent's points. The Baron yelled, "Somebody guard that man. He's running wild."

St. John's was facing another Kentucky powerhouse in this 1951-52 campaign. The result was the worst defeat of McGuire's collegiate coaching career, 81-40. At the time nobody could see the storm clouds gathering over the Wildcats. Kentucky would go on to finish the season with 29 wins against only three losses but, the school would be embarrassed by revelations by former players that they and other athletes had received under-the-table payments. The violations were severe enough that the NCAA would force them to cancel their entire 1952-53 schedule.

Such a loss would have been devastating to some teams, but not to this one. McGuire reminded them that, in spite of the size of the score, the game counted only as one loss and the Redmen were still 5-1 with a long schedule ahead. St. John's won 14 of their next 15 games, losing only to Loyola of Illinois, who were in their first season under George Ireland. Loyola finished 17-8, and Ireland began a building program that would lead the Ramblers to a NCAA championship.

A 22-4 record was good enough to earn McGuire's team bids to both NCAA playoffs and NIT for the second season in a row, losing in the quarterfinals to LaSalle.

However, the Redmen's main order of business was the NCAA East Regionals in Reynolds Coliseum in Raleigh, North Carolina. There they would meet Everett Cases's North Carolina State Wolfpack, while top-ranked Kentucky was the easy favorite over Howie Dallmar's Penn State team.

Kentucky had no trouble with Penn State, winning by a score of 82-54, with All-American Cliff Hagan and Frank Ramsey leading the way. The Redmen held off the tenacious Wolfpack on their home floor, 60-49.

There's nothing like a 41-point regular season win over an opponent to boost a team's confidence going into a tournament game against that same team. How confident was Rupp that his Wildcats would prevail? Kentucky had already chartered a plane for the NCAA finals, which were to be held at Seattle, Washington. Hotel reservations were also confirmed.

MCGUIRE: "Our players knew that our experience at Lexington earlier in the season was in no way typical of our team. We had just had a sub-par game against a great basketball team under unusual circumstances.

"If the team ever had incentives, ours did. First, just winning a game was important, and advancing to the finals of the NCAA playoffs made it even more so. Then, there was not only the loss to Kentucky earlier in the season, but the events that surrounded added to the determination of our players.

"We knew that Kentucky would probably have the crowd advantage, because of the geographical location of the game. However, the game at Lexington was the only one of two that we lost on an opponent's home floor during the season.

"Our team arose to the occasion and played its best game of the season against the Wildcats. Great players seem to always hit their peak in crucial games, and this was the case with Zeke Zawoluk. He did everything you could ask of a player, scoring 32 points and holding his own and then some against Kentucky's big inside men.

"The final score was 64-57 in our favor, but the importance of this victory cannot be overstated. It propelled St. John's basketball to a new level. It established us as more than just a good New York City team.

"Statistics tell me that I coached in 784 college basketball games and won 550 of them. Yet some games go down as much more than just entries in a media guide. In looking back I cherish that win over Kentucky right alongside our 1957 NCAA championship victory over Kansas while I was at North Carolina and my South Carolina team's win over North Carolina that gave us the Atlantic Coast Conference championship in 1971."

The NCAA championship tournament at Seattle involved three teams ranked in the AP top ten; St. John's at No. 10, Illinois at No. 2 and Kansas at No. 8. Unranked Santa Clara, which barely squeaked into the Far West regional, was the surprise of the final four. The Broncos had a regular-season mark of 15 wins and 11 losses, but they upset Wyoming, rated No. 10 in the United Press poll, to win the regional.

Kansas was paired against Santa Clara in the first round of the championships, while St. John's was matched against Illinois. Santa Clara, led by future New York Knicks star Kenny Sears, upset UCLA in the first round of the Far West tournament and was considered a darkhorse, along with the Redmen, against higher ranked opponents.

Kansas was led by 6-9 Clyde Lovellette, who was rated the best of the pivotmen of his day and a unanimous All-America choice. His 28.6 points per game average coming into the playoffs was easily best among individual performers. The Redmen's Zawoluk scored at an 18-point pace, below his average of the previous season, but he was known for having his best games against the best opposition.

In a rather unique arrangement, the St. John's and Illinois teams traveled together to the West Coast on a propeller-driven chartered airplane. Of course, that meant a much longer trip for the Redmen by several hundred miles, and the plane encountered severe turbulence in the west. All of those aboard worried less about their up-coming basketball game and more about surviving the trip. After deplaning safely in Seattle, players and coaches were talking more about the plane ride than game strategy.

Both squads had regained their land legs, as the Redmen faced their Illini in the first game at Seattle. It was close all the way, with neither team holding a lead of any size. With the score tied at 59-all in the last minute, Macgilvray made good on a shot from short range, and then stole the ball as the Illini were trying to set-up a game tying basket.

Santa Clara was no match for Kansas in the other semi-final, as Lovellette continued his individual dominance, and the Jayhawks won by a score of 74-55. Therefore, St. John's, which had eliminated both the No. 1 and No. 2 teams in the nation, now faced the eighth-ranked team for the national championship.

Although Kansas had all-around fine talent, the task facing St. John's in this final was similar to one the McGuire would encounter 15 years later against the Jayhawks. In 1957 it would be to stop a great center, Wilt Chamberlain--but this game would find them trying to deal with Lovellette.

Matched against Lovellette, Zawoluk played an inspired game, but he was giving up three inches in height and the Jayhawks center ruled the day with 33 points to Zawoluk's 20. McMahon added 13 points for the Redmen, but that wasn't enough to make a difference, as the Jayhawks took the championship game, 80-63.

Lovellette's 33 points gave him a total of 141 for the playoffs, an average of over 35 per game, earning him Most Valuable player honors. It also gave him a national record 1,888 career points, not much greater than Zawoluk's 1,826, which still ranked third among Redmen all-time scorers as of 1994.

Zawoluk was a consensus second team All-America choice, which was outstanding, considering the superstars of that year. The All-America first team included Lovellette, Chuck Darling of Iowa, Mark Workman of West Virginia, Dick Groat of Duke and Cliff Hagan of Kentucky.

The 1951-52 season turned out to be McGuire's final one at St. John's, although nothing that brought about his departure was in the works at the end of the season.

The McGuires' only son, Frank, Jr., had been born in January, and it was discovered that he had cerebral palsy. The relationship between Frankie and his father throughout the years became a story in its own.

McGuire and the Media

Besides gaining experience in performing as a college coach, McGuire learned a lesson or two in dealing with the media-particularly the New York City press.

MCGUIRE: "How important is media relations? Some coaches rate it 35 to 40 percent of their job. It's the coach's way of communicating with the public. So you can't be fighting the media, because, as we have said before, you will run out of blood before they run out of ink.

"I was fortunate to have some writers with whom I got along very well, and they were most helpful to me. Dick Young with the New York Daily News; Ike Gillis of the New York Post; and Tom Paprocki of the Associated Press. Those are just three that come to mind many years later.

"In 1948 we played City College in Madison Square Garden, and it was my first year as coach at St. John's, and this was a very big game. City College was one of the top teams in the East and had made it to the finals of the East Regional the year before. City College was coached by Nat Holman, who was one of the original Celtics and was an early member of the Hall of Fame.

"Not counting our first game with an alumni team, we had won only two and lost six before the game with City College, but we had been improving as the team became more accustomed to my style of play. We won the game (38-34), and it was close all the way. But it was a big upset for St. John's.

"When the game was over I went to the dressing room and congratulated my players, then I went on to Leone's, where a lot of the writers went after games.

"Pap called me aside and said, 'You feel good, don't you? Well, tomorrow you won't feel so good when you look at the papers.' I really didn't know what he was talking about, but Pap explained it to me.

"Toward the end of the game I had Dick McGuire hold the ball, because we had the lead, and, somehow, that affected the point spread. Pap told me, 'All the boys lost a ton of money.' You wouldn't believe the write-ups we got the next day!

"I always remembered that and played it straight on anything that would affect the outcome of a game. Such as one time when Zeke Zawoluk had an ingrown toenail and could hardly walk, it was so sore. So, we called the wire services and told them that Zawoluk couldn't play. The doctor with Madison Square Garden looked at it, and said, 'This guy is in bad shape-he can't play tomorrow.' So, we reported it.

"The point spread went 'way down, but they lanced Zeke's toe, and he played. So, all the handicappers said, 'The big bum played,' but the game had been taken off the board, so there was no betting on it, fortunately.

"So, from then on, if we had a player, especially a star that wasn't going to be able to play, we always announced it, so we couldn't be accused of withholding information, for whatever reason.

"I always had a policy of allowing the media to talk to the players only about the game itself. Otherwise, I had the understanding that I created the stories and that anything would come from me.

"I've been out of coaching for over a decade now, and during that time the pressure exerted by the media has been more and more. With the increased television coverage of basketball, newspaper writers have had to change their approach. By the time they come out the next day, the game itself is old news, and the newspapers are looking for something else. Mostly explanations of why things happened the way they did. They want to find something that television cameras didn't."

CHAPTER THREE

THE SAGA OF SOLLY WALKER

The telephone conversation between McGuire and Kentucky basketball coach Adolph Rupp concerning the scheduled game between their two schools at Lexington, Ky. was routine. That is until McGuire said, "Adolph, I want to remind you that we had a black kid on our freshman team, and he will be on our varsity next season."

Rupp paused a moment and drawled, "Now Frank, you know you can't bring that boy here."

McGuire calmly replied, "Well, just cancel the game, because he's a member of our team, and he goes anywhere and everywhere we go."

"Now Frank," Rupp replied, "we don't try to change the way you say Mass in church, and you shouldn't come down here and try to change our ways, either." Segregation--or Jim Crow laws--was still very much in force in Kentucky, and there had never been a college game involving an integrated team in that state--or in the South.

A repeat of this conversation between McGuire and Rupp took place again during the summer, with the same position of McGuire--our entire team goes to Lexington, or cancel the game.

The player in question was a young man named Solly Walker, who was the first of his race to play for St. John's. He had played for Boys High School in Brooklyn under Mickey Fisher and attracted the attention of McGuire, who was building a national power at St. John's.

When coaches of other college teams in the city heard that McGuire was interested in Walker, they also began recruiting him.

Walker, now principal of Manhattan High School on 52nd Street, recalls that he was originally most interested in Duquesne University in Pittsburgh. "I was voted the most valuable player in New York City in my senior year, and this attracted the attention of the colleges in the area, but Duquesne was my first choice until Coach McGuire visited with me and my family.

"My parents really liked Coach McGuire, and he convinced us that it would be in my best interest to go to college in New York City. So I decided to enroll at St. John's. The fact that I would be the first black player there was not a concern. In fact, I don't know that it was ever mentioned."

Walker enrolled at St. John's, majoring in business, and he became an important member of the basketball team.

Kentucky was having its usual great basketball season under Rupp, and the Redmen of St. John's posed one of the major tests, as the encounter in Lexington neared. The St. John's squad boarded the train in Grand Central Station and made their way toward Kentucky—a day trip away.

McGuire made no mention of the conversation with Rupp about the segregation policies in the Bluegrass State.

MCGUIRE: "When we arrived at Lexington, I called Rupp, who was a good man just caught in the rules and customs of his place and times. Rupp told me that I should stay out at the freight yard with Solly. Well, that isn't exactly how he said it! I told him that, if Solly couldn't stay with the team, then we'd all get on the train and head back to New York. Otherwise, we're coming to the hotel.

"'All right,' Rupp told me, 'you're on your own.' We didn't run into any more trouble, although Solly wasn't welcomed with open arms! The game started, and on the tip-off two Kentucky players sandwiched Solly and just about killed him. No foul! But he managed to play the entire game, which we lost by about forty points!" *(Actual score: Kentucky 81-St. John's 40)*

Walker recalled that Kentucky was a great team with outstanding personnel, including Cliff Hagan, Bill Spivey and Frank Ramsey. "They were very aggressive—played hard but there was no taunting or any bad comments. They gave a lot, but they could also take it," Walker remembered. "In that game I hit a couple of shots and then I went to the middle and ended up in about the fifteenth row!"

Very quietly, history had been made in this game, as Solly Walker had become the first black player to play on an integrated team in the South.

MCGUIRE: "On the way home I told the players not to say a word about what had happened. And they didn't. After all, I wasn't trying to change anything or make a social statement. However, I always went to bat for my players and insisted that they be treated fairly. I expected them to be loyal to me, and I was loyal to them."

McGuire pointed out that none of his recruiting activities were based on anything other than getting players who were good athletes, could do college work and become good people.

MCGUIRE: "When I became head coach at St. John's following World War II (1948) black players began to appear on some of the college teams in New York. For example, Sherman White was a star for Clair Bee's Long Island team, but the All-America teams were all-white until Seton

Hall's Walker Dukes made the Associated Press and United Press first teams in 1953.

"Before the war a good percentage of the better players in the New York area were Jewish, even at Catholic institutions such as St. John's. In fact, when I started recruiting Catholics at St. John's I was accused of getting rid of the Jews. But actually Joe Lapchick had started that before I followed him as the coach there.

"Well, blacks and whites were always together at Catholic schools, and there was no rule or policy against blacks on their basketball teams; it was just slow developing. Although black players dominate college and professional basketball today, there weren't that many good black players around before the war. Especially good black players who qualified academically for college.

"I never said to myself that we needed to have a black player at St. John's, and there was no pressure from anyone to recruit one. It was really odd that St. John's didn't have one before then. I heard about Solly Walker and went to see him play. After watching him I felt that Solly was the best player around New York that year. The subject of race never came up in our conversations, and, if he was concerned about being the first--and only at the time--black player at St. John's, he never showed it.

"Nobody made a big deal over Solly coming to St. John's. He was simply accepted as a student and basketball team member.

"Things went well for our team after the Kentucky game, which, fortunately, was not typical of our season. Still it wasn't the end of incidents surrounding the presence of a black player on our team.

"We traveled to Raleigh, North Carolina for the NCAA regionals, which was one of four regionals in the playoff format of that day. The regional also involved Kentucky, Penn State and North Carolina State.

"Our train arrived at Raleigh early in the morning, and we were met by an NCAA official. He said arrangements had been made for us to have breakfast at our hotel. When we got to the hotel, the owner or manager said, 'Coach, I can't take care of that boy,' referring to Solly. I wanted to punch that NCAA guy in the face. He should have known.

"I walked over to the chef, and he told me that he could feed us in the kitchen, so Solly and I had a nice breakfast of eggs and fried potatoes in the kitchen."

Walker laughed about the incident, claiming, "We got more food than the guys out front."

Penn State had two black players on its squad--J.C. Arnell and Bill Hardy--who along with Solly Walker, were the only players of their race in the tournament. There happened to be two Catholic priests at a parish in Raleigh--Dominican missionaries--who were friends of McGuire. Their names were Father Tierney and Father Dillon.

MCGUIRE: "I shall never forget them for what they did. They told me that they would take care of Solly and the other two–that they could stay with them. I said, 'Solly, what do you want to do?'"

"They chose to go with the priests; stayed with them and had their meals with them. We didn't even test the hotel, as far as accommodating the black players was concerned."

Again McGuire told his players not to mention what had happened so as not to distract from their true mission in Raleigh, which was two-fold: 1.) To advance to the final four in Seattle and 2.) To avenge their earlier defeat at the hands of Kentucky.

St. John's slipped by Everett Case's host North Carolina State team, 60-49, in the first game of the regional, while Kentucky obliterated Penn State, 82-54, positioning them only three games away from a second straight NCAA championship.

Walker admitted, "What happened at Lexington definitely gave us an extra incentive in the final against Kentucky." The Redmen avenged the earlier loss by downing the Wildcats, 64-57, earning a trip to Seattle.

St. John's defeated second-ranked Illinois, 61-59, and had a shot at the NCAA championship against Kansas, coached by Phog Allen and led by 6-9 Clyde Lovellette, who was a giant of his day. Kansas won the championship game, 80-63, but it firmly established St. John's as a national power and McGuire as a rising star in the coaching profession.

As it turned out, the NCAA final was the last game McGuire coached at St. John's, as he accepted the job as head coach at the University of North Carolina, where he would eventually avenge the NCAA final loss to Kansas.

Solly Walker continued his career at St. John's under McGuire's successor, Alfred DeStefano. Walker was named co-captain of St. John's for his senior season (1954-55), when he was named to the All-Metropolitan New York team and voted the most valuable player for the Redmen. He was picked by the New York Knicks in the NBA draft, but the offer of a $7,500 a year contract didn't excite him enough to entice him to the Knicks' camp.

Unable to land a satisfactory job in the business world, Walker went to work for the New York City Youth Board, teaching and coordinating youth activities. In 1961 he became a school teacher at Thomas Jefferson High School, going eventually into the field of Special Education and, in 1976, to his present position as Principal of Manhattan High School.

Walker's relationship with McGuire has never ended, taking on a new meaning in 1975, when McGuire assisted Walker's daughter, Charlhan. in enrolling at the University of South Carolina Law School. She earned her law degree and is now a director with the Public Service Commission in Scranton, Pennsylvania. She is now Charlhan Walker Davis.

Out of her law school experience came another South Carolina and McGuire connection, as Alex English, who had gone to the airport to greet her for

McGuire when she arrived to enroll at law school, has become a friend of the family. English visits the Walkers in New York on occasions.

Long before his daughter came to South Carolina, Solly Walker had his own Palmetto State connection, having been born at Branchville. His family moved to New York when he was a small child.

Walker said that the willingness of McGuire to help his daughter get into law school is typical of his relationships with people. After Walker's recent installation in the St. John's Sports Hall of Fame, he wrote his aging coach a letter to once again thank him for "always being there when I need you."

"His interest in me as a person, not just a ball player, meant a lot to me and has helped me through my later life. It if were not for Coach McGuire I wouldn't be here," Walker reflected.

MCGUIRE: "In reminiscing over my years at St. John's I look back on those incidents that occurred four decades ago as just stages in the evolution of the great game of basketball. And, for that matter, society in general. When I watch and read about the great black players of today and observe the acceptance they receive--in the South as much as anywhere--I reflect on those times back in the early fifties. That's when Solly Walker and others like him quietly blazed a trail that ultimately revolutionized the game of basketball."

CHAPTER FOUR

TAKING THE TAR HEELS TO THE TOP

While St. John's was basking in the national spotlight after reaching the NCAA finals in 1952, things were not so rosy at the University of North Carolina. The Tar Heels had experienced their second straight losing season under head coach Tom Scott and finished 11th in the Southern Conference regular season standing, failing to qualify for the conference championship tournament. The season also saw them lose all six games against other members of the North Carolina "Big Four," Duke, N.C. State and Wake Forest.

North Carolina fans were getting restless, because they couldn't see much hope of competing satisfactorily against the powerful teams assembled by Everett Case at N.C. State. The Tar Heels had lost 15 games in a row to the Wolfpack.

Frank McGuire's reputation as a basketball coach was greatly enhanced by his great 1951-52 team at St. John's, and it had not gone unnoticed by William Carmichael, chancellor at the University of North Carolina. Carmichael had seen McGuire's team beat N.C. State, 60-49, on the Wolfpack's home floor in the 1952 Eastern Regional and was also present for the regional final when St. John's defeated top-ranked Kentucky to advance to the Final Four.

Carmichael had lived in New York, played basketball at North Carolina and was a Catholic, which enabled him to relate very well to McGuire and his background.

MCGUIRE: "Billy Carmichael called me and asked me if I would be interested in becoming the basketball coach at North Carolina. I knew that Tom Scott had been fired, so I wouldn't be in a position of taking a job away from another coach. I told him that I'd think about it.

"When I was in the Navy I had been stationed at Chapel Hill, so I was familiar with the area and the school.

"Billy Carmichael told me that they needed a coach who could compete with Everett Case, and he felt that I was the coach that could do it.

"I asked myself, 'Why leave New York?' I had lived there all of my life, I had a good job coaching the school where I had graduated, and this is where all my friends were.

_"However, when I thought about it in terms of my family, particularly my son, Frankie, there were some negatives. We lived on the top floor of an apartment building in the Village, while St. John's was over on Long Island. It was very complicated to take Frankie anywhere. He couldn't eat out in New York City.

"When I went down to Chapel Hill to talk about the job, my friend Harry Gotkin went with me. Everything went well, and they offered me the job.

"So, I made the decision to go to Chapel Hill. When I say that I made the decision, I mean exactly that. I didn't ask anybody to advise me on what to do.

"My decision was based on what was best for my family. I didn't think of anything else. We could live in a house for the first time, and have a swimming pool where Frankie could exercise. And we could go around town without it being such a hassle. It was just much better family surroundings than a big city provides.

"As for my professional career, I hadn't given that much thought until the decision was made. Then I wondered if I would be able to get New York players to go south. I didn't have enough sense to think about that before, but the decision was made, and it was up to me to make a success of it."

Once the decision was made to go to Chapel Hill, McGuire then turned his attention to the challenges that were ahead. Although it wasn't in his written contract, it was no secret that he had been brought to North Carolina to beat Everett Case, who had dominated the Southern Conference since he began coaching at State in 1946-47.

McGuire knew that recruiting was the key to accomplishing that goal. While Case built his program with Indiana high school talent, McGuire would depend on players from his native New York metropolitan area.

MCGUIRE: "I knew all of the high school coaches in New York and the style of play they coached—which was similar to mine. It wouldn't be easy at first to convince boys that they should leave a big metropolitan area and go down to a small Southern town like Chapel Hill.

"The first player I recruited from the area was Jerry Vayda from Bayonne, New Jersey, and that proved to be the ice-breaker. A lot of the players from the area were Catholic, but that didn't prove to be a problem, because they had a Catholic church at Chapel Hill, and we had a priest that traveled with us.

"However, in my first season at North Carolina freshmen were still eligible to play on the varsity, a rule that was changed the following year. We did have several good players returning from the previous team—Vince

Grimaldi, Al Lifson, Paul Likins, Jack Wallace and Bud Maddie. Tony Radovich, who developed into a steady performer, was among the freshmen on that first squad."

If Carmichael had hired Frank McGuire to beat Everett Case, he couldn't have been happier after the first encounter between the two as neighborhood rivals. Of course, St. John's had beaten State in the East Regional the previous winter, so McGuire already had a head start, and in January 1953 the two were on opposing benches in Reynolds Coliseum for the first time.

North Carolina defeated State, 70-69, in that historic first showdown between the two great coaches and builders of programs.

MCGUIRE: "I was never really close to Everett Case. Nobody was. He told me that he never wanted to shake my hand upstairs—in public. Let's shake hands down here. He didn't want us to look too friendly in public. He wanted to keep the crowd in the game.

"He wanted to look like we were enemies. 'You sell more tickets that way,' he would tell me."

Although the Tar Heels would finish their first season under McGuire with a 17-10 won-lost record, the early success against State was not typical. The Wolfpack came back by beating the Heels by 21 and 32 points, the latter coming in the Southern Conference tournament, which determined the league's only representative in the NCAA playoffs. That year even the Wolfpack would be denied that honor, as Wake Forest, led by Dickie Hemrick, upset State, 71-70 in the tournament final.

What happened off the court was the most significant development of the 1952-53 season. This is when McGuire's "underground railroad" began to build up steam.

MCGUIRE: "In my last year at St. John's there was a high school junior named Lennie Rosenbluth who had come to play for the 92nd Street YMCA team, which was coached by Hy Gotkin. Hy was a cousin of my good friend Harry Gotkin, and he told Harry about this gangling six foot five-inch boy who he thought was a great prospect.

"At that time the high school coaches in New York City were on strike, so good players, such as Rosenbluth, were looking for any organized team they could find. Many of them had to stick with playgrounds for developing their talents.

"Lennie was good enough to be invited to play in the summer league in the Catskill Mountains, where a lot of college and pro players gathered to work on their games. Rosenbluth was so good that he even attracted the attention of NBA scouts.

"At that time I was considering my move to North Carolina or another institution that had expressed an interest in my becoming the basketball coach there. We had pretty much sold Lennie on the idea of playing for me, wherever I might be coaching, but he still had another year of high

school to complete before he could go anywhere.

"With the high school situation in New York as it was, it was determined that it would be best for Rosenbluth to spend his senior season somewhere else. So he was enrolled at Staunton Military Academy in Virginia for his senior year.

"He came to North Carolina for the 1953-54 school year, but we were now in the new Atlantic Coast Conference, which was entering its first year of competition. The new conference rules did not allow freshmen to compete on varsity teams, so Rosenbluth spent his first year in that type of competition. It was like a man playing among boys.

"Rosenbluth was the first big recruit in our building program, but it would take another good recruiting class to give us the depth and quality of talent we needed to take our team to the next level. And that level was to move us ahead of State in the ACC."

Case had begun "basketball fever" in North Carolina, but the presence of McGuire at the state university raised the temperature, and McGuire predicted that basketball would replace football as the number one sport in the Tar Heel state. Rivalries other than Case versus McGuire were developing, and the crowds were getting more and more into the game.

MCGUIRE: "What they called the Big Four in North Carolina--the University, State, Duke and Wake Forest--were natural rivals. They were not only in the same state, but they were only a few miles apart. Only ten miles separated Chapel Hill and Durham, and Wake Forest was just outside Raleigh before moving to Winston-Salem.

"North Carolina played its home games in Woolen Gymnasium, which would seat around 5,000 spectators at the most. The crowd was very close to the court, so that sometimes worked to our advantage.

"Once when we were playing Wake Forest in Woolen Gym, a group of our football players sat behind the Deacon's bench and really gave them a hard time. We learned that it works both ways, because when we went to play Wake on their home court, the Wake Forest football players came and sat behind our bench. Only they were dressed out in full pads. Some of them even came onto the court for pre-game warm-ups."

McGuire's second season at North Carolina, which was the inaugural of the Atlantic Coast Conference, was still one of rebuilding. Rosenbluth was in school, and he was scoring in astronomical figures for the freshman team, but that was no help to the varsity. The Tar Heels had an overall record of 11-10, including a 5-6 mark in the ACC, good for fifth place in the standings. McGuire went up against Case's Wolfpack three times, losing twice during the regular schedule by margins of seven and nine points. However, the Tar Heels came close to upsetting the 'Pack' in the first round of the championship tournament. State squeaked by, 52-51, and later won the ACC spot in the NCAA playoffs by beating Wake Forest, 82-80, in an overtime final.

While McGuire was laying the groundwork for his program, other major threats were developing within the ACC. In this first league season Hal Bradley's Duke team finished 15th in the AP poll, with a 22-6 record, and Maryland, under Bud Millikan, was 23-7 and ranked 20th.

Meanwhile, the media were looking for anything they could find to build-up the McGuire-Case rivalry. If there was not a handshake after a game, a great deal was made of it. In State's 57-48 win over North Carolina in Raleigh, they held the ball for the final six minutes. There were no rules to prevent that.

When the two coaches failed to shake hands following the game, McGuire felt that it was up to the winning coach to make the first move, and Case insisted that it should be the losing coach. When asked about it, McGuire reminded the media that Case wasn't too big on shaking hands on the court, anyhow, and that he would tell him, "Let people think we're mad at each other."

THE 1954-55 SEASON

MCGUIRE: **"While we wanted to win every game we could in these first two seasons, I knew that it would take time to build solidly, and the recruiting of Lennie Rosenbluth was the real beginning. And, although we still had a winning record in our first ACC season, our real hope was bringing in players who could win championships.**

"Although Rosenbluth joined the varsity for the 1954-55 season, we still lacked the depth of talent to compete the way we wanted to. The answer lay in the freshmen we had recruited that year. In fact, this was one of the best recruiting classes I ever had. It included Tommy Kearns, Joe Quigg, Pete Brennan and Bob Cunningham, all from the New York area."

This new bumper crop out of New York made the McGuire "underground railway" as famous as the one that smuggled slaves out of the South in pre-Civil War days. Someone placed a prominent sign on the University's administration building that read like that of a New York subway station: "Uptown-Downtown."

Uptown or downtown, the McGuire train was obviously running on the right track!

MCGUIRE: **"Rosenbluth was everything we had hoped for during his sophomore season, averaging 25.5 points per game and 11.7 rebounds. He was named to the first team All-ACC and led us to our first winning record in conference games. This was good enough for fourth place, pairing UNC with Wake Forest in the first round of the conference tournament."**

Wake, led by Dickie Hemric, eliminated the Tar Heels, but this didn't dampen their optimism for the future.

The sweetest victory of the year, and the most satisfying for McGuire at that point in his stay at Chapel Hill, came over State at Raleigh, 84-80. The

Wolfpack and Tar Heels had played slowdown in an earlier 47-44 win for Case's team in the annual Dixie Classic, which matched the Big Four against four nationally-prominent teams from other sections of the country. The Tar Heels had beaten Southern California and Duke in the Classic to claim third place, their best showing to date in that prestigious event.

When the Tar Heels returned to Reynolds Coliseum for a regular season game, McGuire decided to run with the Wolfpack, and it paid off. The Tar Heels celebrated after the game by cutting down the nets, a ceremony normally reserved for tournament championships. This underscored the importance of games between the two schools.

The ACC tournament loss to Wake Forest was particularly disappointing, because North Carolina had swept their regular season encounters. However, McGuire could spend a happy summer of contemplating what was to come.

THE 1955-56 SEASON
Only three freshmen came down McGuire's underground railroad for the 1955-56 season, but a stellar class of sophomores from the Big Apple joined Rosenbluth on the varsity.

When *Sports Illustrated* asked McGuire about his ability to recruit in the New York area, which included New Jersey, he answered, "All the people in New York are my friends. Nobody gets paid for helping, but everybody looks out for me. The whole police department looks for players for me. So do the high school coaches, so do the brothers at the Catholic schools. Even the waterfront looks out for me."

The passengers from up East paid dividends with the 1955-56 regular season ACC championship, as the Tar Heels won 11 of 14 conference games and were 18-5 overall. They lost to State in the Dixie Classic, but beat the Wolfpack in Woolen Gym. North Carolina had opened the season with eight straight victories, attracting attention from those who vote in the Associated Press poll, in which the Tar Heels would finish 13th. Three other ACC teams finished in the poll, including State (2nd), Wake (16th) and Duke (17th).

Rosenbluth had another sensational season, scoring at a 26.7 pace and averaging 11.4 rebounds. He was named to the second team All America by AP and UPI and was a first team All-ACC choice for the second straight year. Jerry Vayda was back for his senior season, and sophomores Kearns, Brennan and Quigg completed the Tar Heel lineup.

THE 1956-57 SEASON
The 1956-57 season for the Tar Heels became known as the "McGuire Miracle," and, as it turned out, you might make the work "miracle" plural. The Tar Heels, while rich in first team talent, did not have a deep bench.

Radovich would be eligible for only the first semester, so he would not be available for the bulk of the ACC schedule. Another blow came when Harvey Salz, a promising rising sophomore guard, dropped out of school. McGuire knew this would be a good team, but he projected that 18 regular season victories would be a realistic expectation.

North Carolina opponents had one common strategy, and that was to stop Rosenbluth. It wasn't quite that simple, and even if they did hold the Tar Heel star to a low point total, the supporting cast of Brennan, Kearns, Quigg and Cunningham were capable of compensating. In McGuire's only appearance in Madison Square Garden this season, NYU triple-teamed Rosenbluth, holding him to nine points, but the Violets still lost the game, 64-59.

The Tar Heels rolled up nine straight victories, most of them by one-sided margins, as they prepared for the Dixie Classic. Utah, which was in the process of a 19-8 season under Jack Gardner, was a 97-76 victim of North Carolina in the first round. Hal Bradley's Duke Blue Devils were 87-71 victims in the semi-finals, and the Tar Heels held off Wake Forest and its great guard combination of Jackie Murdock and Ernie Wiggins, 63-55, in the finals. This would not be the last that McGuire would hear from this Wake Forest team.

North Carolina breezed through five straight games after the Dixie Classic, and McGuire enjoyed an 83-57 win over Case's Wolfpack in Reynolds Coliseum. The Tar Heels were now into their ACC schedule and ready to face defensive-minded Maryland on February 5 at College Park.

Their first conference game on the road had resulted in a scare. In Columbia they faced South Carolina, led by the eventual NCAA scoring champion Grady Wallace, in a field house known to visiting coaches as "The Pit." Maryland coach Bud Millikan once said of the South Carolina arena, which was a sunken floor, surrounded by a short wall and iron railing, that it 'looked like they had drained the swimming pool and used it for a basketball court.'

The game would at least school the Tar Heels in something they would face several times before the campaign ended--OVERTIME! With seconds remaining, and the Tar Heels leading the Gamecocks by two points, Ray Pericola picked off a Tar Heel pass and drove in for a basket that sent the game into an extra period. The Heels prevailed in the overtime to escape with a 90-86 victory.

At College Park McGuire's team was greeted by the largest crowd ever to witness an ACC game, as 14,000 jammed into Cole Field House, which had an official capacity of around 12,000. Maryland used a deliberate style of play that tested the patience of their opponents and resulted in their conference-leading record of holding their opposition to an average of 61 points per game.

For most of the game the appropriately named Terrapins kept the game at a turtle's pace and held on to a 53-49 lead with less than two minutes remaining. With no shot clock or five-second rule to force the Terps to do anything risky, it appeared that North Carolina was doomed to its first defeat in 17 games.

MCGUIRE: "We called a timeout and I wanted to prepare my team for the worst. I told them, 'It looks like we can't catch'em. But I want you to do this--be sure not to make any mistakes, and if we lose, I want you to go down like true champions. If we lose--we lose just like we win. Be good losers as well as good winners, and people will think just as much of you.'

"While they were worrying about Rosenbluth we got baskets out of Cunningham and Kearns, and they missed a free throw. The regulation game ended at 53-all, and we went overtime for a second time in the season. Kearns hit a key basket near the end of overtime, and we won the game. (65-61).

"I told the press afterward, 'These guys don't have enough sense to get rattled--nothing bothers them.' And Rosenbluth turned to me and said, 'Coach' we only have 15 more to go.!'

"I guess you'd say that this was the turning point in the season, or at least prepared us for things to come. It gave the team confidence and made them believe that, regardless of the situation, we could come back and win.

"Anytime you win consistently you need to have Lady Luck on your side. She sat on our bench in the next game against Duke in Woolen Gym. Duke came back on a goal by Bobby Joe Harris with 21 seconds left on the clock. This tied the game at 73, but Harris looked at the scoreboard, and the score hadn't been changed from 73-71 in our favor. He thought his team was two points behind, so he intentionally fouled Kearns with 16 seconds left. Tommy made the free throws to win the game.

"This strengthened our belief that we were a team of destiny."

At this point the polls ranked North Carolina number one in the nation, and their 18 wins against no losses made the choice easy. Still the other coaches in the Big Four were not yet convinced. Case said, "They're a fine ball club, but I believe someone will knock 'em off before the end of the season."

Duke's Bradley observed, "North Carolina has a fine team, and I'm glad to see them ranked number one. It looks good for our conference. But I don't think they have a great team. They don't have the experience, and they've had too many scares."

Fortunately for the Tar Heels, "scares" don't count in the won-lost column, and they were reminded of the old adage, "good teams find a way to win, and poor teams find a way to lose." This was a GOOD team in every sense of the word, with one possible criticism.

Observers questioned McGuire's practice of basically playing his five starters, using substitutes sparingly. It was predicted that this would catch-up with the Tar Heels in the latter part of the season and in tournament play, if they got that far.

MCGUIRE: We didn't have a strong bench, but even if we had, I would have done the same thing. Go with my five best. You don't want outstanding players sitting there watching the game."

The Tar Heels had six games remaining on their regular schedule, and they won rather comfortably, with two exceptions. The Wake Forest team that UNC had defeated by eight points in the Dixie Classic seemed to always be able to rise to new heights against the Tar Heels. It was no fluke, because this was a talented Wake Forest team that, as was pointed out earlier, was ranked in the top 20.

North Carolina was able to defeat the Deacons by three points at Chapel Hill and by five at Winston-Salem for their third win of the season over Wake.

Duke players claimed that the scoreboard operator had cost them the game at Chapel Hill, although that speculation would have to assume that the Tar Heels would not have scored in the final 16 seconds and that the Blue Devils would have prevailed in overtime. They vowed that things would be different when McGuire's team came to Durham.

The result of that game was an 86-72 Tar Heel win, ending the ACC season and giving the Tar Heels the top seeding in the tournament in Raleigh. The Tar Heels had performed well on that floor, winning the Dixie Classic and beating State by 16 points. They later routed the Wolfpack at Chapel Hill by 19.

North Carolina had no trouble with Clemson in their opening game of the championship event, beating the Tigers, 81-61. Rosenbluth scored a tournament record 45 points in the victory, canning 19 field goals and seven free throws. Murdock led Wake to an opening round win over State, leading to a semi-finals match-up with the Tar Heels on Friday. Maryland beat Virginia, and South Carolina downed Duke in other first round games.

The battle between UNC and Wake was a classic. Led by Jack Williams, the Deacons kept the game close all the way, and going into the final seconds, the score was tied at 58-all. As the Tar Heels worked toward what could be a game-winning basket, there wasn't anyone among the 12,400 at the game who had any doubt as to who would take the shot.

As the deacons converged on Rosenbluth, the Tar Heels star worked his way into the upper lane, went high into the air and looped in a shot that found the bottom of the net. Again, the team of destiny had found a way to win.

After the game, a fan of Baptist-supported Wake Forest walked dejectedly up to McGuire and commented, "Coach, our Baptists from Wake Forest and your Catholics were having one helluva game, and that Jewish guy had to go and spoil it!"

The tournament final was anti-climactic, although it had the glamour of matching two members of the UPI first All-America—Rosenbluth and Wallace of South Carolina, which had eliminated Maryland in the other semi-final.

Rosenbluth outscored Wallace, 38-28, as North Carolina won easily, 95-75. Rosenbluth had a total of 106 points for the tournament, giving him another all-time record. All five Tar Heel starters were honored on the all-tournament selections, Rosenbluth and Brennan making the first team, while Kearns,

Quigg and Cunningham were named to the second unit.

The ACC tournament victory qualified North Carolina to meet Yale in the first round East Regional game in Madison Square Garden. The Eli, coached by Joe Vancisin, were no match for the Tar Heels, who dominated the game, 90-74. This earned a trip south to Philadelphia to join Syracuse, Lafayette and Canisius to determine the East Regional representative in the Final Four, to be played in Kansas City.

North Carolina outscored Canisius, which was coached by Joe Curran, 87-75, and defeated Syracuse, 67-58, running their record to 30 wins and, still, no losses.

The other teams in the Final Four were Kansas, coached by Dick Harp, San Francisco, whose coach was Phil Woolpert, and Foggy Anderson's Michigan State Spartans. Kansas had won the Midwest regional, San Francisco was the Far West champion, and Michigan State was winner of the Mideast over the third-ranked Kentucky Wildcats.

Although Kansas ranked second in the polls behind UNC, the oddsmakers favored the Wildcats to win the NCAA title. The main reason for this was the presence of seven-foot sophomore Wilt Chamberlain in the Kansas lineup. Chamberlain was in a two-way battle with South Carolina's Wallace for the national scoring title, which Wallace would win by a fraction of a point. The site of the game would also be an advantage for Kansas.

Another "McGuire miracle" would be needed in the Tar Heels' first round game against Michigan State, which was led by All-America and future NBA star Johnny Green. With the score tied at 58 and time running out in regulation, State's Jack Quiggle attempted a buzzer-beater, and the shot was good, but it was ruled that it came after time had expired, and North Carolina had dodged another bullet.

In the first overtime it again appeared that the McGuire streak would end, as Green stood at the free throw line trying to give the Spartans a three-point lead with less than a minute remaining. The shot bounced off the rim, and Brennan grabbed the rebound, drove the length of the court and laid it in to give his team another overtime opportunity. Neither team scored in the second overtime, so a third extra period was necessary.

This time the Tar Heels held the upper hand and escaped with a 74-70 victory.

MCGUIRE: "Even when we were down, I never felt like we would lose. I had so much confidence in that team, because of the way they would always come back, no matter what the situation was. They had more guts than any team I've ever seen. And there's nothing that will take the place of guts."

Led by Chamberlain, Kansas blew out San Francisco, 80-56, and went into their championship game against North Carolina well rested, compared to the Tar Heels, whose starters had gone most of the way through regulation and three overtimes in their semi-final win. Oddsmakers made Kansas an 18-point favorite, obviously considering the fatigue factor and the "home court" advantage of the Jayhawks.

MCGUIRE: "Before the game the media made it appear that it was us against Chamberlain. He dominated the coverage, just as he had dominated games. We talked about that in a meeting we had at about 3:30 the afternoon of the game.

"I looked at Tommy (Kearns) and said, 'You don't have to show up tonight, if you don't want to.' Then I turned to Joe (Quigg) and said, 'Are you afraid of Chamberlain?' Joe answered that he wasn't.

"Then I asked Tommy the same question, 'Are you afraid of Wilt?' He said, 'No.' So I looked at him very seriously and told him, 'Well, you're going to jump center against him.' After that I didn't think much about what I had said.

"After all of the pre-game ceremony and introductions were over we were ready, at last, to play basketball. The teams took the floor, and I looked out and saw Tommy walking over to jump center against Chamberlain. Compared to Tommy, who was barely 5-11, Wilt looked to be about ten feet tall.

"Wilt looked over at me on the bench as if to say, 'Are you crazy? Nobody in their right mind does that.' I had really forgotten about telling Tommy he was going to jump center, but I tried not to act surprised. So Tommy walks over and shakes hands with Wilt, just as though there was nothing unusual about the situation.

"Afterward the media gave us credit for a great psychological move and brilliant strategy. I don't know what effect it had on the game, but Wilt didn't make a basket before we had scored nine points. When the ball went up to start the game Wilt didn't even bother to jump. Years later when I was coaching Philadelphia, Wilt would often mention the situation that started the game.

"In order to reduce the effectiveness of Chamberlain, we sagged everybody on him to deny him the ball. Of course, it was no secret to Kansas what their main objective on defense should be--to stop Rosenbluth. So Dick Harp used a box-and-one on Lennie, with four defenders playing a zone, and the fifth dogging Lennie everywhere he went on the court.

"Our strategy was to play a very deliberate game on offense and not to take anything but high percentage shots. Those shots had to be from outside, because if we had gone inside, Wilt would have blocked every shot. Quigg, our center, was only 6-8, so he was at a tremendous height disadvantage against Wilt, so we had to deny him the ball as much as possible.

"Kansas laid off Cunningham--almost ignored him when we had the ball--because he was a defensive specialist and didn't take many shots. I guess you would say that the strategy of both teams worked, because both

Chamberlain and Rosenbluth were held below their averages.

"The game was close, low scoring, all the way, but we got into foul trouble early in the second half. Quigg had his fourth foul early in the period, and Lennie and Tommy had three each.

"Kansas built up a six-point lead, so Harp decided to protect it by using our strategy and play slow down--to hold the ball and run time off the clock. This actually worked to our advantage, because we had people in foul trouble, and this also allowed us to rest our starters, who had to play most of the game. We managed to close the gap, and we tied it up at the end of regulation to send the game into overtime. However, Rosenbluth had fouled out with a couple of minutes remaining, and we had our backs to the wall.

"The regulation game ended at 46-all, and in the first overtime each team scored only one basket, and we were tied at the end of the period. In the second overtime neither team scored, as both of us played very cautiously and wouldn't take anything but a sure shot, because one miss could be fatal in a game like that.

"With ten seconds left in the third overtime Kansas had a one-point lead, but we had the ball. Quigg had the ball at the top of the key. He faked a jump shot then drove the lane against Chamberlain. As Joe put up a shot a Kansas player reached in and fouled him.

"That put Joe on the line with a chance to tie or put us up by a point. So I called timeout. Joe was a good foul shooter, but he had missed his only other chance earlier in the game. I looked at Joe and said, 'Joe are you nervous?' He answered, 'No coach, but you are!' And he was right.

"Then I said matter-of-factly, 'As soon as we make these free throws, be sure to get back on defense, because they still have some time.'

"Quigg put the free throws in--bing, bing--Kansas came down the court. Nobody had to guess what they were going to do. They tried to pass the ball to Chamberlain, but Quigg, who had four fouls, batted the ball away. Kearns picked up the ball, took one dribble then threw it as high in the air as he could, as time ran off the clock. It was over!

"Asked about the way he ended the game, Kearns said that he had seen Hot Rod Hundley (West Virginia) do that one time at the end of a game.

"We had about 1,500 fans who had followed us to Kansas City, and everybody was celebrating, not only winning the NCAA championship, but setting the record for winning the most games--32--without a loss. Kentucky was 25-0 when they won the championship in 1954.

"I wanted to show my appreciation to our fans, so I threw a victory party in a Kansas City hotel that cost us $1,500. Our athletic director felt that the amount was excessive, so when we got back to Chapel Hill, I had to pay $58 out of my pocket for the roquefort dressing, which was considered unnecessary! But it was worth it.

"When we flew back into the Raleigh-Durham airport we were greeted by a huge crowd of fans and students, who went running out onto the runway and delayed our landing for a few minutes.

"When we got off the plane, the crowd carried several of the players all the way to the terminal on their shoulders. It was a wild scene, but we enjoyed every second of it."

Sometime later, appreciative North Carolina supporters went a step farther by pitching in and buying McGuire a new baby blue and white Cadillac, and the school awarded him a new five year contract with a salary increase.

For Rosenbluth it was a heady end to a brilliant career as he was named national player of the year and, naturally, to every All-America team. He set a number of new UNC scoring records, including 895 points for the season and a 28.0 average, and a career scoring average of 26.9, all of which held up through the 1993-94 season. His 2,045 career points are also still third best for the Tar Heels.

Of course, Rosenbluth was ACC player of the year, ranked second in scoring and averaged a respectable 8.8 rebounds. Kearns was also on the All-ACC first team, and Brennan was named to the second team.

The pro scouts were not exceptionally high on Rosenbluth--nor were they excited about South Carolina's Wallace, who had edged Chamberlain for the national scoring title. Rosenbluth formed a team of former UNC stars and traveled the state of North Carolina, playing exhibitions for two seasons. He later became a high school coach, first at Wilson, N.C., and later in Miami, Fl., where he compiled a 378-126 record at Coral Gables and won a state championship.

Mixed in with a group of Catholics, Rosenbluth was once urged by McGuire to say a "Hail Mary" before taking a crucial free throw. Rosenbluth said that he didn't know how, so Brennan said, "Okay, we'll say the Hail Mary; you make the free throw." It worked!

THE 1957-58 SEASON

To say that McGuire had a hard act to follow in the 1957-58 season would be a masterpiece of understatement. It would be the hardest in the history of college basketball! Rosenbluth was gone, but the other four starters would return--Brennan, Quigg, Kearns and Cunningham. However, Quigg suffered a broken leg and would be lost for the entire season.

Who would take Rosenbluth's place? Nobody. However, McGuire had a talented sophomore, Lee Shaffer, a bulky 6-7 inside player who had impressed with his play for the Tar Heel freshmen. He wasn't from New York, but he came from Pittsburgh, and that was close enough.

The winning streak would end at 37 in Lexington, Kentucky, where they participated in the Kentucky Invitational, along with Minnesota and West Virginia. The Tar Heels beat the Gophers in the first round for their 37th straight victory.

The next night they encountered a West Virginia team that would end this season as the top-ranked team in both polls, and the miracles ended. Led by a sharp-shooting sophomore named Jerry West, the Mountaineers won, 75-64.

Like true champions the Tar Heels bounced back to win the Dixie Classic by downing St. Louis University, coached by Eddie Hickey, Duke and N.C. State. Another streak was underway.

This string ended at six games, as Maryland played a surprising up-tempo game, at least for them, and outscored North Carolina, 74-61, at College Park. This loss would be later avenged at Chapel Hill, but the Tar Heels lost twice to Duke and once to State to finish their ACC schedule at 10-4, good enough for second place behind the Blue Devils in the regular season standings. The Tar Heels did equal their highest single-game point total by beating McGuire's future team, South Carolina, 115-88, in Columbia.

Once again the Tar Heels made it to the finals of the league tournament by beating Clemson and State. Maryland, which had finished fourth in the standings, downed Virginia in its first round game, then upset top-seeded Duke in overtime to face UNC for the title.

Things went well in the first half of the final, with the Tar Heels leading, 31-27, in an expected low-scoring game. However, the roof fell in on McGuire's defending champions in the second half, as the Terps, led by Charlie McNeil, scored an amazing 59 points in the second half to win, 86-74.

The Tar Heels were in monumental foul trouble for much of the second half, as seven of them finished the game with four each. A total of 33 were called against UNC, and the Terps responded by making 40 of 52 free throws. That proved to be the margin of victory.

North Carolina had a 19-7 record to show for McGuire's sixth campaign at Chapel Hill.

MCGUIRE: "We were flying too high and had to come down to earth sooner or later. I believe we lost our chances of repeating as national champions when Joe Quigg went to the hospital. On top of that, his replacement, Danny Lotz, was lost for eight games because of an injury. We just didn't have the depth of talent to compensate for that.

"It was still a good season, and we brought in a couple of freshmen from New York that I felt could really help us the next season. They were York Larese and Doug Moe."

Another member of that freshman team was Lou Brown, who would figure in the Tar Heels' future basketball fortunes, but in a negative sense.

THE 1958-59 SEASON

Brennan and Kearns were missing from the squad, as the Tar Heels prepared for the 1958-59 season, but Shaffer was joined by Moe and Larese to give McGuire a strong nucleus with which to meet the challenges of an ever strengthening conference. Shaffer had averaged 11 points and six rebounds per game as a sophomore, and Harvey Salz, who returned to the University after having dropped out of school, had a ten point average.

McGuire saw his team come out of the starting blocks with a vengeance, winning 17 of their first 18 games. beating defending champ Maryland and taking two games over Case's Wolfpack. The only loss came in the Dixie Classic to third-ranked Michigan State. However, UNC came back to beat fourth-ranked Cincinnati to take third place.

North Carolina finished its regular season with an 18-3 record and tied with State at 12-2 for the best ACC record. In the conference tournament the Tar Heels disposed of Clemson, 93-69, and Duke, 74-71, to reach the final against State, which had beaten South Carolina by three points in overtime and Virginia by three in regulation.

Reaching the championship game assured North Carolina of a bid to the NCAA's because State was ineligible. This was State's third of four seasons on NCAA probation because of serious rules violations concerning the recruitment of Louisiana high school star Jackie Moreland. It was found that State had promised Moreland incentives that included over $200 a year for clothing, an annual gift of $1,000 and a college education for his girl friend.

The tournament championship game proved to be no more than a required formality, as State ran away, 80-56. The Wolfpack seemed to have extra incentive, because of their probation, while North Carolina had it made. McGuire pulled his starters for much of the game to rest them for the NCAA first round game to be played three days later in New York City. A disgusted fan went backstage at Reynolds Coliseum and cut off the lights in protest. It took eight minutes to get them back on.

MCGUIRE: "It wasn't as if we didn't care about winning the game, because we did. Actually State won it with our regulars on the floor. They had a big lead midway through the second half, and that's when I decided to rest my starters. This was Saturday night, and we had to play again Tuesday in New York.

"It was no attempt to take anything away from State's victory. They just seemed to have more incentive than we did and played harder. And, remember, they had a great team. Good enough to be ranked fifth in the nation."

In the East regional the Tar Heels met a Navy team coached by McGuire's very good friend, Ben Carnevale. It was Navy's day, and the Midshipmen prevailed, 76-63, in what was considered the biggest upset of the playoffs.

UPI ranked North Carolina sixth in its final poll, while AP ranked it 20th, as the final won-lost record of 20-5. Larese and Moe were both named to the All-ACC first team, and Shaffer, to the second team, and Larese was elected to the AP All-America third team.

MCGUIRE: "As basketball in the ACC became more and more competitive, the fans became more involved in the games, and this created a very hostile atmosphere. Ugly incidents involving players and fans became more numerous, and this was a big concern of ours.

"A number of fights between players had occurred, some of them resulting in reprimands from the commissioner, and sportsmanship among fans was pretty bad.

"At N.C. State's home games, when they introduced the players, they would turn off the lights and follow each player as he was introduced out to the middle of the court with a spotlight. In our 1958 game in Reynolds Coliseum they started the player introductions, and Pete Brennan was first. As the spotlight followed Pete on the floor, he was greeted by boos from 12,000 spectators.

"So I decided that no other North Carolina player would be subjected to that, and I told them just to stay beside me at the bench. When the second player's name was called out, the spotlight couldn't find him, so it just focused our group at the bench. That didn't keep the crowd from booing, but it wasn't concentrated on any individual.

"Earlier in the season I had taken the public address microphone and asked our crowd to show the Duke team good sportsmanship while they were playing us in Woolen Gym. Unfortunately, Duke came back and won the game--only one of four conference games we lost that year. So our fans thought that behaving themselves might have had something to do with our losing.

"When I came to Chapel Hill the football team would always sit behind the visiting team's bench and give them a hard time the entire game. I put a stop to that and tried to create a more sportsmanlike atmosphere in our gym.

"There were a number of incidents involving other ACC teams, and I'm not trying to say that we were any better than the others. We did make an effort to encourage students and players to be more mature in how they approached the game.

"One incident that didn't involve our team, but at which we were present, occurred in the 1959 Dixie Classic. Cincinnati, which had the great All-American Oscar Robertson, was playing Wake Forest. Robertson and Wake's Dave Budd were involved in a scuffle that received undue publicity, because Robertson was black, and there were no black players on ACC teams at that time. But it still gave our conference some very negative national publicity."

THE 1959-60 SEASON

The most significant newcomer to the North Carolina varsity in the 1959-60 season was Donnie Walsh, a sophomore backcourt player out of Riverdale, N.Y. With Shaffer, Larese and Moe returning, the preseason polls again had the Tar Heels among the favorites to win the ACC championship and present a challenge nationally.

The core of State's fine team of the year before had graduated, and NCAA probation was having a telling effect on Case's recruiting. His top assistant, Vic

Bubas, had been lured away to the head coach position at Duke, and the Wolfpack program was in a downturn.

Wake Forest suddenly became the leading threat to the Tar Heels, as they added two great sophomores, guard Billy Packer and center Len Chappell to Bones McKinney's squad.

Despite back to back losses to Kentucky and St. Louis in the Kentucky Invitational, the Tar Heels put together an impressive season. They lost twice to Wake Forest, which earned a ranking of 19th in the final AP poll, but the only hard-to-understand loss was to South Carolina, 85-81, in the second annual North-South Doubleheader in the new Charlotte Coliseum.

With a 12-2 ACC record, the Tar Heels tied with Wake for the "regular season championship." In the tournament at Raleigh, North Carolina easily defeated Virginia, 84-63, but fell victim to a Duke team that they had beaten by margins of 22 and 27 points during the regular season. Duke won, 71-69, thanks mainly to a 30-point scoring night by Carroll Youngkin who wasn't normally a scorer but was used mostly for his rebounding ability.

The Blue Devils maintained their momentum from this game to upset Wake Forest, 63-59, and win the league's place in the NCAA playoffs. The Blue Devils, who had entered the ACC tournament with a record of 12-10, continued to play well in the East Regional, downing Princeton and St. Joseph's before falling to NYU in the championship game.

Although ranked 14th in the final UPI poll with an 18-6 record, the Tar Heels were again denied post-season play. Larese and Shaffer were both named to the All-ACC first team, and Shaffer was a 3rd team selection on the All-America squad.

However, the real disappointment of the season was a revelation of what had been transpiring off the court over several years. In a widespread investigation of college basketball, it was determined that at least 54 games across the country had been fixed, and 50 players were involved, representing 25 schools.

One of the players charged was North Carolina's Lou Brown, who was identified along with four players from N.C. State. They were granted immunity in return for cooperating with the court in testifying against the accused bribe suspects. The players were later indicted and convicted and given suspended sentences.

A number of men from throughout the East were convicted and given prison sentences.

MCGUIRE: "I was stunned. I had no idea that this sort of thing was going on. There was a point-shaving scandal back in the early 1950's, including the Long Island team coached by my good friend Clair Bee. Clair was heartbroken, and the school was so concerned that it abolished basketball at Long Island for the next six years.

"It was like being let down by a member of your family. They aren't strangers, but young men you look in the eye and believe in. I was just

thankful that only one of ours was involved, but that was one too many."

Reaction to the point shaving scandal prompted reactions notably the almost total confinement of college basketball to college campuses. Even the popular Dixie Classic at Raleigh was canceled, because of the desire to place less emphasis on the game and cool down the emotions of fans and players. It accomplished neither of the latter.

THE 1960-61 SEASON

MCGUIRE: "Going into the 1960-61 season we knew that just having Doug Moe and York Larese in our lineup made us a good team. How good, we didn't know. None of the other players were what you would call stars, but they worked together very well.

"I think we had a smart group of players. Among them were Larry Brown, who now has achieved celebrity status in the coaching profession, and Donnie Walsh, who later assisted me at South Carolina and became a head coach in the NBA.

"We lost two early games against Kentucky in Greensboro and Kansas State at their place, but they both went to the playoffs and Kansas State was ranked in the top five. After a 70-65 win over McGuire's team, Kentucky's Adolph Rupp was highly impressed. "They're well coached and a smart team," he said. "And I think they are capable of going all the way."

The Tar Heels made Rupp look like a prophet by following the two losses with 12 straight wins that began with a 78-70 victory over Kansas at Lawrence.

One of the games in the streak revived memories of the 1956-57 "McGuire Miracle." North Carolina was playing Notre Dame in the Charlotte Coliseum, and the Irish had a three-point lead with a minute and a half remaining. When an official ruled that Larese was fouled in the act of shooting, Irish assistant coach Bill Crosby was called for a technical foul. Crosby had questioned in no uncertain terms the neutrality of Joe Mills, whose twin brother, Jim, also officiated. The Mills brothers were from the Raleigh area.

Larese, an 86 per cent career foul shooter, sank the three free throws in his usual machine gun fashion, and the Tar Heels had a tie at 71-all and possession of the ball. McGuire instructed his team to hold the ball for the last shot, and Moe put it up with a few seconds left. Moe's shot rimmed out of the basket but 6-7 Jim Hudock tipped it in to give the Tar Heels their sixth victory in a row.

However, Rupp's assessment of the Tar Heels' ability to go all the way again became a moot point in late January. UNC officials notified the conference that they would not participate in the ACC tournament to eliminate the possibility of a team that was ineligible for the NCAA playoffs eliminating one or more eligible teams.

The NCAA sanctions against the Tar Heels were imposed when it was ruled that McGuire and his New York recruiting aide, Harry Gotkin, had paid entertainment bills without proper accounting. The assumption was made that they could have paid for entertainment away from the campus of players, high school coaches and/or parents. McGuire and the University denied the assumptions, but, nevertheless, the NCAA ruled against them, making them ineligible for post-season play.

In announcing the withdrawal from tournament play, North Carolina officials again defended the school's innocence, stating that they were guilty only of errors in judgment, rather than violation of NCAA regulations.

If anything, the rivalries between ACC teams were more intense than ever, and several games were interrupted by confrontations or fights between players. One incident took place on February 4 at Durham, where Duke ended the Tar Heels' 12-game winning streak, 81-77. Duke's Art Heyman and UNC's Larry Brown engaged in a fight that erupted in a free-for-all, and it took several minutes for order to be restored.

Earlier Heyman had slapped one of UNC's male cheerleaders on the back of the head, after the cheerleader had touched him. An assault charge against Heyman was later thrown out of court.

As a result of the fisticuffs on the court ACC commissioner Jim Weaver suspended for the remainder of the season Heyman, Brown and UNC's Donnie Walsh, whom game films had shown to be one of the more enthusiastic participants.

Four days later the letdown Tar Heels lost, 89-92, in Columbia to a South Carolina team that they defeated by 24 points in Charlotte. Those were the only two conference losses of the season for McGuire, who achieved the consolation of winning the "regular season title" over second-place Wake Forest.

McGuire also had the satisfaction of sweeping the series with Case's Wolfpack and McKinney's Deacons, along with avenging the loss to Duke in the final game of the season. And that would eventually prove to be the final game of McGuire's coaching career at North Carolina.

The season produced other consolations for the Tar Heels, including a ranking of 5th in the AP poll, All-ACC honors for Larese and Moe, a place on the AP All-America second team for Moe, and a third team spot for Larese.

For the record, Wake Forest won the championship game of the ACC tournament, 96-81, over the Heyman-less Blue Devils, and reached the championship game of the East Regional before falling to St. Joseph's.

CHAPTER FIVE

REFLECTIONS ON CHAPEL HILL

From February to June of 1961 proved to be an eternity for Frank McGuire in terms of what could transpire in that period of time Besides being on the recruiting trail and landing one of his all-time best, several other "fronts" were opened. The prize recruit was Billy Cunningham, who played high school basketball in Brooklyn, developed into one of the Tar Heels' all-time greats and an even better pro player with Philadelphia.

MCGUIRE: "I had known Billy's parents for a long time. His father was a fire chief, and his mother was a teacher. They lived right next door to my sister. There wasn't any recruiting battle over Billy, although I'm sure any college would have wanted him. He had talent that only God can give you.

"So, when it came time for Billy to make a decision on where he was going to college, his father said, 'Billy, you are going to North Carolina.' And that was it."

Meanwhile, the New York Knicks were doing some recruiting of their own. They wanted Frank McGuire to be their coach. They had just completed a season of 21 wins and 58 defeats, the worst record in the NBA. Their coach, Carl Braun, was gone after two seasons, the identical longevity of his predecessor, Andrew Lavanee.

The Knicks came on strong to McGuire. They figured that coming back to the Big Apple would have a strong appeal, and that was a selling point. However, McGuire turned down three offers, and that was enough to convince the Knicks that they were getting nowhere fast.

Not discouraged by his resistance to the Knicks, Philadelphia Warriors owner Eddie Gottlieb began his own campaign. He was also met with little enthusiasm from McGuire at first, but Maurice Podoloff, long-standing president of the NBA got into the act. He met with McGuire and convinced him that his future lay with the pros.

McGuire accepted the position of Vice-President and head coach of the Warriors, and his transition from college to professional coaching had begun. His leap from high school into college had been a sensational success, and

Gottlieb felt that McGuire was just what his team needed to win the NBA championship.

MCGUIRE: "When I went to chancellor (William Aycock) and told him of my decision to go to Philadelphia, we began discussing who would be a good coach to succeed me. The chancellor seemed to lean toward going after a big name coach. That was their decision when they offered me the job.

"I told him that he should give the job to Dean Smith, who had been on my staff for four years. The chancellor said, 'I don't know about that, Frank.'

"I said, 'Well, I know.' And he seemed to take my word for it. And Dean became North Carolina's head coach.

"When I went to North Carolina, Buck Freeman became my assistant--and only assistant coach. However, in 1958 I went out to Louisville for the final four of the NCAA playoffs. They always have a coaches' meeting in connection with that, so most of the head coaches from around the country are there.

"I was talking to Bob Spear, who was the first basketball coach at the Air Force Academy, and mentioned that I was looking for another assistant. He told me about Dean Smith and was very emphatic that he would make an excellent coach.

"Dean had played under Phog Allen at Kansas, and that's a good start. After finishing Kansas Dean went into the Air Force and ended up at the Air Force Academy, where he assisted Spear. So, I talked to Dean about the job, and he felt that it was a great opportunity. And it turned out to be just that.

"At first I had a little trouble introducing him. I would say, 'Meet Dean Smith,' and people would think he was some kind of professor. But he was very serious about learning basketball and was a very hard worker. His job on the staff was to teach fundamentals and work on defense.

"I'll tell you how serious he was about it. One time I was rooming with Dean in a New York hotel, and he walked in his sleep. I woke up and there was Dean hovering over me like he was playing defense--man-to-man. It was because he was so nervous and had defense on his mind.

"While he was developing, Dean never mentioned to me that he had ambitions to become a head coach. But I presume that all coaches worth their salt feel that they could handle the head job, if the opportunity presented itself.

"One of the reasons I had chosen Dean was that I felt that he would fit into the community. He was a Midwest Baptist and had a background that was similar to the people in the area. He seemed to be a bit shy at first--sort of reserved. I think I was able to make him open up.

"After a year, Dean came to me and said, 'When are you going to give me something to do?' I assumed he was talking about recruiting. So I asked him, 'What do you want to do?'

"I didn't need any help in recruiting. All my help came from the outside.

"Players from New York had to be handled differently from, say, a boy from a small Midwest or Southern town. That is what Dean had been accustomed to.

"When I left for the Warriors, Dean found that Billy Cunningham was difficult to handle. So were Doug Moe and Larry Brown. It's interesting that all of them turned out to be successful coaches.

"Cunningham almost got Dean fired at first. Billy wasn't studying, so Dean sent him home. That took a lot of guts. But Billy took correspondence courses and became eligible.

"Moe was one of the toughest players to recruit. He was a funny guy--stubborn as hell. I knew that his father liked Harry Gotkin, and that had a lot to do with Moe coming to play for me.

"It took a while for Dean to get into being a head coach--I believe he had a losing season his first year (8-9), but he caught on fast. One thing he did that was smart. He became very close to the chancellor--played golf with him--and that helped. Before long, Dean could do anything he wanted to. And he did!

"Later on, when I came to the University of South Carolina, Dean and I became rival coaches, but we have always remained good friends. Before games against each other we have stayed up late in the evening talking about old times. But when they threw the ball up the next day, we tried to beat each other's brains out. *(NOTE: After becoming head coach at South Carolina in the 1964-65 season, McGuire's teams lost four straight games to Smith's Tar Heels. After that they faced each other 13 times, with McGuire holding a 7-6 edge. One McGuire victory was in the 1971 ACC tournament championship game, and the last time they faced each other Smith came out on top in 1972 East Regional at Morgantown, W.Va.)*

"Even after South Carolina withdrew from the ACC, and none of the ACC teams except Clemson would schedule us, Dean and I stayed in touch. Dean has been very good about calling regularly since my illness.

"I'm very happy for Dean in the success that he has had. He deserves it, because he is a good person and has worked hard. It is satisfying to me to think that I had a small role to play in helping him to prepare for the opportunity at North Carolina."

In accomplishing what many considered to be McGuire's number one priority when he went to North Carolina–to beat Everett Case–the Irishman can reflect on that with pride. McGuire and Case sat on opposing benches 22 times, with McGuire's teams coming out on top 13 times and losing nine. Five of those losses were incurred in McGuire's first two seasons at Chapel Hill.

MCGUIRE: "When I arrived at North Carolina the school had experienced some football success right after the war, when Charlie Justice was playing. But, as far as basketball was concerned, they were still talking about the Tar Heels teams that were highly successful in the 1920s and were called the White Phantoms. That had to do with their uniforms, I suppose. Nothing to do with race. I guess that name wouldn't be acceptable now.

"In my first four seasons at North Carolina people had become excited about basketball again and were filling up Woolen Gym. We couldn't sell any tickets because of the small seating capacity.

"However, the football team wasn't doing too well over the same period of time. *(NOTE: UNC had a 13-24-1 record during those seasons.)* The administration decided to go out and get a coach who could win and challenge Duke, which was winning big under Bill Murray.

"Maryland was winning even bigger under Jim Tatum and was national champion in 1953. They were going to bowl games every year, which meant money in the school treasury.

"Tatum was a North Carolina alumnus and had served one year as head coach (1942) before going into the service. It is always attractive for a coach to come back to his alma mater, so Tatum took the job.

"His first season at Chapel Hill (1956) was the year in which we won the national championship. Jim's football team had a good year, but all the people in Chapel Hill wanted to talk about was basketball. I don't think Tatum liked basketball, to start with, and it probably grated on him to be playing second fiddle to that sport. He might have been a little bit jealous, but he never let it be known.

"I liked Tatum, and there was no reason that we shouldn't and couldn't get along. We could help each other, because success in one sport at a school helps the other sports, because it is good for recruiting.

"Shortly after we had won the NCAA final in 1957, Jim came over to my office to talk to me. He told me that he had a confession to make, and it was really a surprise. He admitted that he had been silently hoping we wouldn't win the tournament.

"As a matter of fact he told me, 'After the game against Kansas was over, I kicked a hole in my television set. I was so mad, I broke two chairs in my living room. But I've decided that I can't beat you, so I'm going to join you!' And we shook hands right there, and that was it. He even started coming to the basketball games." *(NOTE: Jim Tatum died suddenly in July 1959.)*

"I've been asked why, with all the great teams we had at North Carolina, why players from those teams didn't have greater success in the pros. Actually, Billy Cunningham was the only big success in the pros from among the players I recruited there. Of course, he didn't play on any of my teams, but he was an exception to the rule.

"Good college players don't necessarily make good pro players. Some do, some don't. Lennie Rosenbluth was national player of the year and as good as any playing the game in his position. You can't compare a player like that with a Wilt Chamberlain or a Jerry West. They are different types and called on to play different roles.

"Lennie's style just didn't fit into pro basketball's freelance game. He didn't have the body to play inside and didn't have the speed and ball-handling skills necessary for the backcourt. Also, at North Carolina we played more of a team concept and looked for balanced scoring. Our offense called for a lot of pattern basketball, and both of our guards played outside. They had to be good ballhandlers, but they were what you might call our safetymen on defense.

"We placed a lot of emphasis on defense, and I think this had a lot to do with our won-lost record.

"There were some other fine players on those teams--Moe, Larese, Kearns, Brennan--and a couple of them played some in the pros but were never first-line players or stars.

"Dean Smith's philosophy was somewhat different from mine, but he has continued to emphasize a balanced offense--no super-scorers--and good defense. Michael Jordan was not nearly the great scorer in college that he was in the NBA. In three seasons at North Carolina he averaged well under 20 points a game and didn't even make the all-conference team until his final year.

"Cunningham was a special case. He was someone that took special handling. When Billy was a senior, I went to see North Carolina play Wake Forest, and Wake beat them by something like 20 points. Billy looked absolutely awful. I went into the dressing room and told Billy, 'That was disgraceful--you dogged it.' I really went after him, because when he wanted to, he could be as good as any basketball player in the country. When I said that, Billy didn't even respond."

"I believe when the North Carolina team got back to Chapel Hill, they saw an effigy of Dean hanging from a tree near the gym. That wasn't the only time Dean was hanged in effigy that season.

"Something lit a fire under Cunningham, because he played well during the last half of the season, and the Tar Heels finished strong. Had they not, there was speculation as to whether Dean could have survived. But he did, and he deserved to, regardless of how they had finished.

"After that season, which was Cunningham's last, I called Wilt Chamberlain and suggested that Philadelphia should go after him. Wilt had gone with the Warriors to the West Coast, but he had been acquired by the 76ers from San Francisco. The Philadelphia owners weren't excited about Cunningham, but, as a favor to me, Wilt talked them into drafting him.

"Later, after a game at Philadelphia, I got a call from Wilt, and he said, 'That kid you liked hasn't dressed yet. He's in the dressing room drinking beer!' Wilt told me that all I had said about Cunningham as a basketball player was true, but that he would have to stop drinking beer and smoking in the dressing room. Billy realized what he had to do, and he changed. Then, of course, he was one of the top players in the NBA for many years.

"Players with the talents of Cunningham and Jordan are rare, so I, like any coach worth his salt, always emphasized the importance of academics with my players. Few college players make it in the pros, so they need to be prepared to do something besides play basketball.

"It is much more satisfying to a coach to see his players go on to successful careers as business or professional men, than to see them succeed in the NBA. I have maintained contact with many of the players I coached at North Carolina--particularly those who played on the 1957 national champions. That team became sort of a brotherhood and has even had a couple of reunions.

"Tommy Kearns made millions on Wall Street and is now retired and traveling around the world. But he still calls me and writes me and lets me know where he is. The others stay in touch, too.

"Donnie Walsh, whom I recruited for North Carolina in 1959, became my top assistant coach while I was at South Carolina and did an excellent job. Donnie had a law degree and had an offer from a top law firm in North Carolina, but he chose to stay in basketball.

"After he left South Carolina Donnie was head coach for the Denver Nuggets for three years and is now president of the Indiana Pacers.

"I also established lasting relationships with a lot of people in the state of North Carolina. People who had nothing to do with basketball particularly but liked the sport and supported the University. Chapel Hill was a wonderful place to live, and I still have a feeling of nostalgia about it. Our family was still developing as a family, and we became even closer together in that small town environment.

"While I was there I never developed any close friendships among the opposing coaches, but that's the nature of the business. Hal Bradley (Duke) and I hit it off pretty well, but I think the others considered me to be too much of a threat, because we were beating them. The conference has always had a good group of coaches, not only in basketball but football as well, and they usually managed to leave hostilities where they belonged--on the basketball court or football field.

"But, looking back and recalling the good times and the pleasant memories, quite a number of the best occurred during my years at the University of North Carolina."

CHAPTER SIX

WILT AND THE WARRIORS

Y ou might call it another case of the irresistible force meeting the immovable object, although it would be impossible to determine who was which, or which would prevail. Frank McGuire, the rookie coach of the Philadelphia Warriors of the NBA, was experiencing his first official encounter with the giant of professional basketball–Wilt (The Stilt) Chamberlain.

The meeting took place in Chamberlain's room at the Cocoa Inn in Hershey, Pennsylvania, which is about 80 miles, as the crow flies, from the Warriors' home court--Convention Hall. Ironically, Hershey is the town in which McGuire and Chamberlain would make basketball history a few months in the future.

McGuire found himself in this situation rather reluctantly, as he had turned down the job of coaching the Warriors on several occasions. He had no plans to leave his home and coaching position at North Carolina, where he had completed another great season. His Tar Heels were what is now called "the regular season champion" of the Atlantic Coast Conference with a 12-2 conference record and 19-4 overall. However, North Carolina had withdrawn from the ACC tournament, which then decided the league's one and only representative in the NCAA's 16-team format of that period. What the school termed "errors in judgment" had led to NCAA sanctions, so the Tar Heels eliminated the possibility of an ineligible team winning the tournament. McGuire liked it in Chapel Hill, where he enjoyed hero status, a comfortable lifestyle and an ideal place for a family. However, Eddie Gottlieb, a longtime friend of McGuire, was a persistent individual, and he felt that the Irishman was the one person who could take his group of languishing superstars and mold them into the championship team that he felt they should be. After meeting with the aging president of the NBA, Maurice Podoloff, McGuire accepted the position of Vice-President and coach of the Warriors.

Gottlieb and McGuire were like oil and water in certain respects. Gottlieb adhered to the frugal practices of the cost-conscious NBA owners, while McGuire believed in going first class in everything he did. And the Cocoa Inn at Hershey was nice, but not one he would have chosen for the first meeting with the player many considered the best player in NBA history, even until this day.

MCGUIRE: "If Wilt had any questions about me as a coach, he never mentioned it. I went into the hotel room with a stack of files under my arm and dumped them onto a table. Wilt looked to be even a lot bigger than he seemed when we lined up against him in the NCAA championship game four years earlier.

"I told him that I had spent four hundred dollars calling players and coaches all over the country to ask them about him. And that I had read everything about him I could get my hands on. 'You're supposed to be tough to coach,' I said, 'but I don't believe it.' I guessed that he had never had a coach to treat him like a man and told him that he was obviously a great basketball player who was smart enough to do whatever it takes to win.

"'If I'm wrong, you'll beat me down and ruin my reputation, or I'll beat you down and ruin your career. If I'm right, we'll work together and beat Boston,' I said."

Boston had won the NBA championship for the previous three years and was again the favorite to win the title in the Eastern Division, of which Philadelphia was a member.

MCGUIRE: "Wilt told me that he didn't think that we could beat Boston, because they had too many great players, such as Bill Russell, Bob Cousy and Tommy Heinsohn. I told him that he was right about Boston's abundance of talent, and if you went strictly by the scouting reports, Philadelphia shouldn't beat Boston. Then I said that we couldn't beat Boston, as long as he scored only 37 or 39 points a game, which was what he had done the two previous seasons. 'If you can score 50, I said, 'I think that the rest of the team can do their part and get us even with the Celtics.'

"Wilt looked at me in disbelief and said that there was no way a player could average that much in the NBA. We left it at that."

Neil Johnston, a former Ohio State star who had played for the Warriors through the 1958-59 season, was head coach of the Warriors for the following two seasons, as Gottlieb hoped that Johnston's greatness as a player would transfer into the coaching profession. As had been the case in other such moves, it didn't work to Gottlieb's satisfaction, and he figured drastic action was needed.

He knew McGuire and his reputation for handling players, and he felt that McGuire was exactly what the Warriors needed.

MCGUIRE: "I think the problem was that the Philadelphia players knew Neil too well, as a teammate and an equal. Then, all of a sudden, he was their boss. It is difficult, if not impossible, for someone to do an effective job of coaching his buddies. There has to be a wall of respect between coach and players.

"I wasn't sure how I would be accepted by the players. I had never coached in the NBA and had no NBA playing experience. Yet, I was confident that professional players respond much in the way that college players do. They were just college stars who were now getting paid a lot of money to play. More money than their coach!

"So, when I met with them, I told them that I wanted them to feel free to make suggestions and that, particularly in the early games, I wanted them to decide their defensive match-ups, because they knew their capabilities and those of the opposing players. Then, after I gained the first-hand knowledge, I would begin making the assignments.

"Not too long before our opening game, we had a squad meeting, and I held a basketball and a piece of chalk. I drew a line around the ball, dividing it into halves. I probably shocked the guys by saying that Chamberlain should have the ball fifty percent of the time.

"I even told Guy Rodgers, who was a great scorer, as well as our best passer, that his one job on the team was to get the ball to Chamberlain. After hearing this emphasis on Chamberlain's role, the other players said, 'When it's time to negotiate our contracts with Mr. Gottlieb, and he won't give us a raise because we didn't score enough points, will you be there telling him why?' I said, 'You're damn right I will!'

"My first confrontation with Wilt came when it was time to cut the squad to the allowable number in the NBA, and Wilt had a friend named Carl Green who was trying out. Green was a big guy--about 6-6--and I knew that he was a close friend of Wilt, and when we discussed the tryouts, Wilt would say, 'That guy Green looks mighty good, doesn't he?' I never answered him, but when it came time for the cuts, I cut Green, and Wilt told me I was making a big mistake. I said to Wilt, 'Do you want someone to play, or someone to carry your bags?' Chamberlain never mentioned it again, and Green went on to play for the Globetrotters.

"The result of that was to further clarify our roles--I was to coach the team and make the player decisions. His was to play up to his full capabilities, which were tremendous.

"Fortunately, Wilt seemed to respond to my philosophy and tactics, and I found him to be very coachable--and, if not a coach's dream, certainly not a coach's nightmare, as he had been advertised.

"In our team meeting I had told them that I had never coached anything but a happy team, and that this would be the case with the Warriors. And that this would be based on mutual respect, and each of us carrying our own responsibilities.

"I told them that they were not to argue with officials--that I was quite capable of handling that--nor were they to criticize a teammate. 'So, I have now relieved you of any responsibility for coaching or officiating, so you can concentrate on playing basketball.'"

In his book entitled, *Wilt (Just Like Any Other 7-Foot Black Millionaire Who Lives Next Door)*, Chamberlain expresses his admiration for McGuire: "I'd heard nothing but good things about Coach McGuire, as a coach and as a man, and I was anxious to see if they were true. They were--and then some! He was the finest man and the best coach I've ever played for, before or since.

"He was a brilliant strategist, a master psychologist, a warm, selfless human being, and a guy who always looked out for his players' best interests. Unlike Johnston, he didn't give a damn how much money his players made or how much publicity they got. He figured if he could keep them happy and make them winners, he'd get his share, too--and he was right, or course."

Wilt Chamberlain was almost as famous for his inability to make free throws as he was for scoring field goals, grabbing rebounds and blocking shots.

CHAMBERLAIN: "One day when I was grousing about going two for ten or something like that, Coach McGuire came over and said, 'Look, Wilt, if you were a ninety percent free thrower we might never lose. That would take all of the fun out of basketball, right?' It was bull, but it make things easier for me."

In the first pre-season practices, McGuire shocked the Warriors by sending them through college-type drills. They went up and down the court in squatting, defensive type drills, with, surprisingly, Wilt enthusiastically leading the way like a giant grasshopper. McGuire also sent them through fundamental drills and dribbling races, normally seen only at the high school or college level.

MCGUIRE: "There were certain things in the pros that took a lot of getting used to--some I never could. For instance, in an exhibition game with St. Louis, Clyde Lovellette, who had played for the Kansas team that beat my St. John's team in the NCAA finals, went up to a rookie referee who had made a call that he didn't like. Clyde told the referee that he was something that I won't repeat. The referee called a technical on Lovellette, who responded by saying, 'That makes you two of 'em!'

"Players just don't talk to officials like that, and I made it clear to mine that I would not tolerate it. The coach has to be in control of his players and the game.

"As I have said before, a coach doesn't need to be a dictator, but he does need to be in control. When he says something, the players need to accept it, because he is the coach. That is as far as basketball is concerned. But you do need to handle things in the right way--one that will make your point.

"I had assigned Guy Rodgers to the role of what they now call 'point guard,' but he developed a tendency to dribble too much, a practice that I called to his attention. But he failed to cut down on it.

"So, one day at practice I sneaked in a new ball--with no air in it--just as Guy was going to take it. He took the ball and reacted in shock. I just smiled at him and hold him to try dribbling it!"

McGuire's predecessor had once made a big issue out of the players getting a proper amount of sleep, but their new coach gained their appreciation by taking the attitude that they were professionals and that they would not do anything that would harm their ability to play up to their potential and--most importantly--to win games.

The Warriors also accepted without protest his decision to dress them in matching blazers and slacks, just as he had done with the North Carolina squad. McGuire has always been a stickler for proper grooming--neat clothes, no long hair, and so forth. The Barbers of America once honored McGuire by naming him one of the 10 best groomed men in America.

THE 1961-62 SEASON

The pre-season exhibition games behind them, McGuire and the Warriors faced their first game of the 1961-62 season against the Los Angeles Lakers, who had finished second in their division the previous season and advanced to the semi-finals of the playoffs. They would ultimately win the Western Division this year and lose the championship to Boston in seven games. McGuire's debut was a hard-fought 118-113 loss to the Lakers, as the Warriors began to learn his system under fire.

The main cast for the Warriors consisted of Chamberlain, Rodgers, who was All-American at Temple in 1958, Tom Gola, a LaSalle All-American in 1955, Paul Arizin, a Villanova All-American in 1950, and Tom Mischery, a rookie who had played for St. Mary's. All would average in double figures during the season, except for Rodgers, whom McGuire had assigned the role of getting the ball to Chamberlain as often as possible.

After the opening loss to the Lakers the Warriors won six of their next eight games and followed with spurts of five out of six in late November and 10 of 12 in mid-December. They put together seven-game winning streaks in January and February, but they were not spectacularly successful against the team they had set as target number one--the Boston Celtics.

MCGUIRE: "In spite of their rivalry as players, Chamberlain and Boston's Bill Russell were good friends. They were the two highest paid players in basketball at one time, Wilt being the first NBA player to be given a salary of $100,000. Boston topped it by making Russell's salary $101,000. Those are poverty wages by standards of the 1980s and 1990s, but it was a lot of money at that time.

"When Boston would come to play us in Philadelphia Wilt would have lunch with Russell, which I didn't particularly like, but I wasn't about to try to tell Chamberlain whom he could have lunch with.

"I would say to Wilt, 'How in the hell are you going to play against a guy and be as mean as you're suppose to be, if you've just had lunch with him'. Fortunately, the lunch hour didn't carry over into the games, and Wilt held his own and then some against Russell, who was a great defensive

player and rebounder, but certainly not the offensive threat that Chamberlain was.

"The game that season that captured the imagination of the basketball world took place on March 2, 1962 in Hershey, Pennsylvania, where Wilt and I had held our first one-on-one conference a few months earlier. We were playing the New York Knicks, coached by Eddie Donovan and led by the former Iona College star, Richie Guerin.

"We hated the Knicks and wanted to not only beat 'em but to beat them bad. Before the game I took copies of a couple of New York newspapers into the dressing room and showed our players articles with quotes from some of the New York players about how they were going to run Wilt ragged, because he was so slow and didn't have much stamina.

"Wilt got off to his usual start, except for one part of his game that was completely out of character. He was actually making free throws. Wilt was such a notoriously poor free throw shooter that the other teams didn't mind fouling him. It was almost like getting a turnover. At the half Wilt had hit 13 of 14 from the foul line and had 41 points, but that didn't seem to excite anyone.

"In the second half it continued to be a hard-fought game, but we had moved ahead by 18 points, and a timeout was called. One of the players came up to me and said, 'Coach, do you realize that Wilt has 85 points?' That was already better than the 78 points he had scored earlier for a single-game NBA record.

"If the Knicks were aware of what was happening, they didn't show any signs of it until the crowd caught on and began chanting, 'Hundred, hundred, hundred.' Eddie Donovan called a timeout and told the Knicks to freeze the ball--even pass up good shots to take time off the clock and give Wilt less time to get the additional 15 points he needed. They were determined that Wilt wasn't going to embarrass them by scoring a hundred points by himself.

"We were just as determined that Wilt was going to make a hundred, and we concentrated on getting the ball to him. With 42 seconds remaining in the game Wilt dunked the ball to give him his 99th and 100th points.

"When the game was over fans came running onto the court and there was a mob scene around Chamberlain. The official attendance at that game was only 4,124, but they had seen history made. In fact history was made in more than one way. We won the game by a score of 169 to 147 for a combined total of 316 points for both teams, an NBA record that still stands, as far as I know. As for Wilt, he had been good on 36 of 63 field goal attempts and--get this--28 of 32 free throws. Not bad for a guy who was supposed to be the worst free throw shooter in the league--if not in the history of basketball!

"Although there were just a little over four thousand people at that game, Wilt told me several years later that he had run into at least 20,000 people who told him that they were there.

"But I don't care how many points you score it only counts as one win, and we ended the season 11 games behind Boston in the Eastern Division, giving the Celtics a bye in the first round of the playoffs. That matched us against Syracuse, coached by Alex Hannum and featuring some great players, such as Dolph Schayes, John Kerr and Hal Greer. Of course, this was the team that would eventually move to Philadelphia after the Warriors went to the West Coast.

"We advanced to the semi-finals by beating Syracuse, three games to two, and prepared to meet the Boston Celtics in the next round.

"Boston had beaten us in eight of the twelve games we played against each other during the regular season, but six of those came fairly early in the season, when our players were getting accustomed to my style of play. We felt good about our chances, because we had won four straight from them in the latter part of the season.

"Facing the Celtics, with their great talent like Russell, Heinsohn and Cousy, was a big enough challenge, but we had to go into the series below full strength, as Tom Gola was limited because of a back injury received against Syracuse.

"In spite of the fact that Wilt outscored (33-16) and outrebounded (31-30) Russell, the Celtics beat us by a wide margin (117-89) in the first game. However, we won the second game (113-106) when Wilt dominated Russell with 42 points to Russell's nine.

"We split the next four games, and the series went to a seventh game showdown in Boston. (Boston had won 119-104 in Boston, and the Warriors came back, 109-99 in Philadelphia in the 5th and 6th games.)

"The seventh game, which turned out to be my last one as a NBA coach, was close all the way, but the Celtics won it on a last-second shot."

In that game the Warriors had a 56-52 halftime lead and were ahead 81-80 at the end of three quarters. Gola, who scored 16 points in spite of being hobbled by a bad ankle, fouled out late in the fourth quarter and the Celtics rallied to go up by three with less than ten seconds remaining in the game. Chamberlain drove in and dunked the ball over Russell, who fouled him, and the Warriors had a chance to tie. Wilt made the free throw to tie the game at 107.

This set the stage for Sam Jones' jump shot with two seconds left, and it hit nothing but net to give the Celtics a 109-107 victory and the series. Boston went on to win the championship by beating the Los Angeles Lakers four games to three.

When the final game with Boston was over, Chamberlain went up to McGuire and said, "Coach, you remember at the beginning of the season, when you said we could beat Boston, and I said we couldn't. Well, you were right."

Chamberlain insisted that two disputed calls by an official cost the Warriors the final game and the series with Boston. Once Chamberlain was whistled for being out of bounds, and he insisted that his foot was several inches from the line. The other came late in the fourth quarter, when Chamberlain was called for goaltending on a shot by Heinsohn that Wilt swore was 15 feet away from the basket and in no way could have been on its downward flight.

It was still a great season for the Warriors in their one season under McGuire, and they were already looking ahead to 1962-63 with great optimism. Chamberlain had led the NBA with a mind-boggling 4,029 points and a 50.4 average, along with a league-leading average of 25.6 rebounds. He was named to the all-NBA team, relegating Russell to the second unit, which brought a measure of self-satisfaction to Chamberlain.

In the summer of 1962 Gottlieb sold the Warriors to a group of business men in San Francisco, facing McGuire with the decision of whether to move to the West Coast.

MCGUIRE: "It was not an easy choice for me to make. I had always gotten along well with Eddie, but I wouldn't know what to expect with a new ownership. Looking back, if we had won that last game against the Celtics, I might have gone to the West Coast.

"So one basket in a game made a tremendous impact on my future. That's nothing new in basketball. One goal making a big difference. For instance, the margin of one free throw gave us a national championship at North Carolina.

"Looking at the pros and cons, including where my family would live, I made the decision not to go west. I had never done anything but coach and teach, so I had no idea what I would be doing. But I felt that I would end up coaching somewhere--college or pro."

McGuire's experience with the Warriors and their owner packed a lot of memories into one season. Gottlieb had been founder and player coach of the Philadelphia SPHAS (South Philadelphia Hebrew Association) of the American Basketball League and later the Basketball Association of America. He had finished South Philadelphia and attended the Philadelphia School of Pedagogy (teaching) for four years.

Gottlieb's Philadelphia team was a charter member of the NBA when it was launched in 1949 and, in fact, was instrumental in organizing the new league. He later promoted college basketball double-headers and even organized an overseas tour by the Harlem Globetrotters. He was known as basketball's supersalesman.

Gottlieb moved out of coaching after the 1954-55 season, hiring George Senesky to succeed him, and Senesky's Warriors won the NBA title in 1955-56. Gottlieb died in 1979 at the age of 81.

MCGUIRE: "Eddie was a very shrewd individual, but the had a reputation of wanting to sit on the bench and tell his coaches what to do. When

I took the job I made it plain that I had to be the only coach.

"Before I took the job I was sitting in a restaurant talking to Eddie, and Clair Bee came in. Clair walked over to our table and said to me, 'Frank, don't pay any attention to him. He just wants to use you to sell the team.' That made Eddie mad, but Bee didn't care.

"Bee again said, 'Remember what I'm telling you; this guy wants to sell the team. He hasn't got any money in it.' After the announcement that the team had been sold, I thought back to that conversation with Clair Bee.

"At that time franchises in the NBA were going for about $75,000, and Gottlieb didn't have any money. He had borrowed the money to buy the franchise, which cost about $25,000 originally.

"Think about that cost compared to today's. Someone told me that Billy Cunningham's Miami franchise was worth about $177 million.

"Eddie kept a hands off policy, as far as coaching the team was concerned. But once we were playing the Knicks in Madison Square Garden, and Eddie comes over and asks me shouldn't we give a particular player a chance. I don't remember his name.

"I just stood up and said, 'Now you sit on this bench and you do what you want to! Eddie said, 'I just thought we should see what this guy can do, in case Wilt gets hurt.'

"I said, 'Well, if Wilt gets hurt, you don't have a franchise, so it won't make any difference.'

"However, overall I liked Eddie and didn't have a lot of complaints about how he operated. He was a good man, and, I remember, he never drank liquor. His idea of celebrating after a game was to go out and get a big ice cream cone!

"He was also a big help to Wilt in handling his money. He would give him a certain amount to live on and invest the rest."

CHAPTER SEVEN

THE SOUTH CAROLINA CHALLENGE

Call it happenstance or fate, but the process by which Frank McGuire became basketball coach at the University of South Carolina was most unusual. It had nothing to do with a search committee or even an effort by the school to hire a coach. There wasn't even a known vacancy in the position.

Of course, McGuire was no stranger in Columbia, as the Gamecocks had been playing McGuire's North Carolina teams on a home-and-home basis, and he made speaking appearances in the area, as well. Perhaps some South Carolina supporters had secretly imagined what Frank McGuire could do for the school's basketball fortunes, but it was never placed into public speculation.

For South Carolina it was a case of two people being in the right place at the right--or opportune--time. One of the principals was Jeff Hunt, a Columbia business man who operated a Caterpillar heavy machinery dealership. Hunt had for years been a great supporter of Gamecock athletics--both in spirit and with financial contributions.

Here, in Hunt's words, are the events that drew McGuire to the Carolina campus:

HUNT: "I went to Asheville, North Carolina one morning--flew up there in my own airplane. It was in the winter of 1964, but I'm not sure exactly when. I think it was during the basketball season.

"I flew up there and went to Buck Buchanan's restaurant--called 'Buck's'. It was a real nice restaurant, and we had a private room for breakfast. We had everything you could imagine.

"Buck Buchanan, Baxter Taylor, P.A. Riley and Frank McGuire were in the room. I learned that Buck was a very good friend of McGuire--a big University of North Carolina supporter and a big fan of the basketball team while Frank was coaching there.

"Frank asked me what I was doing there. And I told him that I had come up there to inspect a tractor to see if it was in good shape and to see what I would offer the man on a trade-in. Frank said that he had never seen anybody do that, and it was very interesting to him. He asked me if he could go with me and watch me inspect the tractor.

"So we got into an automobile--I, McGuire, and Pete Riley--and went out to the construction site.

"On the way we were making small talk, and I didn't know much of what to say. I really didn't know Coach McGuire--I think I had met him one time when he was making a speech at the Jefferson Hotel in Columbia.

"So I said, 'Coach, why don't you come and coach the University of South Carolina. And the reaction was quite surprising. Because there was no great reaction. He said in sort of a monotone, 'Well, you've already got a basketball coach.'

"That's the last thing in the world I expected him to say. I expected him to sluff it off. He didn't sluff it off at all. And he acted like, if you didn't have a coach, I'd come there.

"So, I pulled over to the side of the road, and I got serious with him. I said, 'Coach, I don't think we're gonna have a coach very long. The coach we have isn't going to be there very long. I know for a fact that they're going to appoint an interim coach, which they did.

(NOTE: After the 12th game of the 1963-64 season the University of South Carolina appointed Dwane Morrison as interim coach to replace Chuck Noe, who was in his second season as head basketball coach. Dwane Morrison, former Gamecock star, was an assistant to Noe and several years later became head coach at Georgia Tech.)

"McGuire said, 'If they're gonna let him go--and you're sure of that--I'm not out for someone else's job--let me hear from you.'

"I said, 'Give me your phone number. Can I have somebody call you?'

"He said, 'Oh, no. I won't deal with anybody but you.'

"That's when he told me the story of one of the media people in Columbia crossing him up. And, later on, I remember that this particular reporter didn't like Frank. But I learned that at one time the University had made contact with McGuire about the coaching situation and that this particular reporter had leaked it. Frank had backed off after that and didn't want to have any more to do with it.

"I came back, and I called Sol Blatt, Jr., who was chairman of the Athletic Committee of the Board of Trustees. I had known Sol for years. I told Sol we had a chance to get Frank McGuire and was he interested.

"He said, 'Yes, what's his phone number. How do I get in touch with him?'

"I said, 'You can't. He doesn't want to do it that way. He wants to talk to the president of the University. I'm sure he'll talk to you, too. But he wants to talk to you one-on-one--not on the telephone. He wants you to meet him in New York.'

"Sol said, 'Well, when, and where?'

"I said, 'I'll have to call him and find out.' So here I am talking back and forth from one to the other. I called up Frank, and he told me what hotel for the meeting--it was across from Madison Square Garden; I believe it was the New Yorker, but I'm not sure.

"They were supposed to meet him on a Saturday, and Tom Jones (President of USC) went with 'em. However, New York's airports were closed because of the weather and they met on a Sunday.

"It was Sunday night when I got a phone call from Frank, and he told me, 'You're speaking to the new future head basketball coach at the University of South Carolina. But you can't tell anybody.'

I said, 'That's not fair!' Then I didn't hear any more from him until he arrived in Columbia.

"Then one day he called me up and said, 'Come get me. I don't know where I am. Come get me.' So, I met him down at the Sportsman's Restaurant.

"So, I took him out to my house in the country and told him that he could stay there, but it was cold and there were no sheets on the beds and so forth. He went into town and stayed in a motel until he found a place to move in."

MCGUIRE: "After I met with the South Carolina people in New York we scheduled another meeting to take place in Barnwell, South Carolina. Why Barnwell, instead of Columbia? I didn't understand at the time, but it didn't take long for me to find out!

"I didn't know many people at South Carolina, but I did know Marvin Bass, who was head football coach and the athletic director. Marvin had been an assistant to George Barclay while I was at North Carolina, and we became friends. So Marvin was one of the people I called when I was thinking about coming to South Carolina.

"I liked what he told me about the people and the school.

"So, I go to Barnwell, a town I had never heard of, to plot my future at a school whose campus I had never seen. Blatt was there, along with some other trustees, and we talked about the coaching job. Everything sounded fine to me, so I told them that I would accept, and we shook hands. In addition to basketball coach I would be associate athletic director, so that I could have full control over my program.

"As we were leaving the meeting, Sol Junior, which just about everybody called him, turned to me and said, 'Coach, do you realize that we never even talked about a salary.' Well, as I've said many times, I don't make decisions based on money. That part takes care of itself.

"So, I said, 'Just pay me whatever you're paying Marvin. Then build a coliseum that will seat 20,000, and I'll fill it up.' Before I went to that meeting in Barnwell I had already made up my mind to take the job, if they would commit to build a coliseum. The existing field house at South Carolina was built in the 1920s, and would seat only about 3,500 when it was packed. I thought Woolen Gym was bad enough, but this one made Woolen look like Madison Square Garden!

"As far as meeting in Barnwell was concerned, and why people always referred to the chairman of the athletic committee as 'Sol Junior,' it became clear. Sol Junior's father was the most powerful political figure in South Carolina. He was Speaker of the House in the General Assembly, and what he wanted to happen was usually what happened in this state.

"For many years people referred to Barnwell as the state capital, because it was not only Blatt's home, but also the home of Edgar Brown, who was senate majority leader for a long period of time until his death. They called Blatt, Brown and other influential associates 'the Barnwell Ring,' because of the impact they had on what happened not only in the legislature but in other matters around the state of South Carolina. And that included the University of South Carolina, because the legislature elects the trustees that run the school. And, that is why Sol Junior was a powerful member of that board of trustees.

"Any important legislation that Sol Senior wanted passed or rejected in the House, he was usually successful. Not that he was doing anything illegal. It was that he had that much power and influence among the other House members.

"Fortunately, for Carolina, he was a great supporter of the University--and always ready to help. Often that was the only help you needed! On the other hand, anybody who was at odds with the Blatts found out that it could be most unpleasant. Later on in my career at South Carolina I had some first-hand experience with that.

"Although I had never visited the campus, I was familiar with the old field house. It didn't hold many spectators, but I considered it a big advantage for the home team, because the students were so close to the court. Like they were breathing down your neck. In North Carolina we never took South Carolina and Clemson very seriously in basketball. They were what you call, 'white meat!'

"Some of my friends thought I was foolish to take on this challenge, but, from what I had learned, it would be a great opportunity. The big thing we needed was a place to play."

The place the Gamecocks had been playing featured about 15 rows of backless seats forming a square bowl around the court that was about four feet below the level of the first row. It was surrounded by steel railings.

Maryland Coach Millikan observed that it looked as if they had drained an ice rink and were playing basketball on it.

South Carolina's basketball program had been searching for stability ever since Frank Johnson had ended his 16-season tenure in 1958, the year after the Gamecocks had faced McGuire's Tar Heels in the ACC tournament championship game.

Johnson had been succeeded for one season by Walt Hambrick, who had joined him as an assistant two years before from Pikeville, Kentucky Junior College. His star player in Pikeville, Grady Wallace, had accompanied Hambrick to South Carolina.

After a 4-20 season, Hambrick moved over into athletic administration, and Michigan State assistant Bob Stevens took the job. He had apprenticed under Forrest Anderson and brought a basketball philosophy of constant motion offense and man-to-man defense. Stevens followed two losing seasons with a 15-12 record overall and 7-7 in the ACC in 1961-62.

Basketball writers must have considered this a minor miracle, because they voted Stevens the league's Coach of the Year. This was in a season in which both Duke and Wake Forest were ranked among the nation's top 13 teams.

Impressed by Stevens' credentials, Oklahoma offered him their basketball job, and Stevens accepted. The Gamecocks were now looking for their fourth basketball coach in five years.

Along came Chuck Noe, who had experienced some success in tenures at VMI and Virginia Tech. He installed what he called the "Mongoose" offense, featuring a guard spending eons of time in the pivot position. The mongoose had little success against the cobras of the ACC, and he finished the 1962-63 season at 4-10 in the conference and 9-15 overall.

After 12 games of the 1963-64 campaign Noe was breaking even in basketball games, but losing the battle of personal problems that led him up to, if not over, the brink of a nervous breakdown. The decision was made to replace Noe with his assistant, Dwane Morrison.

Morrison had been a star of the USC teams of 1951 and 1952, leading them to winning, though not sensational seasons. Morrison had been a successful high school coach in Anderson, S.C. and did an acceptable job of keeping the Gamecock ship afloat. He even coached ACC wins over Clemson, State, Virginia and Maryland.

He wanted the permanent job as head coach in the worst sort of way, but once the administration learned of McGuire's availability, Morrison didn't have a chance. Several years later he did land the head job at Georgia Tech and even had the satisfaction of winning a game against McGuire in Columbia.

MCGUIRE: "The first thing I needed to do after I got settled down in Columbia was to hire a staff. Once Morrison learned that he would not be considered for the head coaching job, he applied for the job as my assistant. That is not what I had in mind, because I wanted to start fresh--pull the curtain on the past.

"Morrison had friends in the community and at the University, and they began to pressure President Jones to persuade me to hire him. I didn't have anything against Dwane. He was a fine fellow, but not the person for my situation. President Jones kept insisting that I hire Morrison, and I

knew that I couldn't succeed in an atmosphere like that.

"I said to Ginger (Rigdon--McGuire's secretary) one day, 'I'm quitting. Don't say anything, but I'm taking the train to New York.' That's how I left. Doctor Jones called me a day later at my mother's house where I was staying, and said, 'You and I can see eye to eye. Why don't we meet in New York. I have to see you.' So he and his wife drove up, and we went to a restaurant to talk.

"Sol Blatt Senior had told Jones to go to New York and bring me back and not to come back without me. He told him that he could get a new president easier that he could get another Frank McGuire. So Jones told me to hire whoever I wanted, so I came back.

"After that little disagreement Doctor Jones and I got along fine. I liked him, and he was very supportive of the basketball program. So, after that, Buck came down and we began making our plans for recruiting and going into our first basketball season. It was my fifth and, what turned out to be, my last coaching job."

THE 1964-65 SEASON

To face his first season at South Carolina McGuire would inherit remnants of a team that had struggled to a 10-14 record the previous season. First team All-ACC choice Ronnie Collins, who averaged 23.7 points per game, was the biggest loss. Also gone were Jimmy Collins (no relation), 16.2 points, and Bill Yarbrough, 15.0. The leading point-maker available to McGuire from the 1963-64 team was John Schroeder, who had averaged 4.0 points and 3.6 rebounds.

Of course, McGuire had known this going in, and he hit the recruiting trail immediately. It was no mystery to where the recruiting trail would lead--the New York area. The Irishman landed three players who would be eligible for his second Gamecock varsity and form the nucleus for a move into respectability. The three were guards Skip Harlicka of Trenton, N.J. and Jack Thompson of Brooklyn and forward Frank Standard, also of Brooklyn.

There was some help coming up from the previous freshman team, including 6-9 Al Salvadori, whose son played for Dean Smith at North Carolina in the early 1990s, and Gary Gregor, who would have a bout with academics to overcome.

MCGUIRE: "Fortunately, my recruiting was still alive. I had been out of college coaching only two years, so some of the high school players that I was looking at in my last season at North Carolina were just reaching their senior year. And the same help I had with recruiting at North Carolina was still there.

"South Carolina had great fans and great support, but I don't think they really believed that they could compete with the Big Four in basketball. Many of them were greatly surprised that someone with my record of success would take on this challenge.

"I spent a lot of time making speeches and trying to convince supporters that we could accomplish at South Carolina what we had done at St. John's and North Carolina. Their hopes had been raised so often, only to end in disappointment.

"Maybe this helped raise the school's sights in athletics, because several years later they hired Paul Dietzel, who had won a national championship at LSU, to coach the football team, and Bobby Richardson, who had been a star infielder for the New York Yankees, to coach the baseball team.

"After Dietzel and Richardson had joined the athletic staff it made the fans more optimistic. One of the jokes that circulated around Columbia after those two came here was that the University was going to hire Arnold Palmer to coach the golf team!

"Once at South Carolina I had no doubt as to whom I wanted as my assistant. That was Buck Freeman, who had coached me at St. John's and assisted me at North Carolina. Buck knew exactly what I wanted to do, so he was a natural.

"My next major staff move came the following year. Donnie Walsh, who had played for me at North Carolina, finished law school at Chapel Hill in June of 1965 and faced a career decision. He could have joined the law firm of Richard Nixon in Washington or join Buck and me in Columbia. Donnie had helped coach the freshmen at Chapel Hill while he was in law school, so that gave him a head start.

"Donnie was a New Yorker and knew the players from that area. I had known his family for years. Believe it or not, I attended Donnie's Christening back in the early forties. My Christening gift was a basketball! That's what you call getting a head start with a prospect!"

McGuire took what he inherited and began establishing his system, which was completely different from that of his predecessor. Jim Fox, a senior who had transferred from a junior college, led the team in scoring with a 17.6 average, and Salvadori averaged, 11.0, but McGuire was short on productive players. The team was dealt a big blow in January when Gregor became academically ineligible.

Another key player at the first of the season, junior college transfer Jerry Croke, who was averaging 14.2 points per game, was also an academic casualty for the second semester. With that diminished squad, competing with the ACC powers was out of the question.

The Gamecocks dropped their final eight games of the season leaving them with a 6-17 overall record and 2-12 in the conference. Although it was still a loss, the Gamecocks pushed ninth-ranked Duke, the ACC regular season winner, all the way to the final seconds before losing a 62-61 decision in the league tournament at Raleigh.

Meanwhile the freshman team was winning 14 of 16 games, giving Gamecock fans a glimpse of the future. In the spring McGuire would land his highest profile recruit since coming to Columbia. He was Mike Grosso, a 6-8 center from Raritan, N.J. who would later become the subject of controversy over his eligibility at USC.

THE 1965-66 SEASON

The cover of South Carolina's basketball media guide for 1965-66 was what they call a "mug shot" of McGuire and an architect's rendering of a proposed coliseum, to be built on the corner of Assembly and Blossom Streets, adjacent to the USC campus.

The structure that was ultimately erected there bore little resemblance to that architect's rendering, but it was symbolic of the school's commitment to McGuire that he would have a respectable place to play. This was not only important for the future but for the present, because McGuire was able to promise outstanding high school prospects that they would be playing in a coliseum, rather than the cracker box a couple of blocks away.

The media guide quoted McGuire: "We are making progress, and when we get into our new coliseum in a couple of years we hope to have both the basketball team and the schedule to permit us to compete with the best in the country and to bring the best to Columbia to play us."

With the core of his first recruiting class now eligible for the varsity, McGuire was ready for step two in his building process on the court. Harlicka, Thompson and Standard joined varsity returnees Salvadori and John Schroeder, along with Skip Kickey, who had averaged 12 points per game for the freshmen.

Not long into the 1965-66 season Gamecock fans were treated to a preview of things to come. McGuire's sophomore-laden team won six of its first seven games, losing only to N.Y.U. in New York. The fans were really set on fire in the third game of the season, when Duke's second-ranked Blue Devils came into the Pit. Led by Harlicka's 19 points, the Gamecocks fought Vic Bubas' powerhouse on even terms the entire game, and with 15 seconds left Standard broke free, took a pass from Thompson and laid it in to give Carolina a 73-71 victory.

You would have thought that the Gamecocks had won the national championship. Fans engulfed the playing floor, and the nets were ceremoniously cut down. The McGuire era had officially begun.

Although the Gamecocks' record would still be on the minus side, 11-13, they had other significant victories, including a 42-39 nail-biter over Pennsylvania in Philadelphia. They also made it to the second round of the ACC tournament by beating Clemson for the second time in the campaign. Four of Carolina's losses were by four points or less; including a one-pointer to N.C. State and by three points to Duke in what the Blue Devils considered a payback operation in Durham that almost backfired.

While the varsity was showing improvement by the game, Grosso, the blue chip recruit, was having a field day. He averaged 22.7 points and an amazing 26 rebounds, as a new battle developed off the court.

The battle was over Grosso's eligibility to play for South Carolina. A 6-8, 220 picture athlete, Grosso had led Bridgewater-Raritan High School to the New Jersey state championship, averaging 30 points and an unbelievable 31 rebounds per game. In a state tournament game Grosso scored 42 points and had 45 rebounds for what must be some kind of national record.

Over 40 colleges were trying to lure Grosso to their campuses, including ACC institutions, such as Duke. Grosso make a score of 789 on the college board exam. At the time the ACC had a guideline that called for student athletes to score at least 800 on the college board in order to be eligible for a scholarship. The rule was not adapted and made official until May 1966, nine months after Grosso enrolled at South Carolina.

MCGUIRE: "I knew Mike's family very well, and he had made up his mind that he wanted to play for me. When he didn't make the 800 ACC requirement on the college board, he could have gone to almost any college in the country. He could have gotten in academically, and they would have been happy to have him. But he wanted to come to South Carolina.

"His family didn't have a lot of money, but he had an uncle who owned Grosso's Bar and Grill up there, and Mike worked for him on occasions. When Mike decided he wanted to come to Carolina, his uncle offered to pay his tuition until he could establish his eligibility for a scholarship. It could have been a loan, as far as anyone could have known. However, he paid the tuition with a company check--Grosso's Bar and Grill.

"Perhaps he should have just deposited the money in Mike's father's account--be sneaky about it--and let Mr. Grosso write the tuition check. Then nobody probably would have known the difference.

"On the other hand, with Mike's reputation as a basketball player, and the competition among the schools, I'm sure that other colleges were looking for anything they could to keep Grosso from playing at South Carolina. However, Eddie Cameron, the athletic director at Duke seemed to have a particular vendetta against us, and he waged a campaign to have Mike declared ineligible.

"Cameron had almost a lifetime hold on the chairmanship of the conference basketball committee, and he had a lot of influence. At one time he had been Duke's basketball coach, and he was very much interested in the game.

"Right before the basketball season began in 1966 the conference executive committee made a crazy ruling that applied only to South Carolina. It said that if they were suspicious of an athlete at Carolina, insofar as eligibility was concerned, that he would be ineligible until he was proven to be eligible. In other words, guilty until proven innocent!

"That meant that Mike was ineligible, and as far as I am concerned it made a victim out of an innocent boy and a fine athlete mainly because of my relationship with Eddie Cameron and Duke. A couple of months later the NCAA declared Grosso ineligible because of his tuition being paid by a company with which he was not legally associated.

"I was disappointed that I didn't get more support from the University administration and athletic director (Paul Dietzel), and I voiced some opinions as to the motives of the conference, particularly Duke. That didn't set too well with some of our people, and certainly not those at Duke.

"Because of the hard feelings between our school and Duke, the conference ruled that the two teams didn't have to play each other during the season. The two schools agreed that feelings were running too high to risk an incident, so our two games for that season were canceled.

"Losing Grosso was a big blow to my program. He was really my only recruit in his class, which meant we got no help from rising sophomores for the 1966-67 season. I was able to arrange for Mike to receive a scholarship to Louisville, which had a fine program and one of college basketball's great centers, Wes Unseld. Grosso played behind Unseld for a season, then became a starter."

THE 1966-67 SEASON

The good news for the 66-67 season was the Gary Gregor, a strong 6-7 junior, had re-established his eligibility. This provided McGuire a solid lineup of Thompson and Harlicka at the guards, Salvadori at center, and Standard and Gregor at the forward positions. Thompson has been described by McGuire as the best ball-handler he has ever coached, while Harlicka had great shooting range and was also adept at driving to the basket. Standard was a clever player, who was quick enough to use his basketball astuteness to outwit and outquick defenders. Standard was also a fine rebounder, to help out Gregor in that department.

That combination led the Gamecocks to a 16-7 record and 8-4 in the ACC, good enough for third place behind North Carolina and Duke, the latter which they did not play, or course. However, they did split their two games with the Tar Heels and defeated N.C. State twice. McGuire also established a series with Marquette, coached by his former pupil, Al McGuire. The Gamecocks defeated the Warriors in the first round of the Milwaukee Classic, but fell to Wisconsin in the finals.

The Gamecocks didn't meet Duke in the regular season, but as fate would have it, they drew the Blue Devils in the second round of the ACC tournament after beating Maryland in the first round. In an emotion-packed game the Blue Devils edged the Gamecocks, 69-66, as the tournament moved to the Greensboro Coliseum for the first time.

The tournament was won by North Carolina, which was ranked fourth in the final AP poll, but South Carolina, even without Grosso, had firmly established itself as a team to be reckoned with in the future.

Gamecocks Thompson and Gregor were named to the All-ACC second team, and Salvadori had two great games to make the all-tournament first team, scoring 22 points in each of the contests.

MCGUIRE: "My freshman team that year was an interesting one, because I had recruited only one player that would have any impact on the varsity. He was Bobby Cremins, who had played for All Hallows High School in the Bronx but was attending Fredericksburg Academy.

"That same year my good friends Ben Carnevale and John Terry had sons attending and playing basketball at Bullis Prep in Annapolis, Maryland. John also worked with Bob Fulton on the radio broadcasts of our games and was owner of Taylor Street Pharmacy, a store that sold practically everything and was an institution in Columbia. Ben was basketball coach at the Naval Academy for years but was now athletic director at N.Y.U.

"Bullis Prep had a game up there with Fredericksburg Academy, so John, whose son was named Tommy, and Bob went with me to see the game. After the game I asked Bob and John who they liked. Both mentioned this tow-head kid who was all over the floor, diving after loose balls and really scrapping. That tow-head kid was Bobby Cremins and I was also impressed with his hustle and determination. So I told him he had a scholarship at South Carolina, if he wanted it. Well, he wasn't being heavily recruited, if at all, by other schools, so he accepted the offer. That proved to be one of the best moves I ever made.

"Bobby never did score big numbers as a varsity player, but he averaged around 20 a game for the freshman team, because he didn't have other players on that squad who were as good as he was.

"On that freshman team with Bobby were Tommy Terry, Corky Carnevale and Greg Blatt, who was the son of Sol Junior and had played for Barnwell High School. So, basically it was a team that had only one legitimate scholarship player, along with Corky, Tommy, Greg and a few walkons. However, most of my varsity players were just juniors, so it wasn't urgent that I have a great recruiting class.

"After that freshman year Greg became our varsity manager and in 1975 joined my staff as varsity assistant.

"The freshmen didn't win many games, but the four players I mentioned averaged in double figures."

THE 1967-68 SEASON

The cover of the 1967-68 media guide progressed from two season ago, this time featuring a photograph of McGuire wearing a hard hat, framed against the steel beams of a rising Carolina Coliseum. Inside it was pointed out that the new 12,500-seat arena would be ready for the 1968-69 season. So, this would be the final year in the 34-year-old Carolina Field House.

The old structure had been built as a basketball palace, because of the excitement created by the 1932 team that featured major players from a Texas high school team that laid claim to the national championship

Over a two-season span the Gamecocks won 35 games and lost only three, including a 32-game winning streak, still easily the longest in school history

The point is that South Carolina fans had experienced a brief encounter with basketball euphoria, and some of the people who had that experience were still alive to watch the building of a new championship team and a new place to play.

The team that closed out the old field house was a good one. To replace the departed Salvadori at center, 6-7 Gregor was moved into the position, while other help would come from Skip Kickey, who had missed most of the previous year with an injury and had slimmed down his 6-8 frame from 256 to 219 pounds. McGuire had his starting guards, Harlicka and Thompson, back, and Standard was set at forward. That meant moving Cremins from his natural guard position to the other forward for his sophomore season.

The lineup of four seniors and a sophomore eventually led to their being referred to as "four horsemen and a pony." If you had asked any South Carolina supporter or McGuire which team they had rather beat during this season, the answer would have been unanimous--DUKE! After a year's absence from their schedules these two adversaries were on the docket again--home and home. The narrow (69-66) loss to Duke in the 1967 tournament did nothing to cool down feelings between the two schools.

Duke was again a co-favorite, along with North Carolina, to win the ACC title. And the Tar Heels would likely have placed second in a poll among Gamecocks as to which team they would most like to defeat.

The team began the season as though this would be one of heartbreak. After demolishing tiny Erskine, an Associate Reformed Presbyterian school about 100 miles due west of Columbia, the Gamecocks lost by one point at Maryland and by two at Virginia. They would later defeat those teams with ease on their home court.

The team hit its stride after that, once winning eight games in a row, including two lop-sided victories over arch-rival Clemson. Then came the first game against the Blue Devils, led by All-America center candidate Mike Lewis, who would later spend several productive years in the NBA. Fears of overreaction by the South Carolina fans were unwarranted, and it turned out to be just another hard fought basketball game.

The game was almost an instant replay of the 1965 game, in which Thompson had nine assists to go along with 17 points in that 73-71 victory. The result then was the Gamecocks' first ever ranking in the national polls, as they jumped to No. 10.

Again this was a heavily favored Duke team, but again the Gamecocks prevailed, this time by a wider margin--three points--83-80!

Carolina's string of wins ended in the North-South doubleheader in Charlotte, where they lost to State by 13 and to North Carolina by four in mid-February. However, the Gamecocks would end that month with two of the greatest back-to-back triumphs in the school's history. They would have to rank high among the highlights of McGuire's years in the sport.

MCGUIRE: "I've had a lot of teams that were more talented than this one, and teams that won a lot more games. But this one has a special place, because of a number of reasons. First, they were a bunch of over-achievers. I think they got more out of what they had than any team I've ever coached.

"They also showed more heart and more composure under pressure than most teams I've seen. They sort of set the stage for the personality of teams that would follow them. Ready to take on all comers and ask no questions. It was us against the world.

"Maybe it was because of the way the conference treated us about Mike Grosso. Whatever it was, this team had a togetherness that was unusual."

That team chemistry was never more in evidence that on February 24, when McGuire took his team to Durham, where the eighth-ranked Blue Devils were ready to avenge their loss in Columbia and do it convincingly. It wasn't long into the game that coach Vic Bubas realized that the win by the Gamecocks in Columbia was no fluke.

The Gamecocks built up a lead in the second half, then held off Duke in the final minutes to win, 56-50. A sweep over basketball enemy number one at that time was all McGuire could ask. Adding to Duke's agony, the two losses ultimately cost them the number one seeding in the conference tournament.

The best was yet to come. Four days later the "four horsemen and a pony" trotted into Chapel Hill to meet the Tar Heels, then rated No. 3 in the polls. While McGuire had dictated a slow pace against Duke, he felt that he could run with the Tar Heels, even in their own gym. North Carolina had a highly-rated sophomore named Charlie Scott, who would be a key figure in Gamecock-Tar Heel battles.

Dean Smith had another sophomore on his squad--Eddie Fogler, whom McGuire had also tried to recruit for South Carolina. In 1993 Fogler did land at South Carolina but as head coach. Fogler apprenticed under Smith, then had successful coaching tenures at Wichita State and Vanderbilt, taking those teams to post season play during all seven years that he coached them.

North Carolina had won 20 straight games in Woolen Gym, but this did not intimidate this USC team, which seemed to thrive on big challenges.

The game was one that Gamecock fans of that day will talk about as long as they can reminisce. Both teams ran, and both teams scored, as the lead see-sawed. With a minute and a half remaining, it was South Carolina that held an 81-80 advantage. Just as important was the fact that they also had possession of the ball, and there were no restraints placed on holding the ball. This is what McGuire told his team to do.

During a timeout called at that point the Tar Heels looked over their choices of whom to foul. That was easy. Cremins, a sophomore and a 59 per cent free throw shooter. So foul Cremins they did, but the strategy didn't work.

Cremins canned six of seven foul shots, as everybody in the packed gym screamed in his ears and waved their arms. South Carolina had been the beneficiary of another "McGuire miracle," 87-86. When the Gamecocks arrived back at Columbia airport that night they were greeted by around 10,000 fans, who celebrated long into the night. At last they were no longer the "whipping boy" of the ACC.

Herman Helms, sports editor of *The State* in Columbia, eulogized the team's amazing accomplishment and quoted McGuire, "It is something you hope for and pray for and dream about, but it doesn't happen. Beating Duke and North Carolina back-to-back on their home floors when they're got great teams. It just doesn't happen, but it did. If anybody had come to me and told me it would happen, I would have said, 'Listen fellow, you're crazy. It was a thousand to one shot.'"

After the great win at Chapel Hill the Gamecocks came home to face an improving State team that would later make it to the finals of the ACC tournament before losing to North Carolina. The Gamecocks lost a 55-54 heartbreaker to earn the fourth seed in the tournament. They blew out Virginia, 101-78, in the first round of the event, which was played in the Charlotte Coliseum for the first time. In the semi-final the Gamecocks lost another down-to-the-wire battle to North Carolina, 82-79 in overtime, but it was still clear to the rest of the conference that McGuire was back.

In the other semi-final that evening Duke and N.C. State made ACC tournament history for absurdity. Although Duke had beaten State twice during the regular season, Bubas chose to have his team stand around and hold the ball most of the game, holding the ball for 14 minutes without moving it at one point. The strategy paid off with a 4-2 halftime lead for Duke, but State blew it open in the second half to win by a 12-10 score. That game gave other ACC coaches notions that they would be unable to resist in the future.

The better-than-expected season and the big wins gained McGuire third place in the voting for league coach-of-the-year behind Smith and Bubas, both of whose teams had finished in the top ten nationally. In the All-ACC voting Harlicka was a first team choice, while Gregor and Standard were both named to the second team. Gregor and Thompson were first team all-tournament selections.

Harlicka, who averaged 21.8 points per game, was the first round draft choice of the Atlanta Hawks, while Gregor, whose scoring average was 17.9, along with 12.9 rebounds, was picked by Phoenix.

The place of "the four horsemen and the pony" in the progression of the Gamecock basketball program had been firmly established, as they had demonstrated to their fans that the school was now competitive in the ACC. South Carolina was no longer considered "white meat!"

The interest created by McGuire's success at Carolina had radiated throughout the Palmetto state. Basketball goals were sprouting in backyards and playgrounds, little leagues were formed, and high schools began to place more emphasis on the sport.

His success also forced arch-rival Clemson into upgrading its basketball program and facilities, as Littlejohn Coliseum on that campus followed the completion of Carolina Coliseum.

CHAPTER EIGHT

THE ROCHE-OWENS ERA

What most people consider to be the best three teams in the history of the University of South Carolina basketball, had three basic leading men--John Roche, Tom Owens, and John Ribock. They were three different types in personality and talents, but they blended into the mind, muscle and nervous system of Gamecock teams of seasons ending in 1969, 1970 and 1971.

Roche and Owens were from New York City, while Ribock spent his high school days in Augusta, Georgia. The other two positions in the starting lineup during their three varsity years were held by four or five different players, but Roche, Owens and Ribock were the constants on those teams.

MCGUIRE: "Roche and Owens were both playing for LaSalle Academy, and both attracted the attention of college recruiters, but most seemed more excited about Owens than they were about Roche. John and Tommy were very close to each other, and there was a lot of speculation that they would end up at the same college.

"John's father was an examiner for The Chase Manhattan Bank in New York, but even with that family background, he still played a lot of "street" basketball and later on a CYO team. He was sort of a skinny kid, but he had developed good basketball skills and seemed to really have a mind for the game. Roche was recognized more for his defense than for his offense.

"Owens was the only good 'big man' in the area--he was about 6-10, but he downplayed that, because he wanted to be a forward, where his chances of playing pro ball would be better. I wanted both of them, because they seem to work well together--inside and outside.

"My friend Jack LaRocca, who helped me in New York, called me and told me to come up, that John was ready to sign. When we got there John's mother said that she wanted John to go to Duke.

"I turned to John and said, 'What am I doing here?' He had told me himself that he wanted to come to South Carolina.

"Mrs. Roche said, 'I received a call from Vice-President Nixon. He said that Duke is a fine school.'

"I said, 'Nixon is a loser!' And John told his mother, 'Duke is a good school. But so is South Carolina. I've decided on South Carolina.'

"So, I signed him that night."

McGuire was successful in his double catch, signing Owens. None of this attracted much in the way of media attention at that time, because recruiting of high school players didn't receive the coverage then that it does now.

This kept the Roche-Owens high school combination intact for their college careers. Off the basketball court they had a lot in common, both being good students and both having to ride the subway to LaSalle from their homes some distance away.

Roche, who would be known for his blank expression on the court that concealed the raging fire within, sometimes teased his college coach about his recruitment. "You really wanted Tommy, not me," Roche would say. "You only took me so that you could get Tommy!"

Whatever truth there was in that statement is debatable because nobody can remember the time when McGuire didn't consider John Roche the greatest thing that ever happened to basketball. At least his world of basketball.

Perhaps their common Irish-Catholic background bonded them either closer together, but, whatever it was, there was a near-reverent feeling between the two. One comment concerning Roche that was attributed to McGuire was, "I wouldn't trade the dirt under his fingernails for anyone else's soul!"

When critics questioned his practice of keeping the ball in Roche's hands so much, rather than giving equal time to other talented players on the team, McGuire would reply, "John is the best I've ever seen at controlling a game. He won't be here forever, and while I have him I'm going to take advantage of him."

McGuire observed that in intra-squad games, if Roche were on one team, it would win by 20 points. Move Roche to the other team, and it would win by 20. In his 29 years of coaching college teams, McGuire had many fine players, and a coach hesitates to single out any one player over the others. But if you held a gun on him and told him he had to pick the one that he considered THE BEST, it would no doubt be John Roche.

MCGUIRE: "There have been a lot of great basketball players who can use their individual talents to strengthen a team. However, a truly great player is one that makes all of the players around him play better–lifts them to a higher level than they would be without him. That was John Roche."

Roche's ball-handling and dribbling ability were legendary. If he didn't invent the behind-the-back dribble while racing down the court, he perfected it and popularized it. With nothing to limit the time of possession by a team or individual, Roche could control the ball by himself for about as long as he chose. Many feel that the creation of the five-second rule was a reaction to John Roche.

MCGUIRE: "John had such great self-confidence, and it rubbed off on the rest of the team. Even in a game he would talk to the guy guarding him--nothing unsportsmanlike but definitely cocky. He would say, 'I'm gonna go,' meaning he was going to go to the basket, and then he would move, and the defender couldn't do much about it. He was a mean competitor. Not a mean person. Just mean on the basketball court. I can see why fans of the other schools hated him."

The third piece of McGuire's recruiting puzzle that year was John Ribock, a 6-8, 230-pound, two-time Catholic All-America high school player for St. Thomas Aquinas in Augusta. Ribock had scored 28 points and grabbed 28 rebounds in the Georgia all-star game and was named the outstanding player.

College recruiters were lined-up outside the Ribock home. John had lived a traveled life, as he was the son of an army mess sergeant. Ribock looked as though he would be better suited for the position of tight end on a football team, but McGuire courted him to become what is referred to now as a strong forward. Strong was an apropos reference to Ribock. If a brawl broke out, you would want Ribock to be on your side.

Ribock's role would evolve into that of a rebounder, rather than a scorer. But with Roche and Owens, and later Kevin Joyce, on the team, that was enough scoring power.

The fourth catch for McGuire was Bill Walsh, an All-New York City prep star at Mamoroneck who went to Frederick Military Academy. A left-hander, Walsh was a good ball-handler with an excellent outside shooting range. A perfect compliment to Roche at the guard positions. Walsh was a bit short at six feet, but he had excellent speed.

Walsh would become an academic casualty after his sophomore year, but he would be a valuable member of the starting lineup while he lasted.

THE 1968-69 SEASON

It didn't take long into the 1967-68 season for Gamecock fans to learn that something special about the school's freshman basketball team. When the Biddies, as they were called, played preliminaries to varsity games, there would be almost as many spectators on hand as there were for the main event. In a single game against Lefty Driesell's highly-regarded Davison recruits Roche put on a clinic to lead his team in a blowout before a packed field house.

McGuire's prize crop accomplished astronomical statistics as a team and as individuals. Roche averaged 21.5 points per game, while Owens was even higher at 24 per game, along with 17.6 rebounds. Ribock averaged 16.7 points and 14.5 rebounds, while Walsh had a 16.4 scoring average. The foursome had a combined average of 79 points per game, enough to win most of the time.

Adding to the excitement for South Carolina basketball fans was the fact the Carolina Coliseum, the long promised arena, was scheduled to be ready for the opener with Auburn on November 30, 1968. With a seating capacity of around

12,500, the facility would be the largest on a college campus in the Southeast. The $10 million facility included a tartan playing floor, which was supposed to eliminate dead spots and provide extra protection against injury. Years later a removable wooden floor was brought in and installed over the old tartan surface for basketball games.

It didn't take long, or a lot of imagination, for the coliseum to be affectionately called "the house that McGuire built."

To basketball fans and the players, it seemed that the first game of the 1968-69 season would never arrive. The anticipated debut of the star freshmen, who would start along with Cremins, finally took place. Cremins, although only 6-2 would continue to play forward in order for Roche and Walsh to be in the guard positions. Ribock would be the center, with Owens at the other forward position.

The Coliseum was packed and the game was preceded by things that usually happen in opening ceremonies, and the first tip-off in the new arena finally took place. Nobody remembers who won the first tip, but the game itself was one to remember.

Auburn coach Bill Lynn had his own fabulous frosh, John Mengelt, a 6-2 guard from Indiana, who was starting his first game of a distinguished varsity career. Mengelt would become an All-Southeastern Conference star and play in the NBA for Cincinnati.

Carolina's super sophs were in control most of the first half of the game, leading the Tigers by ten points at the intermission. However, Auburn rallied behind Mengelt and junior forward Ronnie Jackson to overtake the Gamecocks and finally take the lead at 49-46 with only 1:12 remaining in the game. Cremins was fouled in the act of shooting, and he made the first of two free throws. Fortunately, for the Gamecocks, when the second shot bounced off the rim, Owens sliced through to tap it in and tie the score at 49-all.

When Auburn failed to score, Carolina had possession with 49 seconds showing on the clock. Roche controlled the ball for much of that time, and with time running out, he made his move to the top of the key. Fans would see hundreds of Roche jump shots in the arena, but none would appear any prettier than the one he launched with just a couple of seconds left. It was actually not much to look at, as it caught the rim of the basket, bounced to the backboard and then through the net, as the Coliseum crowd roared. The Gamecocks had escaped with a 51-49 win.

And what a way for Roche to begin his career--a last second shot to give the Gamecocks a victory. And the other sophomores lived up to their billing, as Owens scored 16 points and grabbed 14 rebounds, while Ribock added four points and nine rebounds, and Walsh, six points. Roche scored in double figures, 14 points, as did Cremins, 11.

With that the Gamecocks launched what many Gamecock fans still refer to as "the Roche-Owens" era.

One thing that was reinforced in that first game was McGuire's belief in playing his five best players most of the time. In this case it was part philosophy and part necessity, because the drop from the floor to the bench was considerable.

Before the season ended the Gamecock starting lineup would be called the "Iron Five," because they got little rest. Cremins, Ribock and Roche played the full 40 minutes against Auburn, while Owens was able to rest for all of two minutes, while Walsh sat down for four.

That starting five would score 96 per cent of Carolina's points for the season and get 86 per cent of the rebounds. Only in case of foul trouble could the starters expect any amount of rest.

After the opener the Gamecocks were thrust headlong into their ACC schedule, facing Wake Forest at Winston-Salem. The Deacons had one of the nation's most highly publicized sophomores in Charlie Davis, one of the pioneer black players in the ACC, and like four of the Gamecock starters, he was a New Yorker.

Roche prevailed in that first meeting, scoring 25 points, as South Carolina hit crucial free throws down the stretch to win by a 68-63 score. Already North Carolina's Big Four were getting nervous about this new threat to their dominance of the conference.

The Gamecocks lost a conference game to Maryland and a non-conference battle with Driesell's fifth-ranked Davidson Wildcats. Those would be the only two losses in the first 12 games, and South Carolina would, for the first time ever, become firmly entrenched in the rating polls. During that stretch they won the Quaker City Classic by beating Rhode Island, St. Joseph's and LaSalle, and Roche was the unanimous choice for the tournament's most valuable player.

In late January the Gamecocks made a road trip to independent Florida State, an odd inclusion in a schedule that featured mostly ACC opponents, with a couple of state teams intermixed.

The Seminoles were coached by Hugh Durham and were led by future NBA star Dave Cowens. From the outset McGuire continually protested what he considered one-sided officiating.

MCGUIRE: "I told Bob Fulton before the game that we were gonna get screwed, and those officials made a prophet out of me. At one point, near the end of the game, Cowens, who was twice as big as Bobby Cremins, went charging toward the basket and ran completely over Bobby, who was just standing there. They called a foul on Bobby, and that was about all I could take.

"I told the official what I thought of the call in no uncertain terms, so he called a technical on me. I said, 'That's one,' and the official said, 'What did you say?' I told him that he couldn't count, and told him to give me another one. He did, and I said, 'That's two.' He kept on calling

technicals until he got to seven. At that time they hadn't installed that rule about two technicals and you have to leave the game.

"There was less than two minutes remaining, so I told my team to come on to the dressing room, so we left, and the game was over. They were ahead by about ten points, anyhow.

"Years later I saw Dave Cowens out in Las Vegas, and he was laughing about that game. He said, 'Coach, I think that official is still back there calling technicals!' He might be, for all I know."

In the month of February the Gamecocks faced the challenge of eight games against ACC opponents, four of which were played in Carolina Coliseum. On the first of the month the Gamecocks' number one antagonists, the Duke Blue Devils, came to Columbia, and this brought the first head to head competition between Owens and Duke's highly touted sophomore, Randy Denton, a 6-10 center who played high school basketball in Raleigh. Although Denton had a big weight advantage over his Carolina counterpart, Owens dominated the first meeting by controlling 21 rebounds, as the Gamecocks won, 64-57.

That was the beginning of a frustrating career for Denton, as far as his rivalry with Owens was concerned. Against Carolina Denton was on the losing end five times in seven games. All three seasons he placed behind Owens in the battle for the ACC rebounding title, won by Owens each year.

Two nights later Roche had his highest scoring game, hitting for 33, as the Gamecocks routinely downed Wake Forest, 73-62. Walsh made the biggest impression, however, scoring 16 points and holding the high-scoring Davis to single digits. Five nights after that the Gamecocks headed for Durham to face the harassment of Cameron Indoor Stadium, named for the man who engineered Mike Grosso's ineligibility.

Roche and Owens again put on a clinic, as John hit 10 of 16 field goal attempts and 17 of 21 free throws, for 37 points, while Owens had 26 points on 9 for 11 shooting and 13 rebounds. This gave McGuire his second straight regular season sweep over Duke, probably number one on his hit list, as Carolina won, 82-62.

Roche and Owens had played together so long that they could read each other's mind. Often Roche would drive for the basket off of a pick by Owens, and, depending on a defender's commitment, would either continue and lay the ball in the basket, or flip it over his shoulder to Owens, and let him score.

Roche had an uncanny ability to dribble inside, cut along the baseline and work his way between defenders to score what appeared to be easy layups. His outside jump shot was classical, but a shot that he made off a dribble came almost from the hip, as he would loft soft floaters in sort of a pushing motion. Whatever he did seemed to work more often than not.

In the second highest point total of their three seasons, the Gamecock sophomores led a massacre of Clemson at Clemson, 106-79, as Owens scored

29 points and Ribock had one of his best games with 19. Ribock was not a habitual scorer but continued to improve in his contributions in rebounding. His average of seven per game ranked him seventh in the conference at the end of the season.

The victory at Clemson led into the North-South Doubleheader at Charlotte, where the Gamecocks faced North Carolina on Friday and State on Saturday. The Tar Heels were ranked second in the polls and were led by Charlie Scott, a New Yorker who played opposite Roche and who had made the All-ACC team as a sophomore. Owens' top Tar Heel rival was Lee Dedmon, a 6-10 soph from Baltimore who would be featured in the most famous play in USC basketball history in a couple of years.

The game against North Carolina was "the John Roche show," as the Gamecock star appeared to be motivated to new heights by the one-on-one challenge from Scott. Before the game ended in a 68-66 South Carolina win, Scott would be sent to the bench in frustration, as Roche "owned him" in a 38-point performance that eliminated any doubts that he would become one of the all-time greats of the ACC.

Columbia sports editor Herman Helms overheard a North Carolina friend of McGuire tell him after the game, "Frank, if you keep this up, those people down there in South Carolina are going to elect you governor." McGuire replied that he would prefer to keep on coaching.

The following week the sign in the Columbia sandwich shop that had read, "McGuire for Governor," had been changed to, "McGuire for President."

Following the loss to South Carolina Dean Smith added his accolades to those already accorded Roche. "If he played that well, South Carolina could beat UCLA." Quite an opinion in the context of UCLA having won two straight NCAA titles and would add three more. Smith also proclaimed that the Gamecocks were now favorites to win the ACC title.

That prediction by Smith didn't require a lot of research, because the Gamecocks were 8-1 in conference games and would add another win the following night, when they pried the ball away from State often enough for a 45-35 win. The only consolation State got out of that was holding Roche to 13 points, his lowest production of the season.

McGuire's Iron Five had a nine-game winning streak going into a return game with North Carolina in the Coliseum. This time the Tar Heels prevailed, 68-62, but it was a lot closer than that. With less than two minutes remaining the Gamecocks trailed by only two points and had possession. Their chances went down the drain when Roche was called for a controversial offensive foul, not only giving North Carolina the ball but taking Roche out of the game with his fifth personal. Little satisfaction came from the fact that Roche had again claimed a personal victory over Scott, whom he outscored, 22-13.

South Carolina lost another nail-biter, 67-64, against State at Raleigh, costing them a tie with North Carolina for what is now known as the regular-season championship.

Seeded second in the ACC tournament, the Gamecocks routed Maryland, 92-71, in the first round but ran out of steam against Duke, 68-59, in the semi-finals at Charlotte.

The Gamecocks were invited to the NIT in Madison Square Garden and defeated Southern Illinois 72-63, in the first round, as Roche had 26 points, and Owens, ten rebounds. Luck would be against the Gamecocks, however, as Walsh was lost for the game with Bobby Knight's Army team when he received a severe cut in his left leg when a revolving door at a hotel shattered around him.

The loss of Walsh, who was averaging 12.7 points per game, left a big gap in Carolina's offense, not to mention taking away a key defensive player. With a fourth of their offense out of action, the Gamecocks were victimized by the defense minded Cadets, and South Carolina's first-ever trip to post-season basketball play was over.

McGuire, nevertheless, had put South Carolina, not only on the map, but on the main road. The 21-7 won-lost record marked the first time South Carolina had won 20 or more games in a season. The choice for ACC Coach of the Year was no contest--McGuire received 78 votes to Smith's 22.

Player of the Year honors went to Roche, who outpolled Scott, 56-39, and he was a first team all-conference choice, while Owens was named to the second team. Roche's 23.7 scoring average was second in the league, and Owens led the rebounders with 13 per game. Owens was also ninth in scoring at 16.4, as Ribock was seventh in rebounds at 9.3.

Scott, who led North Carolina to fourth place in the final AP poll but whose scoring average was over a point below Roche's, was critical of the voting for Player of the Year, claiming that he should have received it and that the vote was racially motivated. Of course, Roche clearly outperformed Scott in their two games against each other, which might have influenced the decision.

By finishing 13th in the final AP poll, the Gamecocks had not only excited their followers but had gained the attention of the national media. With all five starters returning for the 1969-70 season, big things would obviously be expected of McGuire's newest basketball empire.

THE 1969-70 SEASON

The underground railroad produced two freshmen who would become significant additions to future teams and stopped off in Virginia to take another one aboard. Tom Riker, a 6-10 center from Hicksville, N.Y. who played for St. Dominic's Prep, was a high school All-American and recruited by at least 150 colleges before casting his lot with McGuire.

Bob Carver was an All-City choice for Archbishop Molloy, which would later send down Kevin Joyce and Brian Winters. The third highly recruited freshman was Rick Aydlett, who was Virginia's high school player of the year at Blacksburg.

As the Biddies clawed their way through freshman and junior college competition, Riker averaged 26.6 points and 18.3 rebounds, while Carver had a 16.5 scoring average, and Aydlett, 12.0.

The addition of this new talent to Carolina's varsity did not go unnoticed by the national press. When the basketball magazines hit the newsstands and the wire services later did their pre-season polling, South Carolina was generally ranked as the No. 1 team in the land. That, of course, was another first for USC athletics, but McGuire knew first hand that nobody remembers pre-season rankings--only post-season.

The NCAA allowed colleges to begin their formal practices for the season no earlier than October 15, and this was the date that McGuire assembled his formidable squad. He announced that the public was invited to watch the first practice session, and almost 10,000 took him up on it.

The only damper on the optimistic atmosphere was the knowledge that one of the last year's starters, Walsh, had been declared ineligible for failure to meet academic requirements. This created a vacancy in the backcourt, which would be filled by Cremins and allow Owens to move to the forward position, where Cremins had filled in. Riker was more of a natural center than Owens, while Ribock would remain in his forward position, and Roche, of course, at guard. With Carver and Aydlett available McGuire could now go to his bench with more confidence, although he would not drastically change his five-man philosophy.

Some new excitement had been created in the ACC with the coming of a new "name" coach. Maryland, which had suffered through two 8-16 seasons under Frank Fellows, hired Lefty Driesell away from Davidson. His job was to make the Terps contenders again in a conference that was getting stronger by the year.

A new (old) threat was looming in the ACC race, as Norman Sloan, who had come up through the coaching ranks through Presbyterian College (SC) and The Citadel, had developed N.C. State into a team to be reckoned with. With Driesell at Maryland and Smith at North Carolina, the conference was accumulating quite a roster of marquee names.

The Roche-Owens act was at its best at Auburn, as they led an 86-64 drubbing of a good Auburn team. Owens had 27 points and 17 rebounds, while Roche had 25 points, as Riker made his first start as a varsity player.

The Gamecocks experienced a horrible shooting night, 33.9 per cent, against Tennessee in a packed Carolina Coliseum, and the Vols took advantage of it to lead, 55-54, with seconds left. Roche tried a game-winner at the buzzer, but it bounced off the rim, and a stunned crowd filed out of the arena.

McGuire repeatedly had said that a loss could relieve the pressure from his players. He held on to that philosophy following the Tennessee defeat. If the Gamecocks could shoot that poorly and lose by only one point to a team that good, it wasn't all that discouraging.

Roche's attitude was, "Well, I'd rather lose to them than North Carolina," which said a lot about the rivalry that was building between the two neighboring state universities.

After demolishing little Erskine (SC) and East Carolina, the Gamecocks faced Virginia at Charlottesville in their first ACC encounter. Virginia's strategy was to play slowdown and stop Roche, which they accomplished, as the Gamecock star attempted only six shots. Owens supplied the scoring punch, 23, and controlled 11 re-bounds, as the Gamecocks coasted, 62-51.

In his first meeting with Driesell at Maryland, McGuire orchestrated a 101-68 blowout in Cole Field House behind 29 points by Owens and 27 by Roche. Riker was beginning to assert himself, as he grabbed 17 rebounds and scored 18 points against the Terps. In a rare display of sportsmanship from an ACC crowd, Maryland partisans gave the Gamecock starting five a standing ovation when they left the game toward the finish.

After Carolina ripped Long Island University, 89-52, in Madison Square Garden, Blackbird coach Roy Rubin called the Gamecocks "the most powerful team I've seen in my nine years of coaching."

In New Orleans, where the Gamecocks traveled for the post-Christmas Sugar Bowl Classic, newspaper writers introduced a comparison between Roche and Pete Maravich, who was in the final season of his dazzling collegiate career at nearby LSU. Roche obliged by hitting 14 of 19 shots for 31 points and dishing out eight assists in an 85-52 verdict over New Mexico. Incidentally, under statistics rules of the period, a pass had to be directly responsible for a basket in order to be credited as an assist. Nowadays all a player has to do is "hit an open man," and if that player scores, an assist is scored.

This set up a championship game against a top ten Notre Dame team, led by sensational Austin Carr. A 36-point performance by Riker kept the Gamecocks in the game, but Carr led the Irish to a 75-71 lead with two minutes remaining. Roche had been held in check for most of the game, but in the clutch he was at his best. He scored two straight field goals to tie the score, and after a Carr basket, hit on a one-and-one with 14 seconds left to send the game into overtime.

In the extra period it was "the John Roche show," as the Gamecock ace scored Carolina's final six points in an 84-83 victory. That gave him 25 points for the evening, as Owens led the rebounding with 14.

Earlier in the season Roche had sustained a rib injury that required him to wear a special harness in order to play. That injury had become aggravated, as the Gamecocks faced their January schedule, which thrust them into the bulk of their ACC schedule.

Several of their ACC rivals decided that slowdown tactics against the high-scoring Gamecocks would be worth a try. That strategy didn't work either. North Carolina, Maryland and Virginia tried to play keep-away, but the results were the same--double digit losses.

Clemson's Bobby Roberts allowed his team to play, and the Tigers were clobbered twice, 97-76 and 99-52. Bitter rival Duke fared little better, falling by 12 and 17.

In a non-conference encounter against Temple in the Palestra in Philadelphia, Roche took three shots in the first half, and Carolina trailed by five. In the second half John exploded for 25 points in the first ten minutes, and his team moved on to a 79-71 victory.

Davidson, now coached by Terry Holland, came to town to face a Gamecock team that had won 17 in a row. USC led much of the game, but when Owens was charged with his fourth foul one minute into the second half and Ribock and Riker had four each shortly thereafter, the Wildcats took advantage of the situation. They took the lead late in the game, then converted three straight one-and-ones to hold off Carolina, 68-62.

That was one of two losses by the Gamecocks during the regular season, which saw them go through the entire 14-game ACC schedule without a loss. The South Carolina football team had the same experience during their ACC schedule in the fall, going 6-0 against the league. No other school has ever accomplished such a back-to-back two sport sweep.

The 14-0 ACC record made the Gamecocks a runaway top seed for the conference tournament over second place North Carolina and N.C. State, each with 9-5 records. That paired them against Clemson in the first round, and this time Roberts decided not to run with the Gamecocks. It almost worked. It took two free throws by Roche with eight seconds remaining to rally his team to a 34-33 win.

Wake Forest upset Duke in the first round and earned the right to challenge Carolina. The Deacons proved to be little competition, but with 12 minutes remaining and Carolina ahead by 20 points, Roche drove down the lane and stepped on the foot of a Wake defender, severely spraining his right ankle. The Gamecocks won by 16, but a dark cloud gathered over the Gamecock camp, as they prepared for the championship game with North Carolina State.

This was a Wolfpack team that USC had beaten by 16 points the previous week. However, Roche, who had a badly swollen ankle on ice the entire night before, was hobbled in warm-ups for the game. McGuire would probably not have used any other player under those circumstances, but he likely believed that Roche playing on one leg was better than anybody else playing on two.

South Carolina had an 11-point lead with eight minutes remaining in the half, so State's Sloan instructed his team to hold the ball. And hold it they did--for six minutes. Finally, with two minutes to go, McGuire decided to send his team after them.

Star forward Vann Williford worked his way inside for a basket, and State followed with another quick goal off an intercepted inbounds pass, and South Carolina's lead was cut to seven at intermission.

State worked its way back into the game in the second half and managed a 35-all tie at the end of regulation. Roche's shot at the buzzer was off the mark, and he had another shot at a game-winner as the first overtime expired.

With 22 seconds remaining in the second overtime, Carolina had a 39-38 lead and the ball. As Cremins took the inbounds pass from Roche, the Wolfpack's Ed Leftwich took a swipe at Cremins and knocked the ball out of his hands, driving for a layup that put his team up by one. After a hurried shot the Gamecocks fouled, and two free throws put the final margin at 42-39.

McGuire couldn't protest the "no call" on the steal from Cremins that gave State the victory for fear of a technical foul. However, when it was over he followed official Steve Honzo off the court, letting him know in definite terms what he thought. When Leftwich knocked the ball away the impact left Cremins with a sprained finger and little doubt that he had been fouled.

However, the team that many observers predicted would go all the way to the NCAA title was on the sidelines. And they departed amidst the jeers of most of the crowd of 11,000-plus who were not Gamecock supporters. Resentment by the rest of the ACC against South Carolina was growing.

After the loss to State, McGuire was quoted: "We wanted to win this game for John, because he has won so many for us. But it wasn't to be."

State's fine sophomore Paul Coder was among the more charitable members of his team toward Carolina and Roche. He said, "I couldn't believe it when he came out for the game. One of the doctors who saw John at the hospital said that there was no way he could play on that leg. How can you help but learn something from a guy like Roche? I know he plays for South Carolina, but damn if he isn't something else."

Roche's ankle was placed in a cast, and he went around with the aid of crutches for six weeks following the ACC tournament.

MCGUIRE: "John has more guts than anyone I've ever seen, and when he went down and didn't get up I knew he was badly hurt. He had to spend the night in his game uniform.

"John was determined to play. There was no way we were going to keep him off the court. However, John was just not himself, but he gave it all he had. (Roche hit only four of 17 shots and scored nine points.)

"We decided to use a two-on-two zone to keep John from having to chase someone with two good legs, and it was working fine, but we just didn't get the point production we needed."

Ironically, a tournament victory for the Gamecocks would have placed them in excellent position for the NCAA playoffs, as the East Regionals were to be hosted by South Carolina. As it was, State came to Columbia and found no hostile greeting in Carolina Coliseum but still lost its first game to St. Bonaventure, 80-68.

MCGUIRE: "This was one of the best teams I ever coached, and if Roche hadn't injured his ankle, I honestly believed we could have gone all

the way. At North Carolina I brought in Kearns and Rosenbluth to win the national championship, and I felt that Roche and Owens could do the same for South Carolina. That chance went down the drain when Roche stepped on that Wake Forest player's foot."

The Luck of the Irish was absent this go-around.

What follows is an excerpt from a review of the 1969-70 season, written for *The State* newspaper by McGuire:

"Our margins of victory against ACC opponents was phenomenal. Coach after coach, and I'm one of them, has said that there is simply no way a team can win all its regular season games in this tough league. But our team did it, and this will remain a great memory for me.

"I would have to say that this season we accomplished the principal aim that I had when I came here as a coach six seasons ago. My aim was to put the University of South Carolina on the basketball map and to make Columbia the capital of the basketball world. In order to do this we had to overcome many heartaches and headaches, and it took a tremendous amount of work, sweat, blood and tears on the part of all our players and our entire coaching staff.

"I think this was probably the greatest year that I have ever had as a coach. . .I can't say enough about our fans. They usually give an award in the ACC for the most courteous and most sportsmanlike crowds, and I don't see how we could ever miss getting it here in Columbia. . .they certainly proved at the State-St. Bonventure game in the Eastern Regional that they are truly big league fans. . . . They treated the State team with courtesy and dignity, and I am very proud of them for that."

The Gamecocks reaped many post-season awards and were ranked sixth in the nation in the final ratings. However, being host to the East Regionals cost them a bid to the NIT, as being host disqualified the Gamecocks from any other post-season play.

McGuire was named national College Coach of the Year by the Metropolitan New York Writers. However, reflecting the anti-South Carolina feeling among North Carolina sports writers, McGuire placed second to State's Sloan for conference Coach of the Year honors.

Roche was again named ACC Player of the Year, but it was by the narrowest of margins over the Tar Heels' Scott. In spite of all the slowdowns by Gamecock opponents Roche averaged 22.3 points per game and Owens, 15.9. Owens was again the ACC rebound leader with a 14.9 average. Both Roche and Owens were the first team choices in the All-ACC voting.

To show for his sophomore season, Riker had an average of 13.8 points and 9.0 rebounds.

The 25 victories and only three defeats was easily the best record ever by a South Carolina team, particularly when you consider the competition.

Although the United States Basketball Writers Association honored Roche with a place on its All-America first team, AP and UPI relegated him to the second unit. In the commentary in *Look* magazine, Roche was called "the most unselfish player of the year, and maybe the decade."

Both Roche and Owens were named to the 1970 Academic All-America team chosen by College Sports Information Directors of America. This underscored McGuire's professed emphasis on academics among his players.

History was also being made off the court during this 1969-70 season. Casey Manning was the first black player to be given a scholarship to play basketball at the University of South Carolina. The 6-2 Manning averaged 33 points per game at Dillon High School and was the state's prep player of the year.

Having spent the summer in basketball camp in the New York mountains, Manning already knew most of the USC players. Dillon is only 100 miles from Columbia, so he would also be playing close to home at South Carolina.

However, the most prominent recruiting coup for McGuire was Kevin Joyce, the top choice on *PARADE MAGAZINE's* high school All-America team. As the star of Archbishop Molloy High School in New York City, Joyce led his team to a three-year record of 68-5, averaging 34 points and 18 rebounds during his senior season.

He was coached by Jack Curran, who played for McGuire at St. John's. For the Biddies, Joyce averaged 25.3 points and 15 rebounds per game, while Manning had a 16.3 average.

Another prep All-American, seven-foot Danny Traylor from Winston-Salem, N.C., had an 18.3 scoring and 15.6 rebounding average for the freshman team, as it won 12 of 16 games against tough opposition. Jimmy Powell, another All-New York City choice at St. Helena's made this a solid recruiting year for McGuire, and the future of South Carolina basketball loomed brighter than ever.

Only Cremins would be lost from the great 1970 team, and Joyce appeared ready to take over in the Gamecock backcourt without any loss of ability. That would prove to be an understatement. What would be most difficult to replace was the leadership shown by Cremins, along with his defensive play. He usually was called on to guard the other team's

MCGUIRE: "One day during our 1969-70 season I turned to my wife, Jane, and said, 'Who do you think is the heart and soul of this team?' She gave the answer I expected, 'John Roche.' I told her, 'No, it isn't John Roche. It's Bobby Cremins.' Bobby had so much heart and determination that it rubbed off on the other players. And that's why he was named captain of our team that year and the following year."

·

THE 1970-71 SEASON

Six weeks after the ACC tournament Roche finally had his ankle out of a cast and could again look ahead—not back. "This is the longest I've ever gone without playing basketball," he said. "I'm already looking forward to next year. I think we're going to have a great team."

Sports writers and coaches across the country seemed to agree with John. They voted the Gamecocks the nation's No. 2 team, behind UCLA in the pre-season polls. They would have a chance to prove their mettle early in the season, hosting Auburn, playing at Notre Dame, coming off a 21-8 season, and coming back home to contend with Duke.

With the addition of Joyce and Traylor, McGuire had a more comfortable situation in the matter of depth. This gave him a total of eight players who would see extensive playing time, including returnees Roche, Owens, Riker, Ribock, Carver and Aydlett.

McGuire's offensive philosophy was well known: "When in trouble, go to Roche." Opponents' defensive philosophy was just as familiar: "Stop Roche." The latter was not quite that simple, and if they experienced some success, it wasn't always that smart. McGuire had other guns in his arsenal.

That was proven in the opening routine win over Auburn, 86-69, as the Tigers held Roche to a comparatively low 17 points, while Owens and Riker scored 28 and 23, along with dominating the backboards.

The much publicized match-up with the Irish in South Bend was enhanced by the competition between two All-Americans, Roche and Notre Dame's Austin Carr. Roche clearly won the day, scoring 32 points, including a perfect 16 for 16 from the free throw line. The Gamecock star, who had converted a school record 41 straight free throws the previous season, made ten in a row down the stretch, as the Irish fought to overtake the Gamecocks.

Thanks to that clutch accuracy, Carolina held on for an 85-82 victory and had passed its first big test with flying colors. Carr scored 27 points, eight below his average, but most of them came after Carolina had built a commanding lead.

After demolishing Duke, 98-78, McGuire welcomed a relatively new adversary, Maryland's Lefty Driesell, to the Coliseum. The Terps weren't much competition for the Gamecocks in basketball, as the final score of 96-70 would indicate. However, an extra-curricular incident marred relationships between the two teams.

With less than five minutes remaining the outcome had long been decided, so McGuire had his starters on the bench to give other players some game experience. For reasons unclear Aydlett and Maryland's Ray Flowers were involved in a scuffle under the basket.

MCGUIRE: "With that players from both squads ran onto the floor and it was a free for all. While officials attempted to calm things down Lefty ran out into the middle of things. When it was all over Lefty claimed that Bobby Carver held him, and Ribock hit him.

"When we looked at the films the best we could determine was that Lefty was swinging away and hit himself in the mouth. I don't think it was much of a blow.

"But Ribock weighed 240 pounds and was a powerful man. If he had hit him, I doubt that Lefty could have walked off the floor."

Driesell disagreed, claiming that he had a split lip and that his film told a different story. He was quoted the next day, "I'm out there trying to break up the fight, and McGuire's standing over there smiling and straightening his tie. If I was McGuire I wouldn't bring my team to College Park."

When the floor was finally cleared officials George Conley and Joe Agee ruled the game over with South Carolina winning by the score that existed when the interruption occurred.

From a basketball standpoint the game underscored USC's scoring balance, as Owens led with 28 points and 17 rebounds, while Roche and Riker scored 17 each, and Joyce, establishing himself as a new threat, had 14 points.

On the road again, against Virginia Tech, Riker tipped in a last second missed shot to give Carolina a 78-76 win. Tech's leading point producer was Allan Bristow, who would ultimately become coach of the Charlotte Hornets of the NBA.

Once again inspired by coming home to New York, the Gamecocks swept to the championship of the Holiday Festival in Madison Square Garden, beating Cornell (83-60) and Providence (102-86) to reach the final against Western Kentucky. This Western Kentucky team would eventually reach the Final Four of the NCAAs and rank seventh in the polls.

With the Hilltoppers concentrating on stopping Roche, Joyce made them pay with a 25-point performance, as the Gamecocks held off a late rally to win, 86-84, and give McGuire his first Holiday Festival trophy. Roche, who had 35 points against Providence, Riker, with 19 rebounds against the Friars, and Joyce were named to the all-tournament team.

The Gamecocks remained undefeated with an 81-53 win over Clemson, but their nine-game streak ended at Chapel Hill, where the Tar Heels used foul shooting down the stretch to widen a four point lead into a 79-64 win. It was Carolina's first ACC regular season loss since March 1, 1969 at N.C. State.

After disposing of Temple, the Gamecocks went to College Park, a place that Driesell had warned them not to come less than a month before. The demand for tickets in Cole Field House was the highest since McGuire had taken his North Carolina team there in 1958.

If they were looking for good basketball, the crowd didn't get their money's worth, because the Terps held the ball for practically all of the first half in an effort to draw McGuire out of his zone defense, a strategy which North Carolina had used in its win. This time the Irishman held fast, and took a 4-3 (correct) lead into the halftime intermission. It appeared that the Gamecocks had survived the hostile environment and the Terp slowdown, leading 30-25 with only 16 seconds remaining in overtime. However, a Maryland lay-up and two straight interceptions of Gamecock inbound passes, resulting in scores, enabled the Terps to pull off a miraculous 31-30 win. As Maryland fans paraded around the floor with Driesell on their shoulders, the Gamecocks were being pushed and hit by others as they attempted to escape to their dressing room.

This type of reception is what the Gamecocks would become accustomed to on ACC courts for the remainder of the season. At Charlottesville two nights later a technical foul was called on Virginia's fans for throwing things at McGuire and the Gamecocks, who led the slowdown Cavaliers, 49-48, with time running out. The Cavaliers chose to hold for an all or nothing shot—Barry Parkhill took it with seven seconds left, and it fell for a 50-49 upset.

After exam break the Gamecocks didn't have to wait long to introduce the Cavaliers to reality in Columbia. By virtue of their win over Carolina in Charlottesville the Cavaliers had been ranked 15th in the polls. The Gamecocks erased that illusion with a 92-70 victory that saw McGuire make extensive use of his bench. Aydlett tied Joyce for scoring honors with 20, and Carver had ten in the easy win.

The traditional ACC welcome awaited the Gamecocks, as they entered Duke Indoor Stadium, where an overflow 8,800 expressed their dislike for their guests. The Blue Devils, who were enroute to a 21-win season delighted their constituency with an 82-71 victory.

Back home against Furman, Roche set an all-time single-game scoring record for the Gamecocks, with 56 in a 118-83 win.

Clemson, whose new coach, Takes Locke, was an advocate of slow-down basketball, put on the brakes when the Gamecocks went to Littlejohn Coliseum. The Tigers made a run to overcome a nine-point USC lead late in the game, but Riker hit three key free throws to preserve a 47-44 win. Roche's 23 points represented almost half the Gamecock scoring.

Carolina downed Davidson in Charlotte before returning home for two crucial ACC games against N.C. State and North Carolina. State was disposed of, 79-63, in a foul-filled game in which Roche scored 41 points on 17 for 22 field goal accuracy. The Gamecock star turned it up a notch to compensate for the absence of Joyce, who was out because of a leg injury.

The rough contest with State was just a warm-up for the visit from Smith's Tar Heels. With Joyce still on the sidelines. Roche continued his scoring streak, 32 points, as South Carolina defeated the ACC leaders, 72-66, before an overflow 12,717 in the Coliseum. The game was marred by 57 personal fouls, six disqualifications, 84 free throw attempts and two technical fouls against Smith.

After beating NCAA-bound Houston, 88-71, the Gamecocks routinely handled Wake Forest (84-64) at home, State (82-69) and Wake (88-73) on the road to end the regular season at 10-4, second to North Carolina's 11-3. Highlights of the road wins were Roche's 37 points against State, and Aydlett's 29 in the win over Wake Forest. In the latter game USC hit a school record 44 of 57 free throw attempts, including 11 each by Aydlett, Roche and Owens.

This sent the second-seeded Gamecocks into the ACC tournament at Greensboro, where they met the Maryland team that had victimized them with the unbelievable ending at College Park. This time there was no miracle, and Carolina eliminated the Terps, 71-63, as Joyce returned to the lineup, and Owens and Roche scored 18 points each. McGuire used a pressing man-to-man defense this time to prevent any possible Terp slowdown.

In the semi-finals Roche hit only one of his first 16 shots but came back strong in the second half to finish with 19, as Sloan's Wolfpack was brushed aside, 69-56. This set up a championship final with North Carolina, which had beaten Clemson and Virginia in its first two games.

The first 36 minutes of the game didn't provide classic basketball, but the last four would be firmly etched in the minds of every Gamecock who played in or witnessed the contest. With four minutes remaining, the Tar Heels had a six-point lead and went into Smith's famous "four corners" offense, which was really not offense, but a time-consuming strategy.

This time the usually-effective strategy didn't work for Smith, because they failed to convert on five one-and-ones, as the Gamecocks committed fouls to force the issue. South Carolina took advantage of the Tar Heel misses to move within a point, 51-50, and when Aydlett rebounded, George Karl's missed free throw, the Gamecocks had the ball with 20 seconds remaining.

When Joyce drove to the baseline for a shot he was tied up by the 6-10 Lee Dedmon, and there was a jump ball between the two set-up at the Gamecock end of the court. This was before the rule was changed to give alternate possession on jump ball situations.

MCGUIRE: "We called a timeout, and the clock showed six seconds remaining in the game. Over on the North Carolina bench, I think they were planning the post-game celebration--they already had the scissors out to cut down the nets.

"With Joyce, who was 6-3 and coming off a bad leg injury, we couldn't realistically expect to control the tap, so we decided that our best strategy was to plan a way to steal it when their 6-10 guy controlled it. So, they lined up for the jump, and I guess Dedmon was a little complacent about it.

"The official threw it up, and Joyce went like he had springs in his legs, and he managed to tip the ball toward our goal to Owens, who was inside the circle. Tommy grabbed the ball, wheeled around and laid it in the basket to win the game. There was still two seconds on the clock, but they didn't have much of a shot at it, so we had the game, 52-51.

"From North Carolina's standpoint their mistake was violating a rule of sports that you never concede anything. They were so confident of controlling the jump ball that they didn't have anybody on defense under our basket, and there was nobody there to stop Tommy from driving in for the layup. You always have somebody in there. All you want is the ball, and the game is over."

A season of disappointments and running a gauntlet of crowd abuse at ACC arenas had come to a happy climax.

In the aftermath of the dramatic ending at Greensboro there were different versions of what happened on the jump ball. Dedmon insisted that he controlled the tap but hit it in the wrong direction. Joyce, who had not started the game and scored only one basket, felt that "he got a piece of the ball." Replays indicated that Joyce's hand sent the ball toward Owens. UNC's Smith seemed to agree that Joyce did get his hand on the ball.

Statistically, Owens won the battle of the 6-10 players, out-scoring Dedmon, 14-12, and outrebounding him, 19-7. Roche led both teams with 18 points and was named to the all-tournament team, along with Owens. Riker was named to the second team and Roche tied with Dedmon for the tournament's most valuable player award.

Again the anti-South Carolina sentiment was evident in voting for ACC coach of the year, dominated by North Carolina media. In spite of winning the conference championship and coaching the Gamecocks to a sixth-place finish in the AP and UPI rankings, McGuire didn't even figure in the voting, which was won by Smith, with Virginia's Bill Gibson placing second. That sentiment was underscored in the Player-of-the-Year voting, in which Wake Forest's Charlie Davis was a wide choice (86-30) over Roche in the voting.

The rejection of Roche for the honor was in the face of South Carolina's 20-and 15-point wins over Wake during the season, and Roche's selection to the UPI All-America first team. Several other All-America teams, including *Basketball Weekly*, listed Roche on their first team. Seventeen NBA coaches selected Roche for the annual College All-Star first team, while Davis was named to neither first or second team.

After the emotional and physical strain of going through the ACC season and tournament, Roche and his teammates would be exposed to one more hostile crowd. That took place in Raleigh five days after the dramatic event in nearby Greensboro.

The Gamecocks faced a Pennsylvania team that had won 27 games without a loss and ranked third in the nation. McGuire's men, with ACC fans, other than their own, pulling for the Quakers, held a one point halftime lead. However, they experienced a miserable second half and were outscored substantially in a 79-64 Penn victory.

Thus ended the Roche-Owens era at South Carolina, a tumultuous three years that would bring the elation of accomplishment as a team and as individuals. It would also leave the scars of hostility from schools around the conference.

Afterward, when asked if he had to do it again if he would play in the ACC, Roche answered, "I'd play anywhere for Coach McGuire. As far as the ACC, I still don't know exactly what I think of it. I'm going to have to sit down awhile and think about it.

"I know a lot has been said and written about my conduct. But maybe people should try to look at our side of it. If they could read our mail and get some of our phone calls, they might understand. The thing that was important to us was that the people of South Carolina were behind us, and they have been. They read some of the things that were written about us in other places, and they know we're just sticking up for the people of South Carolina."

An example of the receptions that Roche received around the ACC took place at Wake Forest, where students and the Demon Deacon mascot took a dummy wearing Roche's jersey number (11) and stuffed it into a commode at midcourt prior to the game. USC won the game, 88-73, as Roche could probably still hear the cheers of many in the crowd at Charlotte when he injured his ankle against Wake Forest the previous year.

Roche was later quoted, "By the time we were seniors, I don't think I was alone in feeling that we had had about enough of playing in the ACC."

However, the Gamecock seniors could look back on many more good times than bad. Their 23-5 record and No. 6 national ranking for the 1970-71 campaign brought their three-year varsity won-lost record to 69-15, a winning percentage of 82.1, easily the best in the school's history.

Roche set a number of individual USC records, including most career points (1,910), most points in a single game (56 vs. Furman), most consecutive free throws without a miss (41) and best free throw percentage in a game (16 for 16 vs. Davidson and Notre Dame).

Owens established a career field goal percentage record (.501), highest rebound average (13.3) and most rebounds in a three-year career (1,116).

Roche was selected in the first round draft by the NBA, with a choice of Phoenix or Kentucky, while Owens was picked by San Diego in the fourth round, and Ribock, by Boston in the eighth. Roche eventually signed with the New York Nets of the ABA, while Owens went to Memphis in that league. Ribock did not sign with the Celtics, but played professionally in South America and later, Europe.

Later in the year McGuire was given the most meaningful vote of confidence that can be received from the University Board of Trustees--an extension of his contract through the year 1980! At this point in his coaching career McGuire ranked third among active coaches in terms of winning percentages (72.1%) behind Kentucky's Adolph Rupp and UCLA's John Wooden.

In closing the curtain on a great era in South Carolina basketball, the University officially retired Roche's jersey number--11. It became the second such retirement at South Carolina, as Grady Wallace's No. 42 had been retired in 1957.

Roche expressed the sentiments of the departing seniors when he commented, "They've been great friends to us down here, and I'll always remember them. It will always be like a second home."

CHAPTER NINE
LIFE AFTER THE ACC

The realignment of college athletic conferences in the early 1990s was nothing new, and the University of South Carolina had been an active participant in such changes. When the Gamecocks became a member of the Southeastern Conference in 1992 it was the fifth time they had changed their banners, as pertained to the sport of basketball.

The Gamecocks became members of the Southern Conference in 1922, a year after the league was chartered, and they remained in the Southern when several members left to form the base for Southeastern Conference. The Southern ultimately grew to an unwieldy 17-member league that included a strange mixture of institutions, and there was no way members could play each other every year in any sport—much less football and basketball.

During the 1952-53 school year South Carolina athletic director Rex Enright played a leadership role in discussions by seven of the Southern Conference schools about forming a new league. Those discussions led to the withdrawal of those seven schools to form the Atlantic Coast Conference. Along with South Carolina, charter members of the ACC were Clemson, Duke, Maryland, North Carolina, North Carolina State and Wake Forest. A year later Virginia joined to bring the membership to eight.

Dr. James T. Penney, University of South Carolina biology professor and the school's faculty chairman of athletics, had the honor of being elected the ACC's first president.

South Carolina's affiliation was firm and relatively happy for 16 years, but in 1969 the school's head football coach and athletic director, Paul Dietzel, joined Clemson in an effort to relax admission standards which placed them at a competitive disadvantage in recruiting against schools in other conferences across the country.

The ACC required that, in order for a student to be eligible for an athletic scholarship, he had to score 800 on the Student Aptitude Test and project a 1.6 grade point, based on the student's high school grades. The NCAA guideline required only the 1.6 grade point average, and that is the guideline that Clemson and Carolina wanted adopted by the ACC. Both schools were rumored to be on the brink of withdrawal from the conference.

In the spring of 1971, when it was evident that the ACC would not budge on its academic stance, South Carolina, at Dietzel's urging, notified the conference that it was withdrawing as of August 15 of that year.

With this action South Carolina became independent, joining a small number of major all sports institutions, notably Notre Dame, Penn State, Florida State and Miami, without a conference affiliation. This presented immediate scheduling problems in basketball, without much time to act. All of the ACC schools, with the exception of Clemson, refused to play South Carolina in basketball.

The withdrawal didn't affect the football schedule, as a visit to South Carolina resulted in good financial reward, as the Gamecocks always drew big crowds in Columbia.

McGuire was surprisingly successful in lining up an attractive schedule that included home games against national powers such as Niagara and three top ten teams from the previous season, Marquette, St. Bonaventure and Notre Dame. On the road the Gamecocks would play in the Quaker City Classic and face Auburn, Iowa and Houston, which made the NCAA playoffs.

Despite the absence from the schedule of six natural rivals, McGuire felt that he could maintain the momentum of the past few years and build new rivalries. Some feared that attendance at home games would suffer, but that would prove to be a false alarm.

THE 1971-72 SEASON

To enter his first year as an independent, McGuire could count on returnees Riker, Joyce, Aydlett, Carver and Traylor, all of whom had considerable varsity experience. They would be joined by leading members of the 1970-71 freshman team, led by Brian Winters and Ed Peterson.

Peterson was an All-Metropolitan Washington guard out of Silver Spring, Md. and had led the freshman team with a 29.3 scoring average.

Again South Carolina ranked high in the pre-season polls, even without Roche, Owens and Ribock, and once again they were destined to fulfill the prophecy by the media.

Enthusiasm for the basketball program remained sky high during the first year as an independent, and the average attendance at home games was 12,327, less than 200 per game below the record 1970-71 crowds. Home crowds at no ACC school were even close to those that saw the Gamecocks in Carolina Coliseum.

Success on the court continued, also, as the Gamecocks compiled a better won-lost record, 24-5, than they did the year before (23-6) when they won the ACC title.

The development of the seven-foot Traylor and return of Riker enabled McGuire to use a double pivot, with Aydlett at forward, and Joyce and Winters at the guard positions. That lineup gave McGuire height, size and firepower with which to face a challenging year.

After an easy (84-63) home win over Auburn, the Gamecocks went to San Francisco for the Cable Car Classic, which they won by beating Santa Clara (77-66) and California (67-59). No other non-west coast team had ever won the event.

After disposing of Virginia Tech at home and Pittsburgh on the road, McGuire again took his team to the Quaker City Classic, which the Gamecocks had won in 1968-69. Fairfield (87-60) and Boston College (86-64) were no match for the Gamecocks, but Villanova was a different matter. The Wildcats, who were ranked 15th in the final polls, overcame a 28-point, 15-rebound performance by Riker to hold on for a 77-76 win when Joyce's last second shot went into the basket but spun out.

Second-ranked Marquette invaded the Coliseum in early January to challenge the fourth-ranked Gamecocks before a national television audience. The game was a classic, although marred in the first half by a fight that resulted in Riker and Marquette's Bob Lackey being ejected. Riker suffered a broken hand when he landed a blow to Lackey's head, and that set-off a brief free-for-all that the media compared to World War II.

However, the hotly-contested game continued, with Al McGuire's Warriors holding a 36-30 lead over his former coach. Traylor took up the inside challenge in Riker's absence, and Peterson came off the bench to hit seven straight long-range shots to move the Gamecocks to a 69-68 lead in the final moments. After hitting a field goal and two free throws Marquette held a 72-71 lead and Joyce's attempt at a game-winning basket was blocked.

By defeating Manhattan, 116-78, the Gamecocks compiled the third highest point total in their history, as Traylor scored a career high 37 points and grabbed 20 rebounds. With Riker lost for several games, McGuire received balance scoring from Winters, Aydlett, Carver and Joyce.

Carolina edged St. Bonaventure and moved past Niagara in the Coliseum, where those two teams had played in the 1970 NCAA regional. That sent the Gamecocks to a Chicago match-up with Iowa, which rode a 40-point performance by Rick Williams to a 91-85 upset.

Moving to Madison Square Garden, Riker fully recovered from his broken hand to score this all-time high 42 points in a 100-77 victory over Fordham. Traylor had 15 rebounds and Joyce and Aydlett, 15 points each in the win.

McGuire's squad kept their bags packed and returned to Chicago Stadium, where 18,000-plus fans watched them hand Northern Illinois one of its four defeats of that season, 83-72. The Gamecocks were true on 27 of 31 free throws, as they moved up to 6th in the AP rankings. That was followed by a 98-64 rout of Stetson in Columbia.

At Clemson Riker and Traylor led the Gamecocks to a hard fought, 62-58 win, followed by easy home wins over DePaul and Davidson. On the road again, Carolina disposed of Nevada-Las Vegas, but fell to Houston, (95-85).

After beating Davidson in Charlotte, McGuire saw his team score an impressive 109-83 victory over Notre Dame. Carver had a career high 21 points and Riker added 31 to lead the Gamecocks.

With a bid to the NCAA playoffs in hand, USC moved past Creighton, 81-64, as Joyce had 22 points. The regular season came to a close with a 77-64 margin over Clemson, as Joyce again had 22.

In an NCAA tournament pairing at Williamburg, Va., Carolina edged Temple, 53-51, when Joyce drove the middle and went between two Owl defenders to score the winning basket with six seconds left. That created an East Regional engagement with North Carolina at Morgantown, W.Va.

With Joyce and Traylor in early foul trouble, the Tar Heels broke open the game with a 19-5 spurt at the end of the half and moved to a 92-69 win over their former ACC rival. The format of that era called for a consolation game between the semi-final losers, and the Gamecocks ended their year on an upbeat by avenging the Quaker City Classic loss to Villanova, 51-42.

McGuire's 24 victories against only five losses earned final rankings of 6th by AP and 5th by UPI. Another great season had seen the emergence of new star performers. Riker, who was named to the AP All-America first team, led the scoring averages at 19.6, followed by Joyce (18.3), Traylor (12.8), Aydlett (9.8) and Winters (8.3). Riker was also a first round pick by the New York Knicks in the NBA draft.

McGuire's first post-ACC recruiting class was not productive, as none of the 1971-72 freshmen made significant contributions to future varsity efforts. The most interesting recruit was George Felton, who came out of All Hallows High School in New York and was Carolina head basketball coach from 1986-1991.

THE 1972-73 SEASON

Proselytizing would pickup for the 1972-73 class, as several future starters (Alex English, Mike Dunleavy, Bob Mathias and Mark Greiner) would enroll and become eligible to play on the varsity as freshmen under revised NCAA rules. This would be good news for McGuire who would be without departing seniors Riker and Aydlett.

MCGUIRE: "We had already set up our freshman schedule for that season, and it would have been a good team, but as it turned out the rule change helped us. English started every game for us, and Dunleavy was in the starting lineup for all but the season opener.

"English played for Dreher High School in Columbia and was being recruited by a number of colleges, although, at that time, this wasn't the hotbed of basketball. Alex was the first player to come out of Columbia

with the potential of developing into a player of national prominence.

"Casey Manning was the only black player on our squad, so the recruitment of black athletes by us and other Southern colleges was still something new. Some of the black leaders in Columbia took Alex under their wings and wanted to advise him on what to do. Whether they had a lot of influence on his decision, I can't say.

"I do remember that the Dreher coach was a Duke graduate, and he wanted Alex to go to Duke. One thing that helped was that Sue Floyd, wife of assistant athletic director, Ralph Floyd, was the art teacher at Dreher. Alex liked art, and Sue was able to put in some good words for us. That probably would be an NCAA violation today, because the rules are ridiculously strict as to who can talk to a prospect.

"Fortunately, Alex chose to come with us, and it was a good decision for both of us. He blossomed a lot faster than anyone had expected. He represented Carolina very well, on and off the court, and continued to do so after he finished college and went into the NBA.

"Dunleavy was another one of my New York City recruits. He played for Nazareth High School, which was coached by Jim McMorrow, who played for me at St. John's. Mike was a late bloomer in high school, but he became a complete player as a senior and was selected on a number of all-star teams. Fortunately, we got an early start in recruiting Mike, because of Jim McMorrow, and by the time other schools became aware of him we were already involved."

The Gamecocks opened their season against Tennessee's Southeastern Conference co-champs at Knoxville and were beaten, 55-45. This would be the first of three games that would find McGuire without Brian Winters, who was suffering from mononucleosis.

Winters played in the first home game and scored 15 points, joining Joyce (18), Traylor (17) and English (13) in double figures. After wide-margin wins over Michigan State and Georgia Southern in the Coliseum, McGuire had settled on a lineup of guards Joyce and Dunleavy, forwards English and Winters, with Traylor at center. All would average scoring in double figures throughout the season.

Greeted by 16 below temperatures at Salt Lake City, USC fell to fourth-ranked Providence, 79-64, as Carolina's shooting accuracy was also below freezing. The Gamecocks gained consolation by beating host Utah, as Manning and Dunleavy took up the scoring slack with 16 points each.

The Gamecocks lost to Virginia Tech, fifth-ranked Marquette and Notre Dame on the road and to St. John's in the finals of the Holiday Festival but won their 10 remaining home games and six away to earn another bid to the NCAA playoffs.

The most significant of the victories was against fifth-ranked Indiana before the usual 12,000-plus fans in Carolina Coliseum. The unbeaten Hoosiers, coached by Bobby Knight, built up a huge first half lead, as Joyce failed to score a field goal in the first 12 minutes. From that point on Joyce put on a clinic for the visitors.

The Gamecock captain had 16 points by halftime, cutting the Indiana lead to ten points. Joyce didn't cool down during the intermission, scoring 25 points in the second period, putting Carolina ahead for the first time by hitting a basket with less than two minutes remaining. He had scored almost half of his team's points in an 88-85 upset that put the Gamecocks solidly in the national rankings.

A nine-game winning streak that followed the loss at Marquette ensured McGuire of a fifth straight season of 20 or more wins and a third straight berth in the NCAA tournament.

At Wichita, Kansas the Gamecocks downed Southwest Conference champion Texas Tech, 78-70, as Joyce (21), Traylor (16), English (15) and Dunleavy (11) led the balanced scoring that was typical of the season.

This moved the Gamecocks to Houston for a meeting with Memphis State, a team that would eventually reach the NCAA title game, only to fall before UCLA. Future NBA star Larry Kenon led the Tigers to a 90-76 victory to eliminate Carolina. The Gamecocks bounced back to win the consolation game over Southwest Louisiana, 90-85, bringing McGuire's final record to 22 wins against seven losses, giving the Gamecocks their fifth straight 20-plus-win season.

The final UPI poll ranked the Gamecocks 16th, the fifth straight year that McGuire's teams were numbered among the top 20 in the nation. Joyce's 20.4 average led the scorers, followed by English's 14.6, Traylor's 12.8, Winters' 11.5 and Dunleavy's 10.4. As of 1994 only three teams in the school's history had five players in double figures.

The two seniors on the squad, Joyce and Traylor, finished their varsity careers on high notes. Joyce was named second team All-America by AP, UPI and the National Association of Basketball Coaches. He was drafted by Indiana of the ABA and was beginning to make an impact in his second season, scoring 1,210 points and averaging 14.9. However, a severe leg injury ended Joyce's promising pro career the following season. Joyce's jersey number 43 was retired by the University, as he joined Roche and Wallace in receiving that unique honor.

Because he followed Owens and Riker, Traylor probably received less credit than he deserved for his accomplishments. During his three varsity seasons he averaged 10.1 points and 8.2 rebounds, leading the team's rebounding in 16 games and scoring in five.

English, a great leaper, shared the rebounding with Traylor, averaging an identical 10.6 per game.

A significant addition to McGuire's coaching staff for this season was Bobby Cremins, who captained the 1969 and 1970 teams. Cremins had been working for a hotel in New York City and served on the coaching staff at Point Park College. He rejoined McGuire as a graduate assistant for the 1972 season. The following year he became a full-time assistant coach.

In the summer of 1972, Joyce was the first USC athlete ever to be named to the United States Olympic team, participating in the historic and tragic games in Munich, Germany. The U.S. lost its first ever Gold Medal game to Russia in a highly controversial 51-50 decision to Russia. In that game the Soviets were the benefits of two weird calls. With only three seconds remaining Russia was twice unsuccessful in completing full-court passes for attempted shots, but both times the officials gave the Soviets the ball again. On the third chance the Russians made a desperation shot and were awarded the Gold Metal.

The shocked Americans refused the Silver Metal, convinced that they had rightfully won the Gold. This was the event during which Mideast terrorists seized a group of athletes representing Israel, ultimately ending in the death of all.

On a happier note, in May, McGuire was named to the South Carolina Athletic Hall of Fame, which honors sports figures for outstanding contributions and accomplishments.

The following month Buck Freeman, whose association with McGuire went back to his college days at St. John's, announced his retirement. However, it was made plain that Freeman would remain involved with McGuire as a consultant and would continue to live near the USC campus.

The vacancy was filled by Ben Jobe, who had served as head coach at South Carolina State College in Orangeburg for the previous five seasons. Jobe would also be the first black coach on a Gamecock basketball staff, and the second in any sport. Oree Banks had served as coach of the scout squad for Paul Dietzel's football team.

The second vacancy on McGuire's staff had been created when Bill Loving, who had been on the staff for six years, resigned. Loving had done most of the scouting of future opponents of the Gamecocks, along with assisting with recruiting.

THE 1973-74 SEASON

Only one of the freshmen brought in by McGuire for the 1973-74 season would figure prominently on future varsities. He was Nate Davis, who at 6-4 was a tremendous leaper, as indicated by his average of 18.2 rebounds in leading Eau Claire High School of Columbia to the AAAA state championship his senior year. His 17.6 scoring average also figured in his selection as the state's Player-of-the-Year.

Another freshman, Ed Lynch of Miami, Fl., became a star at South Carolina but not in basketball. After a sparsely active freshman year, Lynch devoted full attention to the Gamecock baseball team, leading them to the championship game of the College World Series in 1977. *(Lynch became general manager of the New York Mets in 1994, after having pitched for them in the 1980s.)*

Davis filled out the starting lineup for McGuire, joining Winters, English, Dunleavy and Mathias, while Greiner became "the first man off the bench."

Because the Gamecocks continued their prominence in national ratings and played highly respected opponents from around the country, the absence of ACC rivals from the schedule had little effect on home attendance. Even state rival Clemson was off the schedule because of incidents that occurred two previous seasons.

Even so, the Gamecocks would continue to be one of the top schools in the country in home attendance, averaging crowds of 11,107 at their 15 games in Carolina Coliseum. The average the year before was 11,770, and in 1971-72, it had been 12,327, only slightly below the ACC championship year of 12,523.

When the big name schools came to town, however, the fans responded. The Coliseum was full for games with Marquette, Notre Dame, Pittsburgh, and even Toledo in the season opener.

Winters, a great outside threat, went through an entirely healthy season for the first time and reached his full potential. He and Dunleavy complemented the inside scoring ability of English, who received substantial rebounding help from Mathias.

In a 22-5 season the most significant home victories were over Texas Tech, Marquette, Pennsylvania, Dayton, Pittsburgh and Houston, while Carolina downed Michigan State, Villanova and Georgia Tech on those teams' home courts. McGuire returned to Madison Square Garden to record wins over Fordham and Seton Hall as part of doubleheaders in January.

The most dramatic victory came over third-ranked Marquette, which later reached the championship game of the NCAA playoffs. Al McGuire's Warriors overcame a 32-25 Carolina halftime lead to move ahead midway of the second half, after which the lead see-sawed. With 29 seconds remaining, Greiner, who was a smart defensive player, took a charge from a Warrior, and the Gamecocks had possession and a chance to win. As the seconds ticked off, Winters dribbled to the top of the key, sprang into the air and sent a picture perfect jump shot into the bottom of the net with two seconds showing for a 60-58 Gamecock win.

Winters had 23 points in a win over 15th-ranked Pittsburgh, and 25 in beating Villanova in Philadelphia. These were prominent in his final season's average of 20 points per game.

English had his highest scoring game, 37 points, in a narrow, 72-68 loss to fifth-ranked Notre Dame, while Dunleavy had 20 in a victory over Michigan State and 24 in the Garden game with Seton Hall.

Again the Gamecocks concluded their season in the NCAA regionals, meeting Furman in the first round at Philadelphia. The two South Carolina teams traveled the 500-plus miles to the City of Brotherly Love to play before a crowd of 1,042. The uninspired Gamecocks had an atrocious shooting game and fell to the Paladins by a 75-67 score.

Still McGuire had another nationally-ranked team to his credit, finishing 19th in the AP poll and 16th in UPI's ratings.

Winters became the school's 13th player to score 1,000 points or more during a career, compiling a three-year total of 1,079. He was drafted by the Los Angeles Lakers, who could have been looking at him as a successor to Jerry West, who had just retired from the Lakers. However, Winters was traded to the Milwaukee Bucks the following season and began a distinguished eight-year run with that team. Brian had a career scoring average of 16.8 points per game, and when he retired from the Bucks, the organization honored him by retiring his jersey number.

Winters began a coaching career as an assistant at Princeton, was on the staff of the Atlanta Hawks in 1994, and was named head coach of Vancouver's new NBA Team in 1995.

During the season McGuire and the basketball world were saddened by the death of Buck Freeman on February 14, 1974 in Columbia's Providence Hospital. He was 74 years old.

MCGUIRE: "This was a tremendous loss to me. Buck was a coach's coach, one of the great basketball coaches of all time. He won games because he actually knew more about the game than the other coach.

"He was the first big-time basketball coach in New York and was one of those responsible for increasing interest in the sport and raising it to a higher level, not only in New York, but across the country.

"He was invaluable to me, first as a coach, and later as an assistant who made a major contribution to the success of my teams at North Carolina and South Carolina. He was not only a fine teacher of fundamentals but a positive influence on the lives of the young men who were fortunate enough to come under his guidance.

"I'm grateful for the impact he had on my life."

THE 1974-75 SEASON

The departure of Winters from Carolina left a big hole in the lineup for McGuire to fill. Returning was Dunleavy, who had an excellent sophomore season, averaging 16 points, and English, who was second to Winters in scoring at 18.3 and averaged a team leading 8.8 rebounds. Davis, Greiner and Mathias were also available for the 1974-75 season, so there was a good nucleus to form the basis for another strong team.

The Gamecocks would be bolstered by 6-9 Tommy Boswell, who had played for Jobe at South Carolina State but had transferred to USC following his sophomore year. He had to sit out the 1973-74 campaign but had two more years of eligibility. Boswell would play only one season, however, as the Boston Celtics made him their first draft pick in 1975, moving him into the NBA.

McGuire also brought in two freshmen who would have impacts on future Gamecock teams. One was Jackie Gilloon, a fancy ball-handler and outside shooter from Memorial High School in New York City. An All-America prep player, Gilloon's most impressive credential was being selected over future pro great Moses Malone as MVP of a post-season high school all-star game.

Golie Augustus, a 6-6 forward out of Columbia's Keenan High School, cast his lot with McGuire after receiving the award as the state's top prep player.

Another highly rated prospect, Billy Truitt, a guard out of Lackawanna, N.Y., was an academic casualty after his first year in school.

McGuire missed another 20-win season by an eyelash. The final 19-9 record was excellent by most school's standards and merited an invitation to the NIT, but two one-point overtime losses prevented the Gamecocks from reaching the 20-win goal. The first came against St. John's (78-77) in the Ocean State Classic at Providence, R.I., and the other was 66-65 heartbreaker to Notre Dame at South Bend in a nationally-televised game.

The most significant victory came over 12th-ranked Princeton in the Carolina Classic in the Coliseum. After beating the Tigers by a 65-48 score, the Gamecocks faced LSU, which had beaten Duke in the first round. Carolina outscored Dale Brown's Tigers, 77-64, as freshman Gilloon received the tournament's most valuable player trophy for his scoring (14 and 17 points) and playmaking.

The biggest home crowd of the season, 12,655, saw the Gamecocks lose a down-to-the-wire, 68-65, nail-biter to 11th ranked Marquette in another game that was televised nationwide.

There was another slight drop in home attendance in the Coliseum, where an average of 10,739 fans saw the Gamecocks play. This still placed South Carolina high nationally in that respect.

The Gamecocks' string of six straight seasons ranked in the nation's top 20 teams came to an end, but the 19-9 record was good enough for a bid to the NIT. The Gamecocks disposed of Connecticut, 71-61, in the first round, but nationally-ranked Princeton avenged the loss to USC in the Carolina Classic by an 86-67 score.

Boswell's 16.5 scoring average and 8.7 rebounds led the Gamecock statistics, and that inspired him to declare himself for the NBA draft. He went with Boston and played in the NBA for five seasons.

Following Boswell in the scoring averages were Dunleavy(16.3), English (16.0), Davis (11.6) and Gilloon (6.9), who also had 122 assists.

The Gamecocks had one coaching change prior to the season, as Cremins went to Appalachian State College at Boone, N.C. To replace him McGuire chose Greg Blatt, son of long-time USC trustee Sol Blatt, Jr. Blatt had served the three previous years on the staff of the College of Charleston.

THE 1975-76 SEASON

McGuire went into the 1975-76 season as the second winningest active coach in college basketball. His 25-year record of 471 wins and 179 losses for a percentage of .725 ranked him behind only DePaul's Ray Meyer, who had 509 wins but a lower percentage (.627) than the Gamecock coach. He had won his 200th victory at South Carolina against Canisius before, ironically, the smallest USC crowd in the history of Carolina Coliseum, 7,831.

The departure of Boswell left McGuire without a major inside scorer and rebounder. English, at 6-8 and 190 pounds, and Mathias, only 6-7, would have to shoulder the responsibility.

With Dunleavy and Gilloon at the guards and Davis at a forward, the Gamecocks appeared to be competitive but were without the depth of talent that was featured on previous McGuire squads.

The Gamecocks would prove to be over-achievers, winning 18 games against nine losses, and were deprived of another 20-win campaign by a one-point loss at Nebraska and a two-point defeat at South Florida. They won 10 of 13 home games, including Carolina Classic tournament victories over Yale (100-66) and Oklahoma State (70-61).

Among the Gamecock home victims were Oklahoma and Temple, while they scored a 95-86 win over Villanova in the Holiday Festival in Madison Square Garden. Other impressive road victories came over Villanova in Philadelphia and Pittsburgh.

Two of the Carolina losses were at home--to second-ranked Marquette and a 90-83 loss to Notre Dame in Columbia.

In spite of another fine record against a schedule of prominent opponents, the Gamecocks were not invited to the NCAA playoffs or the NIT. English had a sensational senior year, scoring 610 points and averaging 22.6. He also averaged 10.6 rebounds to lead the team in that category.

English's 1,972 career points was still a USC all-time record in 1994, and his 1,064 rebounds ranked third. English was named to several All-America squads, and the University recognized his place in basketball history by retiring his jersey number (22). English joined Grady Wallace, John Roche and Kevin Joyce in that respect.

Dunleavy's 397 points and 14.7 average brought his career point total to 1,586, ranking him fourth in the USC record book. Both English and Dunleavy moved onto successful playing careers in the NBA. English had ten great seasons with Denver and scored a career total 25,343 points to rank in the top ten of all-time NBA scorers. After a final season with Dallas, he became an executive with the NBA Players Association in New York City, but he continued to make his permanent residence in a suburb of Columbia.

Dunleavy continued in the NBA as head coach of the Los Angeles Lakers in 1991-92 and then joined the Milwaukee Bucks as their head coach in 1992-93.

THE 1976-77 SEASON

For his 1976-77 team McGuire had some big holes to fill in his squad. Lost from the previous years' squad were two of the school's all-time scoring leaders, English and Dunleavy, along with the rebounding strength of Mathias and defensive value of Greiner.

He would have to get immediate help from incoming freshmen, notably Jim Graziano, Mike Doyle and Kenny Reynolds, three more imports from the New York area. Graziano, an All-America prep center from Farmingdale, was one of the most highly recruited players in the country. He figured to make an immediate impact in the pivot, with his 6-9, 230-pound physical attributes.

Doyle, a 6-4, All-New York City guard, was counted on to replace Dunleavy, while Gilloon was solid at the other backcourt position.

Karlton Hilton, a 6-6 forward out of Anderson (SC) Junior College was expected to move into the vacancy created by the departure of English, while Nate Davis was getting star billing at the other forward post.

With a lineup that included only two players with college experience, the Gamecocks faced an imposing schedule. During the season they would face top-ranked Michigan, No. 3 Kentucky, No. 7 Marquette, which ultimately won the NCAA championship over North Carolina, No. 10 Notre Dame and No. 11 Alabama (twice). That gave them seven games with teams ranked among the best 11 in the nation and those games would result in seven of the team's 12 losses during the season.

Probably the Gamecocks' best game of the season resulted in a loss. Over 10,000 spectators and a national television audience saw Carolina battle Michigan's No. 1 Wolverines down to the wire before falling by four points, 90-86. Davis had 28 points, and playmaker Gilloon had a surprising ten rebounds to lead the Gamecocks in that category.

Nationally-ranked Alabama outlasted the Gamecocks, 67-62, in the finals of the Carolina Classic, which drew a disappointing 5,072 fans just two days before Christmas.

The Gamecocks best wins were over Georgia (74-73) in the consolation game of the Sugar Bowl Classic, 54-49 over Nebraska at home, and 49-48 over Temple in Philadelphia.

Graziano and Doyle had a creditable season for freshmen, averaging 13.2 and 8.9 points respectively. Davis led the team in scoring at 15.7, and Gilloon was third at 9.7, but the Gamecocks struggled to a 14-12 record, which would be McGuire's worst record in 11 years.

Still this team had a special achievement in that it provided McGuire with his 500th victory of his storied career. It came on the night of February 9 in Carolina Coliseum, when the Gamecocks defeated The Citadel, 85-66, in front of 8,016 spectators. This event was officially celebrated on March 22 at a Testimonial Dinner at which Mel Allen, famous sportscaster and "Voice of the New York Yankees," served as Master of Ceremonies.

Many national celebrities attended the event, including author James Michener, North Carolina coach Dean Smith, Long Island coach Clair Bee, St. John's coach Lou Carnesecca and DePaul coach Ray Meyer, who was the winningest active college coach of all time.

The following month the University Board of Trustees voted to name the basketball arena in Carolina Coliseum, "Frank McGuire Arena."

Continuing the string of honors for the Irishman, McGuire received the ultimate tribute on May 2, 1977, when he was inducted into the National Basketball Hall of Fame at Springfield, Massachusetts. Ironically, there were no representatives from the USC present at the dinner, attended by over 500. McGuire was presented by his longtime friend, Ben Carnevale, who had coached at North Carolina and Navy but was now athletic director at William and Mary.

The "event-a-month" streak was kept alive in June, when James B. Holderman became the 36th president of the University. He would become a significant principal in events surrounding the career of McGuire.

THE 1977-78 SEASON

Suffice it to say that there were a series of off-the-court events leading into the 1977-78 season.

On the court the Gamecocks entered the season without their top scorer, Davis, but could call on Graziano, Gilloon, Doyle, Hilton and improving ex-Keenan High School (Columbia) star Golie Augustus. Incoming freshmen included Mike Dunleavy's brother, Kevin, and another guard, Zam Fredrick, who had averaged 30 points a game for St. Matthews High School in nearby Calhoun County.

Doyle, Gilloon, Augustus and Graziano all averaged in double figures to lead a balanced scoring attack, Hilton added inside strength, and the improving Kenny Reynolds gave some backcourt depth, as Carolina won 16 and lost 12.

The more significant victories came over Minnesota, Clemson, Southern California and Notre Dame, all in Carolina Coliseum. Again they faced several national powers, losing to NCAA champion Kentucky at Lexington and taking No. 7 Marquette into two overtime periods before losing, 69-66, at home before 11,876 fans.

After the loss to Marquette the Gamecocks won their final five regular season games to earn a bid to the NIT, which had gone to a new format for playing early round games on home courts of participants before moving into the Garden for the final four. The Gamecocks drew North Carolina State (21-10) in their first round game, and the Wolfpack was given the home floor advantage in Raleigh.

Despite an impressive 25-point performance by Gilloon, State eliminated the Gamecocks, 82-70.

In was the 12th straight winning season for McGuire and his seventh post-season tournament at Carolina, which had never been in the NCAA or NIT events prior to the Irishman's arrival.

The veteran coach was honored during halftime of the February 5 nationally televised game against Marquette, as the University observed "Frank McGuire Appreciation Day." McGuire was presented an oil painting by Columbia artist Ted Hamlin depicting scenes from his 500th collegiate victory.

THE 1978-79 SEASON

The most valuable additions to McGuire's 1978-79 squad were a transfer from Auburn, 6-8 Cedrick Hordges, 6-11 Furman transfer Jim Strickland of Columbia, and Tom Wimbush, 6-6, a graduate of Anderson Junior College. They would prove to be three of the Gamecocks' top six point producers during the season.

Leading returnees from the previous squad were Doyle, Graziano, Fredrick and Reynolds. The emergence of the ACC as a leading basketball league and increasing emphasis on conference affiliation placed South Carolina at an increasing disadvantage in recruiting, and home attendance suffered because of the lack of natural or conference rivals on the schedule.

Only three home games attracted crowds of over 10,000. The opener with Hofstra drew 10,216; 12,404 saw the Gamecocks lose to Clemson (70-65); while a 79-74 loss to Kentucky was witnessed by 10,121.

The season produced a winning record, 15-12, but opponents such as Harvard, Wheeling, East Tennessee, Florida Southern, Georgia Southern, Baptist and Western Carolina had little spectator appeal.

Hordges, who averaged 19.6 points and 10.1 rebounds was the bright spot in the season, and Fredrick began to develop as an outside scoring threat, with a 13.9 average. Doyle continued to be a steady performer, averaging 15.3, but Graziano's effectiveness dwindled to 3.9 points and 3.2 rebounds.

THE 1979-80 SEASON (MCGUIRE'S FINAL SEASON)

Following the season and into the summer there was more off the court and behind-the-scenes maneuvering that set the stage for McGuire's final season of 1979-80. It would prove to be his 14th straight winning season, 16-11, and one in which he would receive many expressions of appreciation, both at home and on the courts of opposing schools.

Even at Clemson, which had been one of McGuire's prime tormentors at one time, honored the coach with a presentation on December 5. McGuire had been indirectly responsible for the Tigers' Littlejohn Coliseum, because when USC built Carolina Coliseum, Clemson responded by constructing a larger arena of its own.

When the Gamecocks played Hofstra on January 30, 1980 in Nassau County (NY) Coliseum, nearby friends and associates took advantage of that only appearance by the Gamecocks in the area to honor their native New Yorker.

St. John's coach Lou Carnesecca was among those present to pay tribute, and the Gamecocks responded with one of their better road performances by winning, 89-62.

The grand climax to the Irishman's career came on February 23, when Western Kentucky's NCAA bound Hilltoppers moved into Columbia for a Saturday night engagement. Earlier in the day McGuire was honored at half-time of the North Carolina-Duke game at Chapel Hill. He told the Carmichael Auditorium crowd, "I just want to get credit for one thing up here: I selected Dean Smith. The AD said 'no,' but I went to the chancellor, and he said, 'Frank, if you think that much of Dean Smith, okay.' Isn't it ironic, I began my coaching career in the ACC at Chapel Hill, and I was there on the day my career ended."

Prior to the opening tip-off against Western Kentucky McGuire was inducted into the USC Athletic Hall of Fame, and, in halftime ceremonies, he was named the University's Coach Emeritus.

The game itself was a fitting end to McGuire's coaching career, a victory over a quality opponent before 11,000 appreciative fans. The Gamecocks jumped to an early lead, but it dwindled to three at intermission. With six minutes remaining the Hilltoppers took a 54-51 lead, but Hordges' field goal and Strickland's free throw tied it at 54-54 with 5:39 remaining.

Believe it or not, neither team scored the remainder of the game, extending McGuire's career another five minutes. Both teams used spread offenses to work the clock in the first overtime, and neither was successful in scoring, adding another five minutes to the Irishman's final game. Both teams came alive offensively in the second overtime, and the Gamecocks outscored their guests, 19-11, hitting nine of ten free throws in the final minute to give McGuire the victory, 73-65.

For the record, Hordges again led the team in scoring with a 19.9 average giving him a career average of 19.7, third all-time best for the Gamecocks as of 1994. Mike Doyle became the school's 8th all-time point producer with 1,360, with Hordges also surpassing the 1,000 career points mark at 1,065. Hordges' play earned him a contract with Denver in the NBA, and he played two seasons in the league.

After the game the players on McGuire's final team presented him a plaque. He later reflected on the many courtesies that had been extended to him: "I keep telling those smart Big Apple types that it can only happen in this section of the country. That down here you get respect and love and devotion. Oh, you'll always have a few people who don't like the way you walk or talk or something. But that's okay, that's easy to deal with. Everybody down here has been so nice to me and my family, and I'll never forget that."

Thus ended McGuire's 42-year coaching career that began in 1936 at little St. Xavier High School in New York City and ended on a February night in 1980. It also was the end of a glorious chapter in USC basketball history—one that raised the sights and expectancy level for Gamecock sports teams of the future. As of 1995 that level has not yet been achieved in the sport of basketball.

Along with establishing a new excitement about basketball at South Carolina, McGuire spread basketball fever throughout the Palmetto state. And the stature attained by the state as a breeding ground for college and professional talent is a lasting monument to the Irishman.

CHAPTER TEN

THE END OF A COACHING CAREER

For Frank McGuire 1977 was a landmark year.

On February 9 he recorded his 500th collegiate coaching victory (vs. The Citadel), and three days later it was announced that he had been elected to the National Basketball Hall of Fame. In March a dinner was held in his honor, with a number of famous people participating. The following month the University trustees voted to name the playing area in Carolina Coliseum "Frank McGuire Arena."

In July it was announced that Dr. James B. Holderman had been chosen as the school's new president, succeeding Dr. William H. Patterson, who had announced his retirement as of the end of the school year. Holderman assumed the office on September 1, 1977, which, as a coincidence, was the day that McGuire's top assistant, Donnie Walsh, announced that he was leaving to accept a job as assistant coach and assistant general manager of the Denver Nuggets of the NBA.

McGuire then elevated Ben Jobe to the position vacated by Walsh. This move was looked on with some disappointment by relatives of Gregg Blatt, who could have also been a candidate for the number two job on the Gamecock basketball staff. Blatt subsequently left the staff to become an assistant coach at The Citadel.

The McGuire-Holderman relationship was one that began even before the two had ever met. At the time of his election to the USC presidency he was serving as senior vice president and director of public policy programs for the Academy for Educational Development, Inc., a national educational consulting firm based in Illinois.

MCGUIRE: "When I went to the Philadelphia Warriors I needed a lawyer, and Ned Irish (Madison Square Garden promoter) said that he knew this lawyer in Chicago that was very good and recommended him. The man's name was Arthur Morse, and we began a relationship that continued even after I left the Warriors.

"One day I received a call from Arthur, and he said that he wondered if I could do a favor for a friend of his. His friend was Arthur Wertz, who was in the real estate business and was part owner of the Blackhawks (National Hockey League team). Morse said that Wertz had a friend named Jim Holderman, who had sent an application for the job as president of the University of South Carolina and could I help him.

"I told him to send me a resume, and I would get it into the hands of the powers that be.

"Wertz was also an agent for basketball players with a reputation of holding out for the last penny. He later represented several of my players, including John Roche, Tom Owens, Tom Riker and Alex English.

"So, they flew down Holderman's resume, and I hand delivered it to Bob McNair. (McNair had been governor of South Carolina from 1965 to 1971 and was still an influential political figure in the State.)

"There was a search committee appointed to select a new president, and it was reported that one of the top people at the University of Alabama had the inside track at the time. However, I don't know all of the thinking of the committee at the time and didn't really care.

"The search committee did interview Holderman, and he impressed them enough to get the job. I learned that my contact played a role in getting an interview for Holderman, mostly as a courtesy. Then he obviously did a good job of convincing the committee that he was the man for the job.

"During the previous year I kept hearing rumors and reports that certain people felt that I had outlived my usefulness as basketball coach, even though we were still having winning seasons. There is no question that my basketball program suffered when the University withdrew from the ACC. It began to affect recruiting, as the reputation of the ACC as a basketball conference grew.

"It was also understandable that home attendance suffered, because none of the ACC teams, except for Clemson, would play us, and even Clemson was dropped from the schedule for several years. All of the problems with the basketball program were brought about by pulling out of the ACC. And I had nothing to do with that. Yet certain people seemed to hold me accountable."

T. ESTON MARCHANT: (*Chairman of the USC Board of Trustees when the school withdrew from the ACC and when Holderman was hired. Marchant resigned from the Board in late 1977 to run for Adjutant General of South Carolina and served in the office until retiring in 1994.*)

"I don't recall hearing from Coach McGuire, verbally or in writing about withdrawing from the conference. I never heard him say that he was for it, and I didn't hear that he was against it. He wasn't one of the people involved in the issue.

"Paul Dietzel (head football coach and athletic director) was the point man in getting us to withdraw. He didn't like the ACC academic policies, and an effort to change them was voted down. He was able to gain a consensus among Board members, and withdrawal from the ACC was an action of the Board. I recall that Tom Jones (USC President) was opposed to it.

"I felt that withdrawing from the ACC was the greatest mistake we made while I was on the board. Afterward I spent the next--I don't know how long--talking to Bob James, the ACC Commissioner, about the possibility of getting back into the conference. Things began to look encouraging to the point that we even had a meeting in Charlotte to discuss it. I don't know why it didn't work. We had presentations from both sides, but we could never get a majority of our Board to agree. Some of the board members didn't want anything to do with the ACC forever."

MCGUIRE: "I spent some time down at Myrtle Beach during the summer and came back to Columbia for the start of the fall semester. Holderman had taken over as president and was having a series of interviews with various department heads. So, I had an appointment to talk with him in his office.

"His first greeting was, 'Coach McGuire, how long do you want to coach?'

I said, 'President Holderman,. are you kidding me? How long do you want to be president? Do you know how you got here? You wouldn't be here if it were not for me.'

"He couldn't believe it."

Several of the trustees had tried to persuade McNair to take the job of president for two to four years, but McNair was in the beginning stages of building what became the state's second largest law firm and said that he couldn't afford that lapse in his professional career.

McNair also recalled that Holderman had another endorsement from Edith Green, a member of the U.S. House of Representatives from California. Green was a member of the Eli Lilly Endowment, for which Holderman had previously served as Vice-President.

During Holderman's interview with the University Board of Trustees he was reportedly asked by one member, "Could you fire a living legend?" --An obvious reference to McGuire. Holderman answered in the affirmative.

There was no move toward firing, but prior to the start of the 1977-78 season Holderman made an effort to remove McGuire from the position of basketball coach. Holderman proposed to McGuire that he step down as basketball coach at the end of the season and become athletic director of the University's regional institutions with headquarters at Coastal Carolina in Conway.

McGuire, whose contract at the University extended through 1980 was only interested in coaching basketball and didn't comment publicly on the negotiations.

One week later Holderman pronounced negotiations with McGuire to be regional athletic director had been closed and that his contract as basketball coach would be honored.

One of the concerns by some over declining attendance at home basketball games was compounded by action of the Board of Trustees in December of 1977. They voted to close the University from December 17 until January 20, 1978 because of the national energy crisis. During that period McGuire's team played six home games, while the student body was away, and it was no surprise that attendance suffered. Over that six-game stretch the average attendance was 4,500, less than half the average of 9,250 for the other home games that season.

However, the issue didn't go away, as behind-the-scenes efforts to terminate McGuire continued. In January there were news reports that some officials wanted to force McGuire to retire because of his age, which would be 65 on November 13, 1978. The University had recently reduced the mandatory retirement age from 70 to 65.

Three professors, Wade Batson, Paul Blackstock and Henry Lumpkin, were suing the University in Federal and State courts over the retroactive retirement policy that would have affected them.

As far as McGuire was concerned, the Board of Trustees said that they were taking a hands-off approach and leaving the matter in Holderman's hands.

On January 22, 1978, a full page ad paid for by people loyal to McGuire appeared in *The State*, urging support for the Gamecock coach. The furor died down, as the Gamecocks played their remaining games in a 15-12 season.

Rumors about a move to oust McGuire again surfaced in the fall of 1979, prompting members of the basketball team to announce that they would quit, if McGuire should be fired. On October 25 the University trustees announced that a negotiated settlement with McGuire had been reached and that he would retire at the end of the 1979-80 season.

McGuire commented, "I'm sad to be leaving, and I don't expect to have a say in naming my successor. They've been interviewing coaches for two or three years now, and coaching under those circumstances has been very difficult and very embarrassing. I have no options to stay at the University--I don't want any options--but I do intend to live in Columbia. I have great respect for this state. I like it here. I like the people. The people of South Carolina have been very good to my son and daughter."

The following day terms of McGuire's departure from the University were announced. It included a financial agreement that would pay him a total of $400,000 to be made in annual installments of $100,000 beginning July 1, 1980. Thus ended rumors, reports and negotiations that led to the Irishman's departure from the University of South Carolina at the end of the 1979-80 season, which produced 16 wins and 11 losses.

It also ended McGuire's stormy relationship with Jim Holderman, who would eventually depart from the University amid accusations of financial impropriety. Holderman resigned in 1990 and later pleaded guilty to charges of using his office for financial gain and was sentenced to serve 500 hours of community service.

#1. *The 1933 St. Xavier junior varsity. Frank McGuire is on the front row, far right.*

#2. Frank McGuire's high school basketball coach, Martin O'Malley.

#3. Frank McGuire's college basketball coach, James A. (Buck) Freeman.

#4. Frank McGuire (28) goes after a rebound in St. John's 34-27 victory over Manhattan before 15,000 spectators in Madison Square Garden on Jan. 16, 1936.

#5. McGuire's relationship with sports cartoonist "Pap" Paprocki goes back to his playing days at St. John's.

#6. McGuire with Bob Zawoluk following Zawoluk's record 65 points against St. Peter's on March 3, 1950.

Three McGuires at St. John's--Al, Frank and Dick.

#8. *As St. John's baseball coach, McGuire took his team to the NCAA playoffs.*

#9. *Solly Walker and McGuire.*

#10. Lou Carnesecca, longtime St. John's coach, played baseball (but not basketball) for McGuire at St. John's.

#11. Tom (Pap) Paprocki.

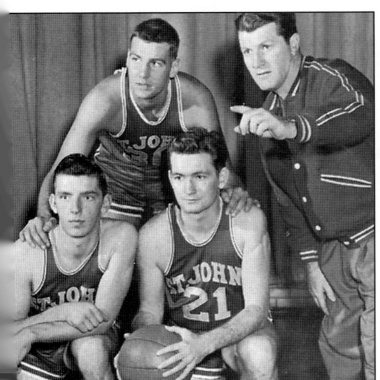

#13. Jack Curran, former McGuire player who produced many future college stars at Archbishop Molloy High School in New York City.

'2. St. John's players Ron Macgilvray, Bob Zawoluk and Jack cMahon with Coach McGuire.

#14. *Long Island University's Clair Bee, CCNY's Nat Holman and McGuire.*

#15. *Frank and Pat McGuire.*

#16. North Carolina All-American Lennie Rosenbluth.

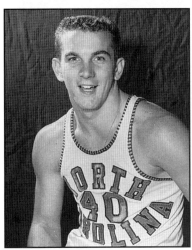

#17. Tommy Kearns jumped center against Wilt Chamberlain in the 1957 NCAA championship game.

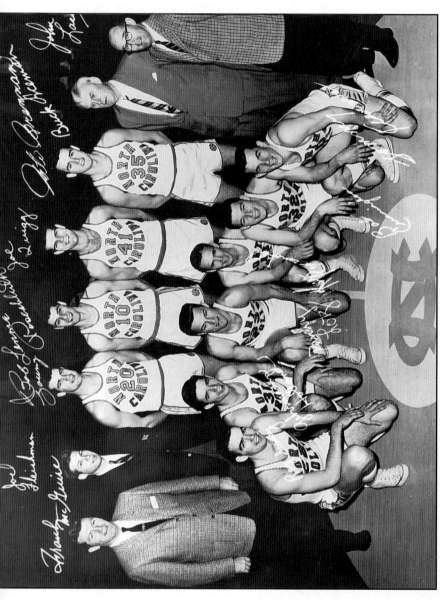

#18. North Carolina's 1957 NCAA champions: Left to right, kneeling: Roy Searcy; Gehrmann Holland, Danny Lotz; Kenny Rosemond, Bob Cunningham and Tommy Kearns. Standing: Frank McGuire; Joel Fleishman (manager), Bob Young, Lennie Rosenbluth, Joe Quigg, Pete Brennan, Buck Freeman and John Lacey.

#19. Tar Heels celebrate their 1957 NCAA finals victory over Kansas.

#20. McGuire displays the 1957 United Press National Champions trophy.

#21. Wake Forrest Coach "Bones" McKinney (left), McGuire and North Carolina Coach Dean Smith

#22. Wilt Chamberlain and Philadelphia Warriors Coach Frank McGuire.

#23. *The 1965-66 South Carolina squad. Left to right, McGuire, Donnie Walsh, Jim Finnegan (14), Frank Standard, Jack Thompson (44), Skip Kickey, Skip Harticka (31), Al Salvadori, Bob Gorgant (21), Bruce Wells, Larry Womack (13), Lyn Burkholder, Earl Lovelace (32), John Schroeder, Charlie Farrell (22), John Fairclough (34) and Buck Freeman.*

#24. Jack Thompson versus Duke at Durham.

#25. Skip Harlicka.

#26. Mike Grosso was declared ineligible to play at South Carolina in controversy over tuition payment.

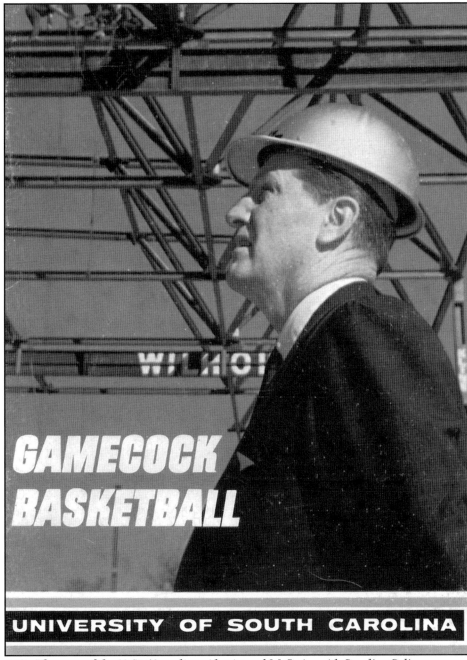

#27. *The cover of the 1967-68 media guide pictured McGuire with Carolina Coliseum construction in the background.*

#28. *John Roche versus Duke at Durham.*

#30. *Buck Freeman (right), McGuire and Donnie Walsh, who eventually became president of the Indiana Pacers.*

#29. *McGuire and longtime secretary Ginger Rigdon.*

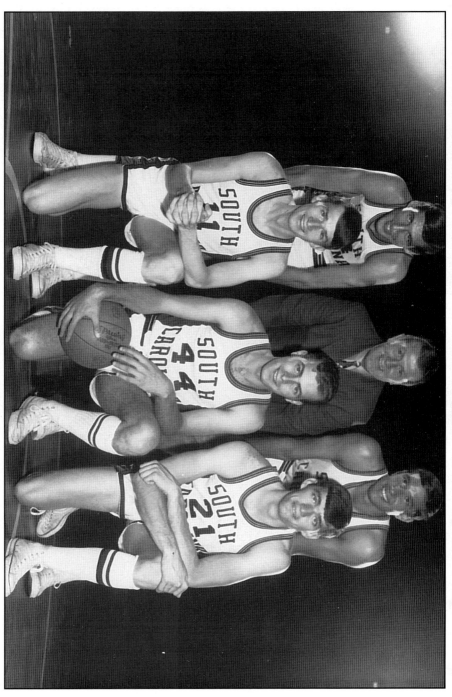

#31. The 1968-69 starting lineup: Kneeling: John Roche, Billy Walsh and Bobby Cremins. Standing: Tom Owens, McGuire and John Ribock.

#32. A view of the Carolina Coliseum arena prior to the first game played there on Nov. 30, 1968. The Gamecocks defeated Auburn, 51-49, on a last-second shot by John Roche.

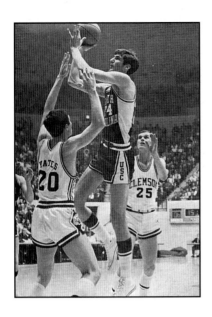

*#33. Tom Owens versus Clemson
at Clemson.*

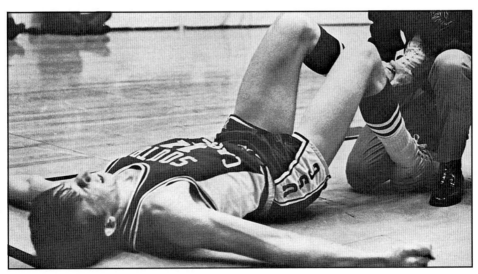

*#34. John Roche suffering a sprained ankle against Wake Forest in the semi-finals of the
1970 ACC tournament at Charlotte, N.C.*

#35. Bobby Cremins.

#36. Tom Riker.

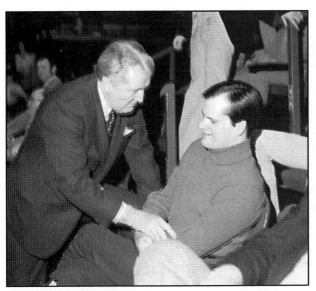

#37. McGuire always paused to greet his son, Frankie, prior to games in Carolina Coliseum.

#38. Kevin Joyce in action.

#39. Tom Owens scores the basket that gave South Carolina a 52-51 victory over North Carolina in the championship game of the 1971 ACC tournament final in Greensboro, N.C.

#40. John Roche rides the shoulders of John Ribock following the 1971 ACC tournament victory.

#41. John Roche received the 1971 ACC championship trophy at Greensboro, N.C.

#42. McGuire with All-American Kevin
Joyce, who played on the 1972 United States
Olympic basketball team.

#43. Brian Winters.

#44. Bob Fulton (right) presides over the retirement of Kevin Joyce's jersey number (43), prior to his final home game

#45. Coach Donnie Walsh stands behind four members of his 1970-71 Carolina freshman team. Left to right, Jimmy Powell, Kevin Joyce, Casey Manning and Danny Traylor.

#46. McGuire with a cake that commemorated his 400th collegiate victory.

#47. Frank McGuire and two of his former players who became successful college coaches--Lou Carnesecca (St. John's) and Al McGuire (Marquette).

#48. With their coach are Mike Dunleavy and Alex English, both of whom experienced great success in the NBA.

*#50. Mike Dunleavy versus
Georgia Southern in Columbia.*

*#49. Alex English in action, with
Nate Davis (53) in the background.*

#51. McGuire was inducted into the Naismith Basketball Hall of Fame on Feb. 9, 1977. Shown with him are friends John Terry and Ben Carnevale, along with his wife, Jane.

#52. McGuire with framed jersey that commemorated his 500th collegiate victory.

#53. *McGuire and former player Bobby Cremins, who became a highly successful head coach at Georgia Tech.*

#54. *After his retirement McGuire directed the programming of collegiate basketball for Madison Square Garden in New York City. Pictured here are McGuire, Garden President Sonny Werblin and Nat Holman, coach of CCNY for many years.*

#55. *McGuire with good friends (left to right) Jack LaRocca, John Terry and Father Tierney.*

#57. The McGuire home at Greenwood Lake, N.Y.

#56. Pat McGuire's parents, Margaret and Charles (of the Ritz) Johnson, at their New York City home in 1944.

#58. McGuire and 1-1/2 year old Frankie at Chapel Hill, N.C.

#59. McGuire's daughter, Carol Ann Morgan, with sons Michael (left) and Patrick in 1980, prior to Patrick's terminal illness.

#60. Pat and Frank McGuire celebrate their 25th wedding anniversary in 1967.

#61. Jane and Frank McGuire exchange wedding vows on June 3, 1972 before Father Jerome Tierney, as McGuire's friend Charles Poole of New York City stands by.

#62. Jane and Frank McGuire, 1977

CHAPTER ELEVEN

"A COACH THAT LET US PLAY"

Years after Dick McGuire had played for Frank McGuire at St. John's, his former coach asked him, "What kind of a coach was I?"

Dick answered, "You were the kind of coach that let us play."

On the surface that may sound rather simple, possibly indicating that the coach did little more than throw a ball out onto the floor and let the players do whatever they chose to do. However, Frank McGuire's philosophy of "letting his players play" is much more involved than that and sums up a style that took him to the pinnacle of his profession.

MCGUIRE: "First of all, I know that players win basketball games. As a coach I never scored a point, grabbed a rebound, made a steal or blocked a shot. It was my job to teach and motivate players to do the many different things that go into a successful team effort.

"Naturally, the better players you have the more successful you can be, if you do a good job of coaching. In college you recruit, in professional basketball you draft and trade, but in high school basketball you take what comes to you out of the classrooms.

"I spent the first 11 years of my coaching career at St. Xavier High School in New York City, and that's the greatest thing that could have happened to me. Coaching is teaching, and on the high school level it is teaching in its purest form. You take a bunch of kids who know practically nothing about the game, and you take that raw material and work with it.

"There is one distinct advantage to high school coaching, as compared to the college and professional levels. The large majority of players who come to you in high school haven't developed any bad habits, because they have no deeply ingrained habits.

"This gives you the opportunity to look over these youngsters and figure out how they best fit into the team concept--what their potential is and where it could best be utilized. Every youngster envisions himself as a scorer, because shooting is the most fun and the most glamorous part of basketball. That's what the spectators see, just as they see the ball carriers, passers and receivers in football; the home run hitters in baseball.

"So, you must take these kids and convince them that the real fun and satisfaction is in playing well as a team and winning. They must appreciate the fact that keeping the other team from scoring is just as important as scoring yourself. And, if you're going to score, you must first have the ball, and you hope it comes to you some other way than by the other team scoring a basket!

"Otherwise you get possession of the ball by rebounding and defense--steals or causing turnovers.

"You have to teach it all to high school players--ball handling, shooting, rebounding, defense, passing and so forth. And it gives you great satisfaction to see them go out and play well.

"I was fortunate to have good players and good winning records everywhere I coached--St. John's, North Carolina, Philadelphia and South Carolina. But I take greatest pride in the fact that my winningest percentage (76%) was achieved as coach at St. Xavier High School.

"What was more important, insofar as my personal career was concerned, is that it better prepared me in the teaching aspects of basketball, which was invaluable at the higher levels.

"If I had my choice of where to coach, without considering the financial aspects, I would choose high school. That's real coaching; it's teaching.

"That's what makes Jack Curran so good. Jack is one of my former players at St. John's and longtime coach at Archbishop Molloy High School in New York City. He has produced a lot of great players, including Kevin Joyce, Brian Winters and Bobby Carver, all of whom played for me at South Carolina.

"Jack had a lot of opportunities to coach at the college level, but he would never consider leaving high school. At his practices they walk on the floor and nobody says a word. They do everything he says.

"Jack was not an outstanding player, but he learned the game of basketball and has obviously been successful in teaching it. Your ability to play a sport doesn't necessarily translate into an ability to coach it.

"An excellent example of that is Lou Carnesecca, who played baseball for me at St. John's but didn't play basketball. Yet he turned out to be one of the all-time great college basketball coaches. In 24 seasons as head coach at St. John's he never failed to take his team to a post-season tournament--18 times to the NCAA playoffs and six times to the NIT. He won 70 per cent of his games and won the NIT five times.

"Lou did well, not because he could play the game but because he could teach it.

"On the other hand it doesn't mean that if you're a great player you won't make a good coach. There are too many examples of great ones who have been great coaches.

"One of the best players ever to play for me was Lenny Rosenbluth, who was the star of my North Carolina team that won the NCAA championship in 1957. Lenny was national player of the year and made every All-America team. However, he wasn't the type of player that could do well in the NBA.

"Instead, Lenny ended up coaching 18 seasons at the high school level, won 75 per cent of his games and took Coral Gables High School to the Florida State Championship.

"Of course, coaching a college team is a completely different situation. Your players are those that you are successful in recruiting, and you try to get the best possible talent you can, because, as I said earlier, players, not coaches, win basketball games.

"In college your players come to you from a number of different high schools and a variety of geographical locations--big cities, small towns. They have played under different systems and under coaches who have personalities and styles that are not the same. Many of the player's basketball habits have been firmly established by the time he reaches college.

"As much as possible, you try to recruit players who will best fit into your system. Some great high school players may not fit into a particular system, and if you recruit a player that doesn't fit into yours, you create a hardship on that player and yourself. Consequently the player becomes unhappy, morale is low, and he doesn't do well in school.

"I always kept that in mind when I evaluated high school talent. I knew the type of player I needed for my system. I grew up, played and coached in New York City, so I was accustomed to the style of play that is prevalent there. I understood their thinking.

"The coaches in the high schools had to use the boys who were in their school, so regardless of their abilities or personalities, they had to school them in their system.

"You get players with varying strengths--some can shoot, others can pass better or jump higher. Others have greater speed. Size and physical attributes have a lot to do with a player and how he fits into your system. I liked the New York City talent, because they had a head start in my system of play. Not that they could shoot any better, run any faster or jump any higher than players from other parts of the country.

"There were a number of things I took into consideration when I recruited players. They had to be good athletes, but I also considered the player's willingness to work hard and learn. I tried to evaluate the boy's personality insofar as being determined to succeed, cooperate and be willing to sacrifice for the good of the team.

"You hope you get players with great talents, such as shooting eye, jumping ability, speed and, something you can't see, great instincts. Then, if you recruit a group of players with these attributes, your coaching job has just begun. It's up to you to mold these individuals into a team that works together to accomplish the goals of the group--not individuals.

"When I was coaching at North Carolina and South Carolina the media made a big thing out of what they called my 'underground railroad.' They were referring to my recruiting connections in New York City, and I did get a lot of players from that area. Rosenbluth, Roche, Vayda, Joyce, Winters, Cunningham, Owens and many others. Sometimes it sounded as if I only recruited players who were either Irish or Catholic or both.

"I did have some fine players with those backgrounds. Yet my biggest star at St. John's, Bob Zawoluk, was Polish, my number one player at North Carolina, Lennie Rosenbluth, was Jewish, and my all-time top scorer at South Carolina, Alex English, was black.

"English was also a good example of the growth of basketball in the South, as he came out of Dreher High School in Columbia. As years went by New York had less of a hold on outstanding prospects. Other sections of the country and small towns began producing great basketball players, too. One example was Zam Fredrick, who played for St. Matthews High School about 25 miles from Columbia. Zam was the NCAA scoring champion his senior year at South Carolina--the year after I retired from coaching.

"Now there is no one great area for basketball recruiting, as there once was--when the Midwest and Northeast were the hotbeds. Many people consider Michael Jordan the greatest player of all time, and he came out of a small town in North Carolina.

"You hope you get a Michael Jordan, but players like that come along very seldom. So you coach to get the best out of every player you have, because even Michael Jordan can't do it by himself.

"There are some things you can't coach, but you recognize those natural abilities and use them to the team's best advantage. There's a saying among basketball coaches that 'you can't teach a player to be seven feet tall,' but you can teach him to use his height for the good of the team.

"There is one thing that you can teach any player--any team--regardless of their measurements or special talents. That is DEFENSE. Defense is a matter of learning fundamentals, mental toughness, discipline and understanding of the game. Defense can also be the most consistent part of the game of basketball. You might have an off night in shooting--and every team does--but you can still win the game by playing good defense.

"I never had the reputation of being what they call an 'X and O coach,' or one who can diagram everything on a piece of paper. I guess that was because of the publicity I received as a recruiter. However, I felt that I had a thorough knowledge of the game and could coach all of the X's and O's I needed to. What I considered more important was who was executing those X's and O's on the basketball court and what their knowledge and motivation amounted to.

"I'll take motivation over X's and O's any day. A good player who is motivated--going all out--is much more valuable to a team than a great player who is half-hearted--not giving a hundred per cent. I always like to use Bobby Cremins, now the head coach at Georgia Tech, as an example of that. Bobby played for me at South Carolina in the late 1960's and was not a highly recruited player. He was a skinny guard on his high school team, but I was impressed by the way he was all over the floor, scrapping for the ball and playing tough defense. He was the only scholarship player on our 1966-67 freshman team.

"When Bobby was a senior he was on a team with John Roche, Tom Owens, Tom Riker and John Ribock--all stars in their own right. That team went through the ACC schedule without losing a game and was ranked sixth in the final national rankings. If I asked someone who the 'heart and soul' of that team was, they would always say it was John Roche. And he was as great a player as I ever coached.

"But there was no doubt in my mind that the heart and soul of that team was Bobby Cremins. Not because of his basketball skills, but because of his spirit and determination that rubbed off on the other players and made us a team.

"Where Bobby's motivation came from, I don't know, but it helped to motivate those around him, and he is still accomplishing that as a coach. I like to think that I contributed to his determination while he was playing for me and later working with me as an assistant.

"There have been in the past--and there are today--many great coaches, and they all have an ability to motivate players. However, there styles might be completely different. There are the psychologists, the cheerleaders, the pushers, the pullers and the preachers. They all have a common goal--regardless of their style--and that is to instill enthusiasm in their players.

"I always felt that it was most important for your players to have confidence in you. You must earn the confidence of your players. They have confidence in a coach they respect. They don't necessarily have to like you, but they usually like a coach they respect. A coach that treats them fairly and doesn't play favorites.

"They need to believe in you and what you are doing. You have to earn their confidence and respect every time you hold a practice or play a game. Your past record as a coach or a player can give you a head start in earning the confidence of your players, because they believe in someone who is a proven winner.

"Players can sense when you know what you're talking about or leading them in the right direction. And when they have that confidence in what they are doing, they naturally perform better.

"I was never much on giving pep talks before games or during half-time intermissions. I was more for getting them in the right frame of mind by assuring them that we could be successful by following a particular game plan or strategy and performing up to our abilities.

"You can't always count on a particular approach to dealing with a team as a team, because all players are not exactly alike and do not respond the same way and to the same things. Some players need to be pushed and challenged, while others need more leading and encouraging. You have to decide how to handle each individual when you are dealing with them one on one.

"Sometimes you have to get tough with the street-type player from the city, while that might not be the best way to deal with someone from a small town in the South. It all boils down to discipline. You've got to be the boss. Your players have to believe in you, and when you ask them to do something, they do it without question.

"Back in 1969 Paul Dietzel, South Carolina's football coach, asked me to come talk to his squad prior to their opening game with Duke. He was really shocked by what I said. I can't remember exactly what it was, but it was not what he expected. He thought I would come in and give sort of a sermon, because that was his style, but it wasn't mine.

"Mine was to challenge them and make them want to go out and beat the hell out of the other team. They were the enemy. I don't know how much my talk had to do with it, but Carolina did win the game. As a matter of fact, they went undefeated in the ACC and won the championship. Interestingly, our basketball team also went through the ACC season without losing. I think it's the only time in the history of the conference that a school didn't lose a conference football or basketball game during a school year.

"At South Carolina, as far as our basketball team was concerned, it was us against the world. Particularly during the seasons when John Roche was playing, and the other ACC teams were really giving us a bad time. That's why my teams always did well on the road. The more the crowd got on them, the better they played. It actually added to their motivation.

"Generally, all other things being equal, the team with the greatest motivation will win.

"However, regardless of the team or the talent, I always remembered that I was a member of the faculty and that I should be a part of my players' overall college education. A very small percentage of college basketball players make it into the professional ranks, so it was my responsibility to see that they earned their degrees and prepared themselves for something besides basketball when they moved out into a competitive world.

"The most satisfying memories of my coaching career are not the national rankings, the national championship, the All-America players or those who made it in the pros. It was to see the far greater number of my players who went on to successful careers in other fields--law, medicine, business, education. To hear from those men and hear them say, 'Coach, thanks for making me do something besides play basketball.'

"It is also important that your players be good people. It is just as important for a basketball player to be a gentleman--honest, caring, helpful, of good character--than for people who are not in the spotlight quite so much. Even more important. For someone to be successful in whatever they choose to do, they must first be a good person. That is basic.

"I have always considered LOYALTY one of the most important--if not THE most important ingredient in human relationships. A coach should be loyal to his players. Go to bat for them--help them in off-the-court situations, just as if they are your sons. Because as long as they are under your care, they ARE your sons.

"Loyalty on the part of the coach breeds loyalty on the part of the players. And this pays off not only in terms of personal relationships, but also in the success of the team. In order for a team to do well, the players must be loyal to the coach, loyal to the team and loyal to each other. Some people call this team chemistry--something like a close-knit family or brotherhood.

"You prepare your team the best you can, but you also realize that it is only one of three participants in the game, along with the opponent and that third party, the officials. It is important to have the proper relationship with officials and understand their role in the game. Some coaches take the attitude that if the call is against their team it is wrong, and if it is against their opponent, it is a good call.

"Officials, like all of us, have their strengths and their weaknesses--their good games and their bad games. And there are some officials that are just better than others, just as coaches and players have varying abilities.

"When you think an official has made a bad call you have to know when and how to protest and when to just let it go. Some officials can tolerate more than others, so you have to take this into consideration.

"One thing all officials have in common is that they do not want to be made to look bad--or 'shown up'--to the spectators. They get enough abuse from the crowd without that--even when they are doing a good job. Still you have to let the officials know that you know it when they blow a call, because most of the time they know it, but they can't change it, or they would lose control of the game.

"One thing you do expect out of an official is consistency. They should call the same things at one end of the court that they call at the other end. So, you try to keep them on their toes and still show them the proper respect. They have a tough job to do. Probably the toughest in the world of sports.

"With all the tugging and pushing and contact that is allowed in the modern game of basketball it is tough to draw the line between legitimate contact and a personal foul.

"There are occasions when you might intentionally over-protest to an official and get a technical foul called. That might seem to be counter-productive, but sometimes it can turn the tide or at least narrow the gap in officiating. I'm sure that no official wants to call a technical foul, and once they do they feel bad about it. Then, perhaps they tend to look at things with greater sympathy for the coach on which they called the technical.

"I can remember a game against Marquette when Al McGuire raised hell with an official for calling a technical on me, protesting that I had wanted the technical. He knew that it is part of coaching strategy. It also assures your players that you are going to bat for them--not just sitting there and accepting whatever happens.

"So, back to the statement at the first of this chapter in which Dick McGuire was quoted as saying that I was the type of coach that "let us play." What he meant was probably a summation of my coaching philosophy. Get the right players for your style of play, teach them what they need to know and motivate them to do their best.

"Then, once the game has started--LET THEM PLAY. After all, they are not a bunch of robots that have to be told every move to make. If you've done your job, you can let them play. Your part during the game is to have the right players on the court, having them in the right defense and to decide the overall strategy during the flow of the game.

"You know that when you let the Bob Zawoluks, the Lennie Rosenbluths, the John Roches and others like them play the game, they can make you a good coach. And, after all, that's the best compensation you can receive.

"The media used to have a lot to say about my personal appearance and the appearance of our players. My philosophy was that these players were more than just athletes--they represented the school off the court, as well as on.

"Our basketball players were idols to the students. If the players had long hair, the other students would have had long hair. If our players had grown mustaches, the other students would have grown mustaches. So I insisted that they be well-groomed.

"This helped to make them feel good about themselves. That they were something special and that they were expected to be the best in what-ever they did. I may have been old fashioned, but it seemed to work for me, and the players appreciated it in the long run.

"In basketball today there seems to be a lot of talking going on during the game by the players. I told my players to keep their mouths shut and to just play basketball. Nothing they could say could speak more clearly than the way they played the game.

"Even on our great teams with John Roche, Tom Owens, Kevin Joyce and Tom Riker--all great players and intelligent young men--I didn't allow any of them to talk to an official. That was up to Bobby Cremins, our captain, and I told him what to say.

"As far as our opponents were concerned, I taught my players not to fear any team, but to respect every opponent. That also carries over into life after basketball, which every player will eventually reach, regardless of how good they are.

"So, when I get to the Pearly Gates, "I'm sure that I will be called on to answer for the influence I had on the young men who played for me, rather than how many games I won. If you can contribute to someone leading a good and successful life, there is no greater victory.

"There have been a lot of great coaches in college basketball, and I doubt that there have been two just alike. Although Dean Smith began his coaching career with me, when he became a head coach, he became his own man--not a clone of Frank McGuire. And that is as it should be.

"John Wooden (UCLA) and Adolph Rupp (Kentucky) were as different as night and day, but they were both highly successful in their own approach to the game.

"The key is to learn as much as you can about basketball, psychology and life itself. Then fit this knowledge into your own personality and capabilities--and the rest depends on dedication, hard work and believing in one's self.

"Then, at the end of the day, if you can look in the mirror and tell yourself that you have done all that you can do--that you have given it your best shot--then you can be at peace with yourself."

PART TWO

MEMORIES OF MCGUIRE
COACH, FRIEND, FATHER, HUSBAND, MAN

CHAPTER TWELVE

AL McGUIRE:
"I OWE EVERYTHING TO COACH"

"**M**y life has been developed by Coach McGuire. If I am wealthy, if I am successful, and I am visible, it's because of one person. And that's Frank McGuire."

Those words came from the lips of Al McGuire, who accomplished all three of the above--wealth, success, visibility.

For a number of years McGuire has served as an analyst on telecasts of college basketball games by CBS-TV and is a much sought-after speaker for banquets and conventions throughout the United States. Those activities keep him busy enough to earn a handsome income without tying him to a workaholic schedule.

Al McGuire is not a blood relative of Frank McGuire, but he places himself in a brotherhood with his former college coach that goes deeper than a biological kinship. Alone in his Pewaukee, Wisconsin (suburb of Milwaukee) office, McGuire reflected on his association with the man to whom he "owes everything."

"Everything" includes a basketball scholarship to St. John's University (1947-1951), a head coaching job at Belmont Abbey College in North Carolina and a head coaching job at Marquette University, where he achieved phenomenal success. McGuire coached the Warriors from 1965 to 1977, winning the national championship in his final game, a 67-59 victory over North Carolina in the NCAA final in Atlanta, Georgia. McGuire was elected to the Naismith (College) Basketball Hall of Fame in 1992, a year before his brother Dick received the same honor.

Guiding Al McGuire through his life and career were a philosophy and code of conduct that he accepted from his mentor.

AL MCGUIRE: "I'd say that the reason I'm in the Hall of Fame--the reason that I cleared the trees financially--is all because of Coach. Nobody else.

"One of the things about Coach was that he was a man's man. He didn't care if you were the Mayor of New York or someone without influence or stature, once Coach took you as a friend, you were a friend for life. He took you when you were dressed like Astor's pet pony on Saturday night, and he accepted you when you had your hair in curlers on Monday morning.

"His friendship was a friendship of almost neighborhood. That meant he went to bat for you. If you called, whatever you wanted, he didn't want to know why. He only went to the whys after you solved the problem. He was that way with his ball players.

"When I was at St. John's, if I got into trouble, he would first solve my problem, and then punch me! He wouldn't be aggressive until after the problem was solved.

"He was loyal to a fault. If one of his friends was going down on the Titanic, he'd go with them. It wasn't this thing of being a politician. It was more that, 'This is my friend, my sphere of influence. These are my ball players, this is my family--this is my neighborhood.' And those were the things that I got from him.

"I'm probably more like Frank than anyone in Frank's sphere. Because I'm really a loner, and Coach was, too. I was never part of his intimate group, perhaps because of the age difference, or whatever it might have been.

"I'm always alone. When I'm with people I get paid. My life has always been that way. If my hair's combed, I'm paid. If I'm with more than five people, someone's paying me.

"With Coach you never had to hold court, and you never acted the way you weren't. I never did anything for Coach out of fear--wet palms.

"He never called you over trivia. It might sound like trivia, but it wasn't. It was important to somebody why he was calling.

"I remember once he called me when I was athletics director at Marquette. He said he had a problem at South Carolina. Because of (Paul) Dietzel they had to drop out of the ACC. He said, 'I don't have a schedule, and I want to play you guys this year.'

"So, I said, 'You've got a date.' No b.s., Frank called, and Frank got. My schedule was full, but I opened up. You don't question it.

"With Coach, whenever he called it was important, or he wouldn't have called. I remember when he was at North Carolina, and I was an assistant at Dartmouth, he came to me about joining his staff. He had just gone 32-0-he had spoiled them at Chapel Hill. He had gone eyeball to eyeball with Everett Case (N.C. State) and Bones McKinney (Wake Forest), and he ended up being the Rocky Marciano or the Joe Louis of the field.

"I said, 'Coach, most anywhere you'd go, I'd go with you. But I will not go to Chapel Hill.'

"Not long after that Belmont Abbey contacted me. I didn't apply for the job--I had never heard of it. The job opened up, the priest called Frank, and Frank recommended me. And that's all it took. I wanted to do my own thing, so off I go to Belmont, where I coached for six years.

"I'll bet that ninety per cent of the things Coach did were out of friendship or some other reason. He had probably done something for Belmont Abbey, and the job opened up, so the priest called Frank. People will never understand the power that Frank McGuire had. But the power was never used for Frank McGuire. Maybe it came back to him indirectly, but that was never the motive. When he got me the job at Belmont Abbey, I'll bet he didn't even get his gas money back.

"Then in 1964 this priest called me from Marquette. Father Orford, who was on the Board. It was Frank that caused it, and that started the calliope of my life. There were no letters to me--no phone call. Coach never called and said, 'I can get you the job.' He didn't operate that way.

"I didn't even know where Marquette was, but he took me from the smallest Catholic school in the country to the largest. Belmont Abbey had two or three hundred, and Marquette had over ten thousand. Notre Dame had only eight thousand, but St. John's might be bigger than Marquette now.

"I didn't know a soul in Wisconsin. I didn't fill out any forms and didn't make out a resume. I didn't call these people or give references. Everything was Coach.

"As a coach, he knew basketball, but he was not an X and O man. His approach was that basketball is won by making a team. He made a family out of the team--you became almost like a city-state, and you're going to fight them. He would form a group that would run through a wall for him. If Coach had told me to hit the Berlin Wall with my head, I would have tried it. You became a neighborhood. The enemy is in the other locker room, and let's don't ever forget that. They're keeping score.

"He used to teach in scrimmages, while most coaches like to teach in practice with different drills--shadow moves--like you set up a box and one. Most coaches like to have almost a classroom, where you sit, and they lecture. And they move around like chess pieces. That's what they call X's and O's.

"Coach liked to teach in action, where you go up and down and sweat. He'd stop and tell you some things, and you'd go right back to scrimmaging. He would talk over the scrimmage, as you scrimmage, which allowed you to learn as you were performing.

"In talking with people like Larry Brown or Bobby Cremins or Jack Curran, I've never seen him take a pencil out and mark something on a table. It was always just conversation. Coach knew that the key to winning was to have the team understand each other. To have a camaraderie and the will to win.

"He made you mentally tough. That was a key term to Coach.

"Coach never went much beyond his 7th or 8th man, and when the game came, the staff would go into the background. He had visibility on the bench--working the officials, working his team and intimidating the other team. Frank was a pro at that.

"You see, Frank and I came from the same background. You fought, and you might get a broken nose, but so what? It was no big deal.

"At St. John's we were playing someone, and before the game Coach says, 'Hey, Al, no fight tonight.' I had been in fights in two straight games, and he thought I needed a rest!

"Danny Finn (member of 1949 St. John's team) and I used to fight so much in practice that one of us had to leave. It was like that everyday. We worked out in this old gym in a terrible neighborhood, and we use to drive Coach crazy.

"But when we got to a game we were just so physical—nothing dirty—just hard nosed. That's just the way we played. When you played for Frank McGuire you always left part of you on the court, or you didn't play for Frank McGuire.

"When my Marquette teams played Frank's teams, it was always a physical game. Our first year down in Columbia (1971) a fight broke out in the first half, and I was always pleased with that fight.

"Most fights are 'buffalo chips,' pushing and shoving, and one guy gets a sly rap. But that was a real fight!"

The fight began when Carolina's Tom Riker and Marquette's Bob Lackey squared off against each other during a free throw situation. As the benches emptied, Carolina security officers ran onto the court to try and stop the fight and to keep fans from entering the court. Order was restored in the game, which Marquette won, 72-71.

AL MCGUIRE: "We thought the people in red jackets were ushers coming to join the fight. But they were security people. That was a real fight. I had one kid named Marcus Washington, about 6-1 and very thin. He ran in twice, and he flew out twice.!

"But you rarely have a good rumble, and it was good to see one.

"Another thing I learned from Frank is that you have to be able to work the officials during a game. One time when I was at St. John's we were playing Niagara at Buffalo, and the refs were screwing us. So, at halftime, Frank grabbed this ref's arm--Frank was very strong--an Atlas. The ref's arm started turning blue, but the audience thought that he was just having a conversation. But he got the message over.

"In our Milwaukee Classic in 1966 we were ahead of Frank's team, and he started getting technical fouls called on him. So, I go over to the officials and say, 'Don't you realize that he's got the crowd on my home court on his side, he's got his team sky high now, and you guys are feeling sorry for him.' And the officials called offensive goal tending on us at the end of the game, and we lost by one point.

"A lot of people didn't understand Frank. They'd see Coach coming into a hotel at eight o'clock in the morning, and they didn't know that he was coming from Mass. They thought that, being Irish. . .You know--God invented liquor so that the Irish wouldn't rule the world. But Frank was coming from Mass.

"With Frank it was either the greatest love affair in the world or the greatest vendetta. He had friends that created a lot of problems, but he never complained.

"Here's an example. Whatever Frank wanted in the state of New York for ten or twelve years, he could have it, within reason. (New York Governor Mario Cuomo had played baseball for Frank McGuire at St. John's.) All he had to do was call the governor. It would have nothing to do with him—it was to help someone else.

"Years ago he did something for, I believe, a black church. I was down there, and I love Southern barbecue, so Frank takes me out for a barbecue sandwich on the way to the airport. While we were at this barbecue place Frank had to make a phone call.

"Someone from that church had called his office and said that they were going to put something about what he had done in the church bulletin. And the reason he was making the phone call was to tell the church not to put anything in the bulletin about what he'd done.

"I'm not sure what it was, but it was something they needed and appreciated.

"Coach had a tremendous sphere of influence—all of these people who loved him. It was a silent group, but they knew, if the phone rings, just get it done. Get it done. It could be a collection for someone in the Bronx who was down on his luck—there was no explanation.

"I know Eddie Fogler *(current head basketball coach at South Carolina)*. I knew his dad, so I always look at these guys as kids. I do think Eddie will be successful, but not necessarily in the same style that Frank did it.

"Because, as I and so many others will tell you, 'There will never be another Frank McGuire.'"

CHAPTER THIRTEEN

TOMMY KEARNS:
FROM PLAYER TO FRIEND

When North Carolina lined-up against Kansas in the final game of the NCAA Championships at Kansas City in 1957, spectators were astonished to see North Carolina's 5-11 Tommy Kearns standing opposite Kansas' 7-0 Wilt (The Stilt) Chamberlain for the opening tip.

That scene captured the imagination of basketball fans almost as much as the Tar Heels' 54-53 triple-overtime victory that climaxed a 32-0 season. The shorter principle in that jump ball recalled that situation as indicative of the state of mind that his coach, Frank McGuire instilled in his players.

Some looked at that strange move as a masterpiece of psychology that influenced the game. However, Kearns reflected differently from his home in Darien, Connecticut, where he lives in technical retirement. However, he still follows a demanding schedule of board and foundation meetings.

KEARNS: "Coach McGuire was such a great motivator, and he made us all feel very good about ourselves. So the fact that I was going to jump center against Wilt was no big deal. That was the way we felt. It didn't make any difference who was going to jump center, we're going to beat you anyway.

"It was mentioned off-handily in the locker room. Buck (Freeman) said something about jumping center against Wilt. I said, 'That's all right with me.' I knew he wasn't serious.

"We went out for warm-ups, and when we came back to the locker room, Coach said, 'You're jumping center against Wilt.'

"As a group we should have lost four or five games that year, but we were still undefeated. We should have lost to Michigan State the night before, but we won in three overtimes.

"Frank Deford wrote in an article in *Sports Illustrated* about ten years ago that we were a blessed team. That translates itself into our being cocky as well. That's the way Coach made us.

"We had a lot of what people called 'miracle wins.' During that season we were behind by four points at Maryland with a little over a minute remaining. Coach called timeout and told us that we had to learn to lose, as well as win, and that if we go down, go down as gentlemen. But we didn't lose, because we made another miracle comeback.

"In the semi-finals of the ACC tournament that season we were tied with Wake Forest with just a few seconds left. Coach didn't call a timeout, because we knew, and everybody in the stands knew, that we were going to Lenny Rosenbluth for the last shot. It was no set play, it was just a case of what Lenny was going to do. When we needed something, Lenny was always there.

"Likewise when we went ahead of Kansas in the NCAA finals, everyone knew that Kansas would go to Chamberlain for the last shot. So we double-teamed Wilt, and Joe (Quigg) knocks the ball away, and I grab it.

"One thing in the back of my mind was that Wilt had blocked several really good shots that I had taken. He just came out of nowhere. So I knew when I got that ball, if I could get it up on the air--it was a real high ceiling--that nobody was going to get the ball in five seconds. And that's what I did. Who knows why you do it. You just do it."

McGuire often expressed great pride in the success that his former players achieved in fields other than basketball. He often cited accomplishments by his former players in the professional and business world. From that standpoint Tommy Kearns is a shining example.

Kearns experienced a brilliant career on Wall Street as a partner in the investment firm of Bear-Stearns. He retired in comfortable financial circumstances at the age of 49. His time is now divided among travel, serving on boards of six corporations and as one of three trustees who oversee investment funds in the University of North Carolina endowment.

KEARNS: "I spend a lot of time at Chapel Hill. We just raised four hundred million dollars for the Bicentennial, so we have close to a billion dollars. Through the years I have become friends with Dean Smith, and we play a lot of golf together. And we shed a tear together at Coach McGuire's funeral.

"I was in Ireland with a group as guest of the Irish government, touring around trying to promote business. I talked to Jane (McGuire), and she said that it was a matter of days, so I got things ready and just came on back.

"When I played for Frank he had a father image and it was a normal player-coach relationship. Then I got to know Frank really well when he went to work for Madison Square Garden. I spent a lot of time with him and got to know him as a friend.

"He was one of the great guys of all time. He had a great way about him, and he knew everybody. For example, Bob McGuire was a friend of mine that I grew up with, and Bob was Police Commissioner for the city of New York for eight or nine years. Bob had gone to St. John's and he always liked Frank.

"We saw a lot of each other and we'd go out together once a month. Frank really knew more about the police department than Bob did. They'd talk about the 23rd precinct, 41st or whatever. They'd just go on for an hour about different people in the hierarchy of the police department, and I had no idea what they were talking about. Bob would comment to me how Frank, being gone so long, knew so much about the department–how the apparatus worked.

"You can imagine, twenty-five thousand people in the department, very complex and had a lot of units. And Frank understood how the whole thing worked.

"He had a soft spot in his heart for Madison Square Garden. To him that was basketball. That's where it started and got its bigtime status. I guess when we played Kansas, that's the first time a game was televised nationally, and a lot of people attributed that to Frank and his charisma. It was really the start of the hoopla that now exists around the Final Four.

"I also know what it is to get on the wrong side of Frank. In the middle of the late sixties Brian Winters was playing for Archbishop Molloy. I had played high school basketball at St. Ann's, which later became Archbishop Molloy, and I met Brian a couple of times and talked to him about Chapel Hill and what a great place it was.

"At that point I did not ingratiate myself to Frank--he got very upset with me. But the fact that I was totally ineffective in my conversing with Brian, and that he did go to South Carolina helped to ease the situation. But I was not in Frank's good graces for a couple of years.

"As far as recruiting went, Harry Gotkin was really Frank's eyes and ears in the New York area. Harry played a very important role for Frank. He loved basketball, and he would see five or six games in a day. He would go from The Bronx to New Jersey, back to Manhattan, to Brooklyn and Staten Island. He knew where the games were, and he knew the players.

"All of the starters on our championship team were from the New York area. Pete Brennan and Joe Quigg were from Brooklyn, Bob Cunningham played for All Hallows, and Lenny Rosenbluth had played for James Monroe High School in New York. There was a teachers' strike during Lenny's senior year, so he went to Staunton Military Academy in Virginia.

"I played for St. Ann's in Manhattan, and Bobby (Cunningham) and I played against each other. I also knew him from grammar school. Bobby had a very serious accident when he was a high school senior. Fell through a window at his home and required sixty or seventy stitches on his right side.

"This is one thing I admired about Frank. Most coaches would have turned their back on Bobby at that point, because it was a serious injury, and you didn't know how he would rehabilitate. But you knew it would be some permanent damage. How extensive it would be was the real question.

Bobby lived at 137th and Amsterdam, and I was walking down the street going to see him. When I got to his apartment Coach was there. And Coach was reassuring Bobby that he still wanted him.

"At the time I was undecided about what I was gonna do--where I was going. But that had a major impact on removing any doubts in my mind about going to North Carolina."

During Kearns' three varsity years at North Carolina, the Tar Heels won 85 per cent of their games, compiling a 69-12 won-lost record. Kearns was a starter all three season, averaging 14.9 points per game during his senior (1957-58) year. He was an All-ACC selection in 1957 and 1958, and a third team All-America choice in 1958.

Kearns recalled that it was a bold move for four New York Catholics to go South for their college education.

KEARNS: "I don't think any of us had ever been south of Baltimore. North Carolina was almost a foreign country. It was beautiful but back then there were signs on bathrooms, 'Colored' and 'White.' There were lines of demarcation, and that was a real shocker to a lot of us who didn't really know what segregation was all about.

"There weren't many Catholics at Chapel Hill, and there was no Catholic Church there at first. They used a hall on the campus for Mass, but later the St. Thomas More Church was built, and I think Frank was a big shaker in making that happen.

"Frank didn't talk to us a lot about our faith, but it was implicit that, although we were on our own, there were still obligations he had to us and our families.

"As a coach, Frank was extremely well known, and he had an extraordinary relationship with the New York press. There was Milton Gross, one of the top writers, who was a great friend of Frank. And Tom Paprocki with the Associated Press. Frank always had a presence here, and although he was removed, he came to the Garden a lot.

"He wore the banner of success. He recruited the best players, and he was a good disciplinarian. By the same token, he let people play more of a freelance game than exists today. There were plays, but you knew what was expected of you. You weren't going to come down and take a twenty-five-foot jump shot. If you did that kind of thing, you'd come out of the game, and you'd get the McGuire wrath for three or four minutes. Then he'd put you back in. You knew the do's and don'ts, but within that you were pretty open with what you could do.

"When Frank went to Chapel Hill, North Carolina was a big football school. They had just gotten over the Charlie Justice hoopla, and they were very successful in the late fifties. Then the football program kinda went sideways, and Frank was brought in.

"I don't think people knew how good Frank was. They knew he was good, but they didn't realize he was going to build what he built.

"One thing Frank demanded was total committment. He didn't want anybody who waffled. There was no middleground with Frank--you were either with him, or you weren't. The lines were clearly drawn.

"He had great character. He was no b.s. guy--what you saw is what you got. He didn't mince words. You knew where you stood with Frank all the time, and that was a great quality of his.

"He believed in what he believed in, and you accepted that and went with him, or you went your own way. He demanded loyalty.

"And those are things that he left for me to take with me."

CHAPTER FOURTEEN

JOHN ROCHE:
SYMBOL OF THE MCGUIRE ERA

Time stood still in the Greensboro Coliseum on Saturday night, March 13, 1971. There were six seconds showing on the motionless scoreboard clock, and North Carolina led South Carolina by one point in the championship game of the ACC tournament.

A timeout had been called, as the Gamecocks' 6-3 Kevin Joyce awaited a jump ball against the Tar Heels' 6-10 Lee Dedmon, and USC fans anticipated the worst. When Joyce outjumped his taller opponent and tapped the ball to Tom Owens for a game-winning lay-up, the most meaningful victory in the school's history was accomplished.

However, to the captain and star player of that team, John Roche, the timeout before the jump ball–when time stood still–produced a memory of his head coach, Frank McGuire, that will far outlast the glow of that triumph on the court.

One report after the game was that McGuire had told Joyce to "jump to the moon," but neither McGuire nor Roche recalled such a remark. Roche remembers McGuire rising above the outcome of the game and speaking to his players in a manner that brought out much deeper considerations.

ROCHE: "I remember that moment very vividly. It stuck with me, because I always felt that this was a game that he wanted to win very much. But I think that he felt more the pain we would experience in having played three years and not winning the ACC tournament.

"He displayed that compassion and empathy to me, and this is not a common trait among coaches, unfortunately, then or now. Despite language to the contrary, they are looking more at their individual achievement–like, 'Gee, its going to be terrible for me, if I lose this game.'

"This was, to me, Frank McGuire conveying to me how he felt about coaching us and how good we should feel about what we accomplished. I remember that when we went over to the bench for the timeout, he knelt down and didn't say anything for a moment. He just looked at us.

"He didn't say anything to us about what to do. We knew that. Try to win the tap and get it to someone for a shot at the basket.

"He told us that in our time here, we had won a lot of games for him. And we had done a great deal for the University of South Carolina and people of the state. And he tied it into the game.

"He said, 'No matter how this turns out, don't forget that.' I think that he felt we were going to lose the game, like we all did. And he was getting us ready for losing the game and going on with whatever we were going to do in our lives.

"Of course, we did win the game, but he had already demonstrated to me that he was much more concerned that we knew how much he appreciated what we had done for the program, than his winning an ACC tournament. I have forgotten the score of the game, but I remember that."

It is probable that most Gamecock fans look at Roche as symbolic of the McGuire era at Carolina. In three varsity years, he led them to a record of 69 wins against only 16 losses, an 81.2 winning percentage, and that includes a 35-7 record in ACC competition. Roche is the school's second leading all-time pointmaker (1,910) and first among players who were ineligible as freshmen and had only three varsity seasons.

Roche was ACC player of the Year in his sophomore and junior seasons and made a number of All-America teams in his final two years as a Gamecock. His jersey number (11) was the second to be retired by the University, the first having been Grady Wallace's (42) after the 1957 season.

Now a partner in a Denver law firm, Roche recalls with great clarity his career at Carolina and his relationship with his coach.

Following the thrilling victory over North Carolina, the Gamecocks lost to Pennsylvania, 79-64, in the East Regionals at Raleigh, N.C. Twenty-four years later Roche reflects philosophically about the finish of his storied college basketball career.

ROCHE: "When we lost to Pennsylvania, a lot of people thought that it was because we were just let down after winning the ACC. And I wish I had that excuse. Winning the ACC was more of a relief than a great joy. I think that I would have enjoyed it more the year before.

"I think we lost in the NCAA because we played a team that was better than us. If we had played them the year before, with the approach and attitude we had as a team, I think we could have beaten them. It's not that Pennsylvania had more talent than we did. They were farther along than we were as a team. And they were the better team. They beat us that night, and they would have beaten us any night."

For the record, Pennsylvania ended the season ranked third in both the AP and UPI polls, while South Carolina was number six in both. The NCAA format of that year involved 28 teams, seven in each of four regionals. Thus, the winner of each regional made it to the Final Four.

During Roche's senior season some of the fans around the ACC expressed a lot of resentment, sometimes bordering on contempt, toward McGuire's Gamecocks. For instance, prior to a game between the Gamecocks and Wake Forest at Winston-Salem, the home team's Deacon mascot went onto the court carrying a dummy of Roche, complete with his jersey number. With the aid of a plumber's friend, the Deacon mascot ceremoniously stuffed "John Roche" into the toilet.

The aggressive, bordering on cocky, personality of the Gamecock players helped to inspire such reactions from the opposing fans.

ROCHE: "Coach established an attitude of 'us against the world.' Whether he did that intentionally to win games, I'm not sure. It was just part of his nature, in terms of having some disputes with people. I don't think he did it as part of a strategy.

"As a coach, he would tell his players how he looked at things, but he did that as a person, and I think the result was that you were up against the world.

"It wasn't always us against the team we were playing, or us against the ACC. Sometimes he was angry about something even closer to home, which kinda brought the team together.

"For example, I think he had pretty well documented disputes with Paul Dietzel (USC football coach and athletics director). And he would comment on those in a way we would feel united, not against another school or a player, but a situation closer to home.

"I think that Paul Dietzel's style was so different from Frank's that I don't think he particularly liked him. So it was a little bit of an attitude in the athletic department. It's not like us against the football program, but I understood that you're not going to get a lot of support from the athletic director at this school.

"It was, like, we're alone here, fighting lots of different things.

"Coach McGuire was a tough guy--looking at some of the things that went on back then. At Florida State, when I was a sophomore, we were down by about ten points with five minutes to go. He gets a technical, and another one and then another one. I remember we were standing there, and it was about five or six technicals.

"And he just turned to us and said, 'We're all leaving--let's go.' He had the ability to have his players do what he asked them to do. When he said to us, 'We're leaving the game,' it was never a doubt. We didn't say, 'Coach, we can still win this game.'

"If that was his call, we were walking off with him. It was a very rough game, and Florida State was a very physical team. There were some very rough fouls. It was a non-ACC game, and we were a lean team. Coach didn't want anyone to get injured--that was part of it.

"If that happened today--can you imagine the headlines. We were a top ten team, and if that happened today, there would be serious repercussions."

Long before he met Frank McGuire, Roche was being shaped by a background that was somewhat similar to his future college coach. He grew up in New York City and was exposed to a tough, competitive environment in the city streets. He attended LaSalle High School, where his basketball coach was Dan Buckley, who had played for McGuire at St. John's in 1948-49. This introduced him to McGuire's style of basketball. Another future Gamecock on that team was Tom Owens, a close friend of Roche.

ROCHE: "I was recruited as part of a pair. It seemed to be understood by everybody that we would go to the same school. In basketball, if you can get a guard and a forward at the same time--that was a big help.

"When I was a sophomore I had hoped I would be good enough to play college ball, and Duke was doing very well, and the ACC was getting a lot of publicity. Tommy also liked Duke, but he was the first one to mention South Carolina to me. He was interested because of his friendship with Bobby Cremins, who grew up in the same area of the Bronx.

"He mentioned South Carolina to me, but at that time the school was on probation. I remember my first comment was, 'You're dealing with a school that is on probation, and I'm a little concerned about that.' However, I also knew that my high school coach had a tremendous respect and affection for Coach McGuire, so we had two personal relationships that started us looking at South Carolina.

"As our senior year went on, and we visited lots of schools, we narrowed it down. We were looking at St. John's, Duke and South Carolina. I liked N.C. State a good bit, and Tommy liked Georgia. But I didn't like Georgia, and Tommy didn't care for N.C. State, so we dropped those. So it came down to Duke and South Carolina.

"When we visited Duke, we didn't feel comfortable, so we decided to visit South Carolina. During the recruiting process I had encouraged my mother to feel comfortable about asking questions to people who came to the house. Sometimes she'd do it--sometimes not.

"Tommy and I decided to go to South Carolina, and we told Coach McGuire and Donnie Walsh (USC assistant coach) that. Donnie had played a key role in recruiting us.

"Frank came to the house, and I had told my mother and father that I had decided to go to South Carolina. My mother had good concerns. Duke was highly regarded, from an educational standpoint, while South Carolina was not as well regarded. So that was in her mind, and she raised that when McGuire and Walsh came up to sign. She might have mentioned Richard Nixon (who attended Duke Law School) had called the house a couple of times.

"That was a time when the relationship between Duke and South Carolina was not the best, so that touched a nerve. And Coach McGuire was a little upset. For years I think he felt that I came to South Carolina over my mother's objections, and that really wasn't the case. She left the decision up to me, and she just wondered if I had made the right decision--a legitimate concern. When I was in the second grade my teacher asked me what I wanted to be, and I put down, 'lawyer.' I chose a college solely based on basketball considerations, but I think I always knew that I wanted to go to law school. Even with a long pro career, which I had. But you retire from that at age 32, and I was fortunate to be able to do something else.

"My main reason for coming to South Carolina was Coach McGuire's reputation. We put scholastic considerations aside. It was not among the elite educationally--like Duke and the Ivy League schools. In the end we felt very comfortable with Donnie Walsh, and when we visited, we liked all the players. Coach McGuire was like one of us. He grew up in New York, like we did, and he was closer to what we knew than the other coaches who came in.

"We went to our high school coach and told him we had narrowed it to Duke and South Carolina, and he told us to go to South Carolina. He said that he didn't know the people at Duke, but that he did know Frank McGuire and how he would treat us.

"Here's a recruiting story. In high school I would study the coaches who came to us very closely. I looked for any signs that we were being manipulated or tricked, or something other than they appeared to be.

"I remember when we were being recruited by Georgia. Kenny Rosemond (assistant coach at USC in 1958-59) was the head coach. He had played for McGuire at North Carolina, and he tried to copy McGuire in his recruiting style and what he would do.

"He picked up Tommy and me once, and before we went to dinner he wanted to drive down and pick up some shirts from a laundry. We drove through a part of town which had, what we call now, a lot of homeless people. Back then they were called the terrible name of 'bums.' We stopped at a light, and a homeless person came across and knocked on the window and asked for a dollar.

"Kenny kinda didn't know what to do--got kind of nervous. He just looked at him and smiled. He didn't roll down the window--wasn't unkind to him--but he didn't give him any money.

"Very coincidentally, Frank McGuire was recruiting us, and we were driving in the city, we stopped at a red light, and the same thing happened. Coach McGuire rolled down the window, took out his wallet and gave him several dollars. He was very comfortable with it and made some comment that indicated some compassion for the man.

"I remembered that very vividly as an indication of something genuine in Coach McGuire. This is no criticism of Rosemond-- was nervous and wanted to do everything right in recruiting us. But I remember how stress-free Coach McGuire was and how well he handled that.

"When we enrolled at South Carolina, Buck Freeman was freshman coach, and we didn't have a lot of contact with Coach McGuire. When Tommy and I got to college we had ideas of how we liked to do things, and they weren't always the way that Buck Freeman looked at it. During our freshman year we would have some conflicts.

"I remember once during practice Tommy and Buck got into an argument, and Tommy walked out of practice–just left. Frank was real angry about that–being disrespectful to Buck–and he took a real active role in talking to both of us, especially Tommy, about that.

"Here's how he set down to me what our relationship should be. Early in my sophomore year we were at practice, and Coach yelled out some instruction. I don't remember what it was, but I was the kind of person who would test to see how far I could go with a coach--as to what I could get away with and could not get away with. He gave me some instruction that I didn't want to follow, and he could see that I wasn't doing it.

"Coach had had experience with players like me--with my background in New York City. And he could see it was a test, as well. We kinda exchanged a few words in practice, and then he took me into the locker room. To me it was a telling moment for my years of playing with him. He looked at me in a way that said, 'This is the way it's going to be, and if you don't like it, I'm the kind who will fight you about it. I'm not just going to tell you I don't like it--we're going to settle that right here.'

"That was his reputation, and he was still young enough to be formidable. I think, at the same time, in that locker room he saw in my eyes, maybe, a similar background to his. If I got upset or angry enough, I would look at it the same way that he would look at it.

"I left that meeting knowing that I couldn't push him beyond a certain limit. And I think he left that meeting with the idea that he couldn't push me beyond a certain limit either. And I think it was very productive.

"During the three years I played for him, just because of basic personality, I might get to the edge of that limit, but I always knew never to go beyond it.

"That was one side of Coach, but when I look at it now, one characteristic that stands out is that he was very funny. Sometimes he intended to be funny, and sometimes not. But when you played for him over a three-year period, some of the funny memories come from his temper and how angry he would get. And what he would do when he became angry. Looking back at it, it was very humorous.

"We're playing a game against Virginia, and they're freezing the ball, and all of a sudden Coach gets up and walks around the entire court. Nobody's watching the game--you had 12,000 people watching him walking around. It was because he didn't like a reporter whom he felt was rooting for Virginia or had some beef against him.

"So now he's in the reporter's face, pointing at him, challenging him. That was very funny, and as he walked back people were throwing things at him, so we run off the court to go after fans who were throwing stuff. The game was stopped, and it was hysterical! He was fun to play for!

"Here's a story that Bobby Carver told me. The year after we left, Bobby was captain of the team. The captains would go out to center court and have a brief meeting with the referees. At this particular game Steve Honzo, who was a well-known official, was the referee. This was one of the first games that Bobby was captain in, and Coach called him over during the warm-ups and said, 'You've got to meet with Honzo, so go out there and tell him he's a son of a bitch.'

"Bobby says he's appalled, and said to Coach, 'But we're just starting the game.' McGuire repeated, 'Go out and tell him he's a son of a bitch.' So Bobby starts the long walk to mid court. Honzo was a dark-skinned man, with his hair slicked back, and he was kinda tall. He's standing there with his arms folded, sorta staring at the ceiling.

"As Bobby is walking out, Honzo is watching him, and Bobby is terrified. On the way, he decided to say, 'Coach McGuire told me to tell you that you're a son of a bitch.' So Bobby's walking out there, and he's about five feet from Honzo.

"I guess Honzo saw Bobby's fear, so he turned to him and said, 'Bobby, I know. I'm a son of a bitch.' Coach had a long relationship with Honzo, getting technical fouls and the like."

Perhaps an association with an incident that many South Carolina fans feel denied them a NCAA championship gave Honzo a negative place in the back of McGuire's mind. It took place in a semi-final game of the 1970 ACC tournament at Charlotte.

Carolina had gone through 14 regular season ACC games without a loss and was favored to win the tournament, which would provide the only berth in the NCAA playoffs for an ACC team. The Gamecocks survived a 34-33 slow-down against Clemson in the first round and had a comfortable lead over Wake Forest in the semi-final that Carolina won, 79-63. With 11 minutes remaining, Roche was driving toward the basket and collided with defender John Lewkowicz.

Roche's left foot landed on Lewkowicz's right foot, and the Gamecock star sustained a severe ankle sprain. Roche recalled that McGuire was upset over his being injured but particularly angry that Honzo had called an offensive foul against Roche on the play.

Roche limped through the championship game against State but was really in no condition to be a factor. Even so, the Gamecocks held a 39-38 lead with 22 seconds remaining and had the ball out of bounds. Roche's inbounds pass to Cremins was stolen by State's Ed Leftwich, who drove for a layup that gave his team a 40-39 lead. A Gamecock foul provided two free throws that added to State's final margin.

McGuire contended that Cremins was fouled by Leftwich in the scramble for the ball, because the Gamecock captain came away with a dislocated finger. Roche had his own version of the entire situation.

ROCHE: "I had sprained my ankle before, but never that badly. In my basketball career I had a number of problems with my left ankle. I broke it in my next to last year in the pros. As a freshman at Carolina I hurt it and was on crutches for a couple of weeks, and, as a sophomore I injured it in an exhibition and was sort of gimpy. But I never hurt it to that extent, and I had never had Novocain in my body. So I didn't know how you could function with that.

"Going into that final game, I had a lot of uncertainty, and that was a problem, because I didn't know how to deal with that. Later on in my career I would have known. But I was just taking it a step at a time. Certainly I couldn't play with Novocain--I could figure that out.

"However, I couldn't feel anything--my foot was like a dead piece of wood. I remember that the injury affected me physically, but worse than that, it affected me emotionally and mentally. And because as players we were given a lot of freedom to make decisions, that affected me.

"When we had an 11-point lead near the end of the first half and elected to come out of our zone, it left a lot of room for second-guessing. However we had beaten State easily the week before (85-69) and had been very successful in pressing them. We wanted to put them away.

"An eleven point lead with the team we had then was enormous because we were very good at protecting a lead.

"At the end I passed the ball to Bobby, and they got it. Bobby takes some blame for it, but actually it was a bad pass. What happened is that I threw it to Bobby, and Bobby could see that a player from State had a clear path to it. He tried to beat him to the spot and got his hand in there and hurt his finger. Bobby had no role in losing the ball, but Bobby, being the way he is, accepts a role in everything. He's quite gallant like that.

"I was too young then to fully appreciate Bobby. When he left (graduated) it was a very major change and had a major effect on the team. Bobby played a very central role in how close we were as a team and how good we were as a team. When he left, the loss was far greater than his talents would suggest. We weren't nearly as good a team the following year as we were our junior year. There was a lot going on, and Bobby helped to keep everyone together and focused.

"In 1970 we felt that we would get to the Final Four and have a showdown with UCLA. Then anything could happen. The Eastern Regionals were played in Columbia, which could have given us an advantage, and the winner (St. Bonaventure) went to the Final Four.

"As a team, we were inclined to put a lot of pressure on ourselves, but during our sophomore and junior years it was still in the concept of being all fun, and we loved it. My senior year, it was all work--it wasn't that I felt great about practicing or couldn't wait for the next game to come.

"When things didn't work out my junior year, that was a very difficult time for me. I think Coach McGuire did the best he could in keeping us focused for the next year, both personally and as athletes. He didn't always succeed in that, because there's only so much you can do. But he could see that there was going to be a shift in the way things were.

"Up until that N.C. State game, everything in basketball was fun for me. My first two years, everyone knew their role-everyone got along very well. We had a common goal and common purposes.

"The following year, we had more good players, and so there were more issues concerning playing time and who would shoot, when and how many shots people would get. And that's most often the case on teams. I learned that in the pros. I was lucky to have played on two college teams when that wasn't the case. That's all I knew at the time.

"Coach McGuire saw that change before we did and tried to deal with it. But some things you can't solve. There's only one basketball and only five places on the floor. There are people who want to play, and maybe personalities don't mesh as well.

"Speaking of me, after that game there was still an element of fun in basketball, but there was also a strong element of work. It's what I did as a job.

"We put a lot of pressure on ourselves, and Frank, by the way he coached, there was a lot of pressure. There was a heightened scrutiny and heightened emotions when we would travel to different arenas. Frank would bring that on himself, very much like Bobby Knight (Indiana) does today. He acted in a way that drew attention to our team by the way he was—the strength of his personality and what was conceived to be a combative attitude by people who weren't supporters of the team that Frank was coaching.

"We were beginning to feel besieged, and Coach felt that some things weren't going our way intentionally. 'They' didn't like the idea of his winning, and there was this anti-Frank McGuire sentiment.

"We lost a game on a very questionable call, and he called us to his hotel room. As we all walked in it was completely dark. There were no lights on, and he was over in the corner of the room, and we all gathered around him.

"And he looks at us and says, 'You know, I don't mind when they put the umbrella up my ass. It hurts, but I can deal with the pain. But what really bothers me is when they open the umbrella and start to pull it out. That's when I can't take it any longer!'

"That was a way of taking some of the heat himself and taking some of the pain away from his players as to the disappointment of losing games. It was part motivation and part personality.

"My senior year in the ACC was pretty rough, and I thought it went too far. We certainly knew when we got there that there was some lingering resentment concerning the Mike Grosso situation. So, when I was a sophomore, we were ready to play Duke all the time—big time! They were a competitor. Later it changed to North Carolina, because they were better."

During the 1970-71 season Carolina's home game with Maryland ended when a fight broke out between the two teams late in the second half. Carolina won the game, 96-70, but the Terps' coach, Lefty Driesell, warned that the Gamecocks would be in for a rough time when they played at College Park later in the year.

There was little abnormal abuse from the record crowd in Cole Field House, but the Terps lived up to their name by slowing things to a turtle's pace and stealing two straight inbound passes for baskets that sealed a 31-30 overtime victory.

ROCHE: "I don't remember that game too much. It was silly. Although they won that game, they weren't very good the three years I was there. That's the only time they beat us.

"Certain schools, we never had problems with because we beat them all the time. We never lost to Clemson or Wake Forest, and Virginia, only once. North Carolina was the dominant presence at that time."

Although Roche was named ACC Player of the Year after his sophomore and junior seasons, Wake Forest's Charlie Davis received the honor in 1971. ACC area sports writers accorded Davis 86 votes to Roche's runner-up 30.

Many South Carolina fans considered this an injustice to their star and accredited it to anti-South Carolina prejudice around the conference area. However, Davis had led the league in scoring with an average of 26.5 points per game, while Roche was runner-up at 21.6.

ROCHE: "Charlie Davis deserved it, and I don't think it had anything to do with anti-South Carolina sentiment. You're talking about individual attitudes of many voters. It's possible that some may have been influenced by personal feelings.

"But take the case of Charlie Scott (North Carolina standout). Charlie was the second black player in the conference, and he was a very outspoken person. I wouldn't be the least bit surprised if there were some writers who voted for me based on racial grounds when I was a sophomore, and Charlie was a junior. You can't look into the heads of the hundred or so media people who vote, but I received the honor over Charlie in 1969 and 1970.

"Charlie played on an extraordinarily talented North Carolina team, and his role was different from mine. On many nights Charlie could get eight points, and the team wins. They're blowing out teams, and he's getting ten or twelve points, because he's playing half a game.

"We needed the contribution of everybody at a high level, so I was in a position to have more outstanding games than Charlie was. That's why it's good to call it 'Player of the Year.' Not the best player.

"That was the flip side when I was a senior. We had so much talent that there were many games where we could win more easily, and we had a deeper bench. Charlie Davis was in a position where he would have to be outstanding every night for his team to win.

"I thought Tommy Owens had a much better year than I did our senior year, so I didn't think I deserved the award that season."

Following his senior year, Roche was signed by the New York Nets, coached by Lou Carnesecca, who had played baseball for McGuire at St. John's. After nine seasons, spread over 11 years, Roche retired from pro basketball to begin a law career.

During the time he also played for Kentucky, Utah, Los Angeles (Lakers) and Denver, where he scored 5,345 points, averaging 11.2 points per game. His best season was 1972-73, when he scored 1,107 points, averaging 14.4, for the Nets.

In 1974 he married Robin Goldstein, who was a classmate at South Carolina, and they became parents of a daughter in 1981. Robin died of cancer in the late 1980s.

Roche was remarried in May 1994, and his wife, Jackie, had a son and daughter from a previous marriage.

ROCHE: "I've been blessed with very wonderful women in my life. My mother and two sisters, to whom I was very close. I was very blessed with Robin, and now Jackie, who is a another wonderful woman."

Roche attended the University of Denver law school during his latter professional years, receiving his degree in 1981. He joined the Denver law firm of Davis, Graham and Stubbs, with whom he became a partner in 1987. Roche is a commercial trial attorney with this firm of over 100 attorneys.

Roche recalls that there were valuable lessons he learned from his college coach that have served him well in his post-college and professional life.

ROCHE: "If I had to characterize it, I would say that Frank coached by putting a lot of confidence and independence into the hands of his players. He allowed his players to make far more decisions than any coach you see today or any coach at the time we were playing.

"If you look at it in terms of developing traits, he was developing in his players a sense of self reliance and independence. He was respecting their ability to make decisions and accept responsibility for those decisions--rather than someone else telling you what to do.

"In terms of living my life, that has been very helpful to me. And that's a part of Frank McGuire that has stayed with me throughout my life."

CHAPTER FIFTEEN

CHAPTER FIFTEEN

BOBBY CREMINS:
THE HEART AND SOUL

Of all the great players who performed on Frank McGuire's college teams, Al McGuire and Bobby Cremins have been the most successful as head coaches on the collegiate level. Al McGuire played at St. John's and won a national championship at Marquette, while Cremins, a South Carolina protégé, has led Georgia Tech to national prominence.

Playing on what many consider Carolina's best-ever team in 1969-70, he was called by his coach as "the heart and soul of the team," because of his spirit and qualities of leadership. Those same qualities have been trademarks in bringing Tech out of the basketball doldrums to championships of the ACC and regular appearances in the NCAA playoffs.

It could have been loyalty to and love for his former coach that led him, in March 1993, to accepting the position as Head Basketball Coach at his alma mater, against a tugging inner resistance. Bobby annulled the agreement after three days, amid considerable media coverage and consternation among Gamecock supporters when he decided to stay in Georgia.

In conversation among Gamecock fans and in the media, it was speculated that the return of Cremins would be the reincarnation of the McGuire dynasty. However, Cremins' college mentor never commented publicly on the events surrounding the decisions of his former pupil and assistant.

McGuire's daughter, Carol Ann Morgan of Columbia, recalls those days.

CAROL ANN MORGAN: "When Bobby was thinking about returning to Carolina, he and my father were talking about it on an almost daily basis. Dad, in talking to Bobby, said, 'Look, you've got a good thing going there in Atlanta. You shouldn't leave. You're making a good income, they love you there. Stay.'

"But for personal and some other reasons Bobby felt that he needed to change. He was going through some personal turmoil. Dad, again, going back to what I said before--he's not an escape artist--there, face it--do it the right way--handle it the right way.'

"But Bobby loved Dad like a father, and Dad loved Bobby like a son. He really loved him as a son. Dad saw a lot of himself in Bobby, and I think Bobby hopes to see a lot of Dad in himself. He wants to emulate him.

"Dad was very proud of Bobby and what he had accomplished. But he knew this wasn't going to be the right move. First of all, he thought that the University was twenty years behind where it should be. It was in a mess. The succession of coaches, or for whatever reasons, it wasn't gonna work. He wasn't the one to come in and rectify it.

"But Bobby, knowing Dad was ill--this was part of the problem--and wanting to eventually come back to Columbia--especially if we got back into the ACC. He wanted to come back and resurrect the school from the ashes before my father died. And he wanted to do this for my dad. That was going to be his gift back to his coach.

"And he was biting off more than he could chew. His life was in a turmoil and the school was in a disastrous state. And my father told Bobby the day before (Cremins accepted), 'Don't come here. Don't do it for me. If it's what you want to do, that's your decision. But, when in doubt, you don't act.'

"That's Biblical. God tells you that. If you don't know what you're doing, don't do it. No guesswork. There was a lot of pressure on Bobby, too. The bandwagon started here--friends and people who knew that his coming here would benefit everybody--from real estate to selling shoes.

"There was so much pressure on him. They got a plane down there the next morning, and they rolled out the red carpet. He was really in a very bad stage of his life. He was burned out, and he was a nervous wreck, and he came. My father said that he was in the right place, but that he had made a bad judgment.

"But I think what was so difficult for my father is that he sat there, and he watched what Bobby was going through. And he knew that it wasn't going to work. He just knew that something was going to go wrong--he could feel it. His heart really went out to Bobby, because he knew what Bobby was doing was for him. And it was all wrong. And Dad felt somewhat responsible for him feeling that he should come here and do what he had to do.

"When it all stopped, and Bobby made the decision to go back, my father wasn't at all surprised. Bobby called John (Carol Ann's husband) and me--we were in Florida--and he was very upset and very concerned. He asked, 'What about your father, Carol Ann, how is he gonna feel about me?

"I told him that my father never abandons his children. And you are one of his children. One of his chosen children. He loves you dearly. He's disappointed for you, because there are so many ramifications.

"But he says for you to go back to Atlanta, rebuild your life there with the athletic department. You make your amends to them, straighten things out and stay put. You've got a great thing going there, stay put where it's working. If it ain't broken, don't try to fix it.

"Bobby listened to Dad, and then he called Jane (McGuire). And Jane told him the same thing. She said, 'Bobby, Frank will always love you. There will never be a day that he won't. He'll be there for you.'

"Bobby punished himself. And when Deedee Salter (very close friend of Cremins in Columbia) died, Bobby wanted to come back to the funeral, and he did. But there was such hard feelings in the community. This is what hurt my father more than anything. On his way from Bridgepoint (McGuire's condominium) to Health South (for therapy) he had to pass certain billboards.

"Dad was looking out the window, and he saw them and asked Jane, 'What is that?'

"She said, 'It's a billboard.' The billboards were the ones that said, 'Welcome, Bobby.' That's when he announced he was coming here. But they had added that symbol--a circle with a diagonal mark--that means, 'No!'

"Dad said that when he came to Carolina, one of the first things he had to do was to get up to the microphone at a game in the old 'snakepit,' when fans were throwing things on the floor. He said, 'I might be a foreigner here, but what I'm trying to do is build a first class basketball team. I want to put you on the map as a first class program. If I'm going to behave in a first class way, I expect you to behave in a first class way. I need you; you need me; this is how we're going to behave.'

"He told Jane, 'I thought I had taught these people, but some of them must have been absent from class. Who in the world would ever think of putting up a billboard with a mark through his name, telling him he's not welcome in the very home where a kid had the crowd standing on their feet with his spirit?'

"When Dad looked at it, he said, 'You know, Jane, if I weren't sick--if I weren't in this wheelchair--whoever thought of those billboards would eat them. Because I ran a first class operation, and that's a low class deal.

"Then he said, 'You know, they may have had the arrow aimed at Bobby, but the one they shot was me. And that's a fine thank you, after so many years of coaching here.'

"It hurt Dad terribly, because it hurt his boy. You might as well have stuck a knife through his heart."

Cremins continued to remain loyal and attentive to McGuire until the end, and he made a financial contribution to a portion of Carolina's new basketball practice facility that was named in honor of McGuire. He looks back at his years in a Gamecock uniform as happy times during which he became well prepared for his coaching career.

CREMINS: "When I came down to Columbia as a freshman--I will always remember my mother buying me a wool suit, which she intended to last me for four years. I arrived in Columbia in August, and it was over one hundred degrees. I never wore that suit again.

"Later I went over to Coach McGuire's home, and I made the mistake of calling him 'Frank.' He didn't say anything to me about it, but he got Donnie Walsh (assistant coach) to straighten me out very quickly!

"Buck Freeman was my freshman coach, and it was a joy to watch him teach. We worked out with the varsity a lot, and I really thought that South Carolina was going to have an incredible team, because we had Jack Thompson, Skip Harlicka, Frank Standard, Gary Gregor, Skip Kickey and, of course, Mike Grosso.

"Mike was a great big man, and Jackie and Skip (Harlicka) were a great backcourt. I was amazed at how good they really were.

"Coach McGuire seemed really excited about the future, and then tragedy struck when Mike Grosso was declared ineligible and had to leave school. It was the first time I had seen Coach McGuire so depressed and upset. I really thought he might quit, because he was so upset at what was happening to Mike. I was just beginning to learn how tough a person Coach McGuire really was.

"Because freshmen were ineligible to play on varsity teams back then, my first opportunity to play with the varsity came in my sophomore season. And, because of Grosso being declared ineligible, I had a great opportunity to start.

"I believe we were on some sort of probation, but, at the same time, we had a very exciting team. The great moment in my entire career came against North Carolina at Chapel Hill. I scored 23 points and had 15 rebounds and managed to make some crucial free throws near the end of the game to ward off a North Carolina rally. (South Carolina won the game, 87-86, over a Tar Heel team that finished the season ranked No. 2 in the UPI poll and No. 4 by the AP.)

"We were a fun and exciting team, but, behind the scenes, Coach McGuire was once again building for the future. He brought in John Roche and Tom Owens, followed by Tom Riker and Bobby Carver, and then Kevin Joyce and Brian Winters.

"Coach McGuire was a great coach. At practice he would talk a lot, and we would scrimmage a lot, but his real strength was at game time. He was big on shot selection and tempo.

"The highlight of my junior year (1968-69) was the opening of the new Carolina Coliseum. It was an honor to be a starter on the last team playing in the old fieldhouse and also a starter on the first team to play in the Coliseum. (Cremins was the only player to hold that distinction.)

"Of course, this was also the beginning of the John Roche era. As we found out during the summer, John was to become a special player in Gamecock history. He started to show us what he had during the summer, and he simply became 'the man.' This was the beginning of some of Coach McGuire's best teams, and his recruitment of Roche and Owens rejuvenated his spirits and hopes of bringing South Carolina a national championship.

"We had a great year (21-7 and ranked 13th in the AP poll) for such a young team, but Coach McGuire was putting everything in place to make Columbia the capital of college basketball. The excitement was there, and everything was about to fall into place.

"Going into my senior year (1969-70) we were ranked number one in the pre-season rankings, and, at times, we seemed unbeatable. We went 14 and 0 in regular season before the disaster in Charlotte. I can remember the play like it was yesterday. After a heart-stopping win over Clemson in the first round, we easily defeated Wake Forest in the semi-finals, but John Roche severely sprained his ankle late in the game. We lost to North Carolina State in the championship game in double overtime, and this was, without a doubt, the most depressed I had ever seen Coach McGuire.

"The loss really hurt me personally, because I so badly wanted to play on Coach McGuire's first ACC championship team (at South Carolina) and, again, bring a national championship to South Carolina. This was the hardest time of my life, and although I didn't deal with it correctly at the time, it was to be a great learning experience for me later on. Whenever I have to deal with adversity now, I always think of that moment.

"Two years later I came back to work on Coach McGuire's staff as Graduate Assistant. I saw the coaching side, and I marveled at how well Coach McGuire handled everything around the basketball program. Of course, getting out of the ACC was very disappointing, but the ACC and South Carolina seemed to be at many odds. It took away from the great natural rivalries and the ACC tradition.

"However, I am very glad now that South Carolina is in the SEC, and I really believe that Eddie Fogler will do a great job for Gamecock basketball."

Cremins was graduated from Carolina with a degree in marketing. Following his two-year stint as McGuire's assistant, he became head coach at Appalachian State, where his teams won three Southern Conference championships.

In 1981 he was hired by Georgia Tech and has become one of the marquee names in college basketball. His Yellow Jackets won ACC championships in 1985, 1990, and 1993 and have participated in seven NCAA playoffs. His team made the Final Four in 1990.

Many great players wore the Garnet and Black under Frank McGuire, but Cremins, above all, exemplified the spirit, loyalty and determination of his former college coach.

CHAPTER SIXTEEN

JUDGE CASEY MANNING:
IN THE SCHEME OF THINGS

In the twilight of his coaching career Frank McGuire was addressing about 400 people in attendance at the annual basketball banquet for the Carolina team at Seawell's fairgrounds restaurant.

"We've had a lot of great players here," McGuire began. "John Roche, Kevin Joyce, Brian Winters, Alex English," the coach named a few that came to mind. "But somebody is here tonight that, in the overall scheme of things, means as much as any of them," he added.

And then he introduced that 'somebody' who was Casey Manning.

Manning was also the first black basketball player recruited by McGuire at South Carolina. He had been a high scorer at Dillon High School, about 90 miles from Columbia, and received attention from a number of colleges, including Carolina's arch rival, Clemson.

MANNING: "I struggled with where I was going, but, in the end, Coach McGuire was the big reason I came to Carolina. At Carolina I could major in about anything, and they had a great basketball team, so I decided that it was my best choice. I had received letters from Wilt Chamberlain and Governor (Robert) McNair about going to play for Coach McGuire, and that didn't hurt.

"The fact that I was the first black player was no big deal to me. Coach McGuire always went out of his way to speak to me, and I felt that he was genuinely concerned about his players off the court, as well as on the court. Perhaps even more off the court than on, Coach was always gracious--always inquired about your family. "He used to tell me Solly Walker stories and Wilt Chamberlain stories. 'You're a pioneer-it's tough.' That sort of thing.

"Sometimes the fans gave me a pretty hard time, and I remember a game up at Clemson when it got real bad. They even had a rope tied to Coach McGuire's chair and tried to pull it out from under him. They did have some highway patrolman right behind our bench, but they did nothing about the crowd.

"After that game Carolina didn't play Clemson for a number of years, but shortly afterward I received a nice letter from the Clemson coach, Tates Locke, apologizing for the way they treated us.

"When Alex English was recruited for my senior season (1972-73), he was actually the second Black to play for the varsity. I had met Alex before he came here, and I had no particular role in recruiting him. The thing I remember is that one day, before the season had even started, I went into Alex's room, and he was literally packing his bags. He was disgruntled about something.

"He said, 'I'm going to Minnesota.' That was one of the school's that was trying to recruit Alex. He said, 'I don't like the way you're being treated,' and went on like that.

"I said, 'Alex, whatever perception you have about me has nothing to do with you, and, in my opinion, in the long run you're better off staying here than going to Minnesota or anywhere else.' We had a long talk, and he unpacked his bags. The rest is history.

"His perception was that I wasn't playing enough, based on my ability. I would have been more successful as an individual player, if we had been playing a more modern game. But we walked the ball up the floor, and it didn't suit my talents--or some of the others who were successful in the system. My strengths were speed and quickness, and I would have been better off in a system that stressed a pressing defense.

"The great thing about Coach McGuire was that he had great players, and he didn't superimpose his philosophy on them. He let them use their individual talents. He was not an X's and O's coach."

"Coach always treated us like men. Didn't try to tell you when to go to bed, when to get up and all that. Like any player, I did want to get more playing time, however.

"One day I was coming out of the Coliseum just as he was getting into his car. I was sorta mad, and I went up to his car and said, "Coach, what do you have to do to get into the game?'

"He looked at me and said, 'Buy a ticket, like everybody else!' That ended the conversation."

After Manning's graduation from Carolina, he spent a year as a field agent for the South Carolina Law Enforcement Division. Then he entered the Carolina School of Law, receiving a degree in 1977. After private practice in Dillon, he served as an Assistant Attorney General in Columbia. He was a partner in a Columbia law firm before being elected to the Circuit Court judgeship in 1993.

Manning recalled that the last time he visited with McGuire was in the fall of 1993, when he accompanied his coach to two of his therapy sessions at Baptist Medical Center.

As he reflects on his relationship with Frank McGuire, Manning can take special pride and satisfaction in his historic role and that McGuire positioned him among the Gamecock greats-- 'in the overall scheme of things.'

CHAPTER SEVENTEEN

MEMORIES OF A COACH

Expect anything when a group of former "Frank's Boys" get together and swap stories about their fabled coach. Tom Riker, who was an All-America pivotman for the Gamecocks in 1972 and also a starter on the great 1971 ACC championship team, was seen as a tough New Yorker, not given to sentimentality. But he expressed the feeling of practically everyone who played under the Irishman.

"One of my proudest monikers is that I'm one of 'Frank's Boys,'" stated the former first round draft pick of the New York Knicks. Four other former Gamecocks nodded agreement, as they rejoiced on this Saturday afternoon, March 5, 1994. The celebration was over South Carolina's 75-74 victory over seventh-ranked Kentucky in the nearby Frank McGuire Arena.

"Seemed like old times," someone said, referring to the many thrilling victories achieved under their coach in the McGuire era. And this was the cue for story-telling time to begin.

The starting team in this gabfest wouldn't have make the final four in basketball, but they could hold their own in a bull session.

They lined up like this:

At one forward was Skip Kickey, a 6-8 forward from Union City, N.J., who played for McGuire from 1964 to 1968 and now owns Dixie Trophies in Columbia.

The other forward would be Riker, a native of Hicksville, N.Y. and who has currently returned to the USC School of Nursing, having already earned a degree some years earlier.

Lyn Burkholder would be the center because, although he is two inches shorter than Riker, he lacked Tom's shooting range. He played high school basketball in Harrisonburg, Va., and was already in school when McGuire became the coach. However, his three varsity years, were spent under McGuire, and he graduated "on time" in 1967. Burkholder earned a degree in engineering and has been employed by Eastman Chemical company for the past 25 years.

The team has three guards, including Casey Manning, Dennis Powell and Bill Gause.

Manning, now a Circuit Court Judge for the 5th District of South Carolina, was the first black player recruited by McGuire for South Carolina, earning his letters in 1971, 1972 and 1973. He was a high scoring performer at Dillon High School (SC) before enrolling at the University.

Powell rode McGuire's famous "underground railroad" down from the Bronx, having played at St. Helena's, and has been an investment banker for 13 years with South Carolina National Bank (now Wachovia) in Columbia.

Gause played his prep basketball at Hammond Academy, a private institution in Columbia, and was on the Gamecock squad from 1975 through 1977. Billy sells medical products for a living and also books speakers and celebrities for the East Coast.

A STANDARD ANSWER

It wasn't long before someone mentioned the name of Frank Standard, who was a member of McGuire's first recruiting class in 1964. A native of Brooklyn, N.Y., Standard had the reputation of being a crafty individual, on and off the court. Kickey volunteered, "Frank could deal you any five cards he wanted to--and often did." Although he was only 6-4, Standard was a double-digit scorer and rebounder throughout his varsity career. He was also a quick thinker.

Once Standard was a guest on McGuire's weekly TV show in a period in which there was considerable controversy over the eligibility of Mike Grosso. When his coach asked him what he considered the main difference between high school and college basketball, Standard immediately answered, "The politics."

Both Kickey and Burkholder were present when the Gamecocks were preparing to face Kentucky in the 1967 Kentucky Invitational tournament at Lexington, Ky. It was two days before Christmas, and the players were in a holiday mood, especially because of their 64-61 upset victory over Cincinnati the night before.

McGuire had called a squad meeting at the hotel at which the Gamecocks were staying to discuss the game plan to be used against Adolph Rupp's Wildcats, who would finish their season ranked 8th in the national polls. The players were well schooled in McGuire's attention to detail and insistence on punctuality when it involved team meetings and practice.

The meeting began, and there was one noticeable absentee--Frank Standard. Several minutes into the meeting, the door at the back of the room slowly opened, and Standard slid through the entrance and toward one of the seats in the rear. His actions did not go unnoticed by his coach.

McGuire stopped his dissertation, scowled in the direction of Standard and yelled, "Where in the hell have you been?"

Without hesitation, Standard meekly replied, "Well, Coach, I ran into this Kentucky fan in the hall and got into a big argument over who is the greatest coach, you or Adolph Rupp!"

The speechless McGuire could only manage a trace of a smile, as he continued the meeting as if nothing had happened.

KICKEY FOLLOWS ORDERS

That incident brought a smile to Kickey's countenance, as he recalled something that had happened the previous evening, during the game with Cincinnati. The Bearcats, coached by Tay Baker, were enroute to an 18-8 won-lost record and were substantial favorites to send South Carolina into a consolation game against Dayton the following night.

KICKEY: "Cincinnati had a big center--I can't recall his name--but he was a great rebounder and tough to defend against inside. About midway through the first half this guy drove for the basket, and as he laid it in, I sorta flicked him on the arm. So, it's a foul, and he makes a three-point play out of it.

"At that point, Coach pulled me out of the game, and I could tell by his expression that he wasn't too happy. He grabbed me by the jersey, and said, 'Kickey, I'm gonna put you back in the game, and the next time that guy drives to the basket, if you don't knock him flat on his ass, you'll never play another minute for me.'

"Now, I don't know how serious Coach was, but I wasn't taking any chances. It wasn't long until this guy drives down the lane, and I body blocked him. It so happened that the benches were at the end of the court, and ours at their end of the court in the first half. So, when I hit this guy he fell right at Coach's feet.

"Coach calmly stood up right over this guy, straightened his tie, looked at me and said, 'Now, that's where he belongs.' Well, maybe not in those exact words, but he made his point.

"I don't think that guy drove for the basket the rest of the game, and it was close right up to the end, but we did pull it out (64-61)."

THE BURKHOLDER REPORT

BURKHOLDER: "Most people didn't realize how interested Coach McGuire was in our academics. He didn't make a big deal out of it publicly, but he always told us that we were at Carolina to get an education, because not many of us would be playing professional basketball. Even if we did, it wouldn't last forever. Just look at the guys around this table. We all have degrees and are using our educations.

"Well, I was majoring in engineering and was having some trouble with a physics course, so I went to Coach McGuire and told him I needed a tutor. So, Coach had someone lineup a tutor, and that really helped me. This was not too long before the mid-term exam.

"Because of the help I received from the tutor, I made an 'A' on the mid-term. Grades were always sent to the basketball office, so they could keep up with how we were doing. So Coach called me into his office and said, 'We're gonna cancel your tutor.'

"I said, 'Why?'

"Coach answered, 'I noticed you that you made an 'A' on your mid-term exam. We don't tutor for 'A's'--we tutor for 'C's.' If you can make an A with a tutor, you can made a C without one.'

"So from then on, I got along fine without the tutor. But Coach was always supportive when I really needed it."

RIKER LEARNS TO SMILE

RIKER: "I considered myself very mild-mannered off the court, but when I was on the court--in a game or in practice--I was a different person. Quick tempered. One day we were having an intra-squad scrimmage, and the competition was pretty intense.

"Coach was always saying to me, 'Tommy, relax. He's just trying to get your goat. Relax.' That didn't come easy with me.

"In this particular scrimmage a couple of things happened that bothered me, and I let out a few curse words.

"Coach called me over and said, 'Tommy, stop cursing at practice. We have some nuns coming to watch us.'

"I said, 'Yes, Coach. I won't.' The nuns arrived, and we kept on scrimmaging. The first rebound, several of us crashed the board, and I let out a cuss word. Coach says, 'Riker, get here!'

"He told me that when he was a young coach at St. John's, sometimes, when things happened that he didn't like, that he would let out a cuss word and grimace--or frown--in doing it. A friend of his gave him some advice. He told Coach that there are always photographers around to take pictures and that when he had to give somebody a piece of his mind, to always smile while he was doing it. 'Smile when you cuss someone out!' So, he sat me down for cussing before the nuns.

"It just so happened that there was a newspaper photographer at this particular scrimmage, and the next day, in the paper, there was this picture taken when Coach was reading the riot act to me. It said, "Coach McGuire is shown giving Tom Riker some friendly advice! And there was Coach, smiling and straightening his tie!"

FREE FOR ALL

Riker also recalled another time when his quick temper created an incident that received prominent attention across the country. It took place on January 9, 1972 when the Gamecocks, ranked fourth in the polls at the time, took on second-ranked Marquette, coached by Al McGuire in a coach versus former pupil match-up.

The game was nationally televised and lived up to its pre-game billing in closeness and intensity. The Warriors held a 36-30 halftime advantage, but that was the largest margin held by either team.

RIKER: "This was a very tense game. We were both ranked high in the polls and we were both Catholic schools. Well, they were officially, and we were unofficially with all the Catholics on our team!

"Marquette was a very physical team--they always were under Al McGuire, and all through the first half they did a lot of pushing and shoving that they got away with. They had a big forward named Bob Lackey, and early in the second half he hit me after the official had blown the whistle on a foul. I don't remember which team it was on.

"When he hit me after the whistle I had just about had it. So I threw a punch at Lackey. It must have landed pretty good, because I broke my hand, and I think he had a cut on his face. Anyhow, he swung back, and that emptied both benches. Here we were in a nationally televised free for all!

(NOTE: Frank McGuire recalls that while South Carolina Law Enforcement Division agents and others were trying to restore order, he and Al McGuire stood together observing the situation. Al turned to his former coach and said, "Coach, I've seen better fights than this in our practices!")

"Both Lackey and I were ejected from the game, but I couldn't have played the second half, anyhow. In fact, I also missed the next three games."

Riker's absence was felt in the second half against Marquette, as the Warriors took a 72-71 lead with only seconds remaining, and Kevin Joyce's jump shot was off the mark as time ran out.

PLACING THE BLAME

All former players present were in agreement that McGuire was an exceptional "game coach" and excelled at adjusting to various situations. They gave him particularly high marks in his ability to "work the officials." One example occurred during McGuire's first season at South Carolina.

BURKHOLDER: "Back in 1965 we were still playing in the old field house, and we were really struggling. Clemson came in to play us and the place was packed, as it usually was when we played the Tigers. One of the officials was Charlie Eckman, who had been officiating in the ACC even when Coach was at North Carolina.

"Clemson was getting the best of us on the floor, but our fans were hanging in there and giving them a hard time. At one point, Eckman called time and went over to Coach McGuire. The fans behind the Clemson bench were very unruly.

"Eckman said, 'Coach, if you don't do something about those fans up there, I'm going to have to call a technical on your team.'

"Coach said in a very calm manner, 'Charlie, those are Clemson fans up there. That's why they're sitting behind the Clemson bench. They know that if they raise enough hell, you'll think they're Carolina fans and call a technical on us.'

"Eckman just walked away shaking his head."

A VISIT FROM SANTA

In December of 1970 the Gamecocks couldn't have been feeling better. They had won their first four games, including a national headliner over Notre Dame at South Bend, a 20-point win over Duke, and a 96-70 blowout over Lefty Driesell's Maryland team in Columbia. The polls ranked the Gamecocks right there with UCLA as the top teams in the early season.

POWELL: "It was late December, and our first game after Maryland was against Virginia Tech up at Blacksburg. We traveled on a bus to Blacksburg and checked into a hotel the night before the game.

"Coach McGuire got up early the next morning and went around knocking on the players' doors, and when they came out he gave them these nice wallets.

"Coach knocked on Riker's door, and there was no answer. He knocked again, and no answer. Then he really pounded the door a few times. By now, most of the guys were standing out in the hall to see what was going to happen.

"All of a sudden this angry voice comes from the room: 'Who the hell is it?'

"Coach says in a sort of disguised voice, 'What do you mean, who is it? Open the door.'

"Again the voice inside yells, 'Who is it?'

"Coach scowls and hollers, 'It's friggin' Santa Claus, stupid! Open the door!'

"The door slowly opens and a sheepish looking Riker peeped out to see Coach McGuire standing there with his Christmas present!"

PASSING THE BUCK

Carolina won its first four games of the 1965-66 season, but their first loss came against New York University, coached by Lou Rossini, a friend of McGuire who had been at Columbia University when McGuire was coaching at St. John's. That was followed by a game against Assumption College at Worchester, Massachusetts.

KICKEY: "Assumption was a Catholic School and had one of my former high school teammates, Tom O'Connor, playing for them. Coach didn't want to lose to this team, and neither did I.

"Coach told us that they had priests refereeing the game, and we might get some bad calls. He was right. Late in the game we had a small lead, and Assumption is bringing the ball up the court. Coach steps out and calls timeout--which you can't do when the other team has the ball. But those officials weren't about to buck Frank McGuire.

"Coach calls us over and says, 'You guys shouldn't lose to this team, so don't throw it away. Just take nothing but good shots. Only good shots, now.'

"We get the ball back and Skip Harlicka brings it down the court. Well, that afternoon I was watching a game on TV and I saw Cazzie Russell make a move where he puts his back to the basket and spins around and makes a jump shot. It was beautiful.

"So, Skip passes me the ball on the baseline about 15 feet from the basket. I wheel around and take the prettiest jump shot you've ever seen! The ball hit the side of the backboard and went out of bounds, so it's Assumption's ball.

"They're coming down the court, and, again, Coach calls time out. And, again, the officials let him do it.

"He calls us over, and he says, 'Kickey, you dumb s.o.b., and he punches me on the chest. Why the hell did you take that shot?' Then he looks over at Harlicka. He punches him on the chest and says, 'And why the hell did you throw him the ball?'

"Fortunately, we held on and won the game (75-69), or I might not have made it back to Columbia."

IN THE ZONE

GAUSE: "When I came along Carolina had withdrawn from the ACC, and the places that Coach McGuire recruited players were different. Basketball was improving in other areas, and it was more difficult to recruit as an independent.

"Coach's best teams came when he had players with similar backgrounds that could relate to each other better on and off the field. We had three black players from Columbia--Alex English, Nate Davis and Golie Augustus--plus guys from the Midwest and New York.

"There wasn't as much camaraderie as there had been a few years before.

"Coach McGuire had decided that, with the type of talent we had on the team, our best strategy was to play a slow tempo game and use a two-three zone defense. This particular season Donnie Walsh and Ben Jobe, the assistant coaches, had handled the early pre-season practices, and they told us we were going to be running, pressing man-to-man team.

"Then when Coach McGuire showed up he said, 'We're going to practice a two-three zone defense, and we stayed at it until mid-February. Then we met Georgia Tech in Columbia, and they were using a running, motion offense.

"We were down slightly at the half, so Jobe and Walsh talked Coach McGuire into going man-to-man in the second half. Tech came out of the dressing room and back-doored us to death the entire second half. They won the game by two points.

"Coach stormed into the dressing room after the game and slammed his clipboard against the wall.

"Then he announced, 'We will never play another minute of friggin' man-to-man!' As far as I can remember, that was the last man-to-man we played that season."

A MATTER OF PERSPECTIVE

In McGuire's first year at South Carolina he inherited a squad that had graduated its top four scorers from the previous season. The third game of that 1964-65 season took the Gamecocks to Winston-Salem to play Bones McKinney's Wake Forest team.

BURKHOLDER: "One of the things I learned about Coach McGuire was that he was always capable of keeping his players focused on the game, regardless of the circumstances. That season I was just a sophomore, and the trip to Wake Forest was our first game on the road.

"We fell way behind in the first half and hadn't shown any signs of being able to mount a comeback. So at halftime, I was wondering what Coach McGuire could tell us to keep us focused in a situation like that. I could tell that Coach wasn't accustomed to being behind like that, but he kept his composure.

"After we settled down in the dressing room, he confronted us very calmly and said, 'Okay fellows, let's go out there and win the second half!'

"I'm not certain that we won the second half, but it was close, because Wake Forest won the game by only 19 points, and we were about that far behind at the half."

MIKE DUNLEAVY LEARNS 'WHAT IF!'

Mike Dunleavy, a hard-nosed guard from Brooklyn who came down McGuire's underground railroad in the 1970's, teamed with Alex English to form the highest scoring twosome in Carolina's basketball history. During his four-year varsity career Mike scored 1,586 points, ranking him fourth among the Gamecocks' all-time scorers.

English, who was in the lineup with Dunleavy from 1972-73 to 1975-76, is the school's all-time top pointmaker with 1,972.

Dunleavy played 11 seasons in the National Basketball Association, starting with Philadelphia, moving to Houston, followed by a season at San Antonio and four years with the Milwaukee Bucks, with whom he ended his playing career. After serving as an assistant coach for the Bucks, Dunleavy was named head coach of the Los Angeles Lakers, taking them to the second round of the playoffs his first season.

After his second year at Los Angeles Mike was hired by the Bucks in 1993 to rebuild that team.

DUNLEAVY: "I had the greatest amount of respect for Coach McGuire, as a man and a coach. He taught me many lessons about the game. I was always trying to pick his brain and understand more about the game.

"I had a penchant for asking questions, such as the proverbial, 'What if?' One day Coach was explaining a strategy, and I asked him, 'Coach, what if they do this?'

"Coach McGuire looked at me and only as he could say it, 'You little Mick. What if! What if! What if my aunt had a beard (or words to that effect), she would be my uncle. You let me worry about the 'what ifs!'

"The whole team fell over laughing, but later Coach told me not to stop asking questions."

Dunleavy's post-college career confirms that he did learn a lot of answers from Frank McGuire.

APPRECIATION DAY FOR JIM FOX

When Frank McGuire became head coach at Carolina Jim Fox was a senior with only a half season of basketball experience at a four-year college. A native of Atlanta, Georgia, Fox had played two years at Gordon Military in Georgia before coming to Carolina.

As a junior he was ruled academically ineligible after 13 games, in which he averaged just 3.6 points and 4.8 rebounds. The 6-9 Fox had regained his eligibility for his senior (1964-65) season and led the Gamecocks in scoring (17.8) and rebounding (13.6).

Fox made great strides under McGuire's tutelage and, with the Irishman's help, made his way through European basketball and into the NBA. He was the first ever Gamecock to make it in that league, playing for seven different teams in ten seasons, averaging 8.9 points and 6.3 rebounds.

FOX: "Coach McGuire's first year at South Carolina was my last. Although that year was not particularly successful, he gave me an opportunity to play and develop. I was an eighth round choice of the Cincinnati Royals, where his friend Jack McMahon (who played for McGuire at St. John's) was the coach. I didn't make the team, but through McGuire's friend Eddie Gottlieb, I signed with Real Madrid in Spain and gained much needed experience. Coach McGuire didn't single me out—he did what he has done for countless people—he gave them an opportunity.

"After a tumultuous year as a junior, during which Coach (Chuck) Noe was relieved and Coach (Dwane) Morrison was interim coach, I found myself working for the South Carolina Highway Department. I was uncertain that I would be going back to school, as my grades were terrible. My supervisor got a call on a job outside of Columbia one morning, and it was from the new coach at Carolina, Frank McGuire. He wanted to see me.

"I borrowed a state truck and drove to the Roundhouse for an interview. I had on work clothes and was quite uncomfortable in front of this dapper New Yorker, who had a national reputation. Coach McGuire was very gracious, stood up to greet me, shook hands, gave me that wonderful smile and soon had me comfortable enough so that I was capable of speech.

"I don't think he had ever seen me play, but he assured me that I was a vital part of the team and that he was looking forward to working with me. I was floating out of the Roundhouse.

"Our first game under McGuire was against Erskine. I had a good game, and the next day Coach McGuire called me into his office. 'I appreciate what you did for the team and our program yesterday.' he said, as he handed me a twenty dollar bill (Fox scored 25 points in a 74-59 victory, McGuire's first at South Carolina.)

"At that time athletes were allowed to sell their tickets as an extra source of income, and I assumed that this was the result of that policy.

"'Coach, there must be a mistake,' I said with hesitation.

"'Jim, there is no mistake. I'm thanking you for your efforts.' he replied, with just a trace of irritation in his voice. It dawned on me after I left his office that this was his way of showing his appreciation for his first win at Carolina. He never again showed his appreciation in a monetary fashion.

"Coach McGuire was a master psychologist. He rarely had to raise his voice to me, as he knew that praise was the better method.

"I believe I was the first basketball player to play in the NBA out of South Carolina. Frank McGuire had a large hand in my getting to that level, and I will always be indebted for his efforts."

A SHOWER FOR DONNIE WALSH

Skip Harlicka, a star guard for Notre Dame High School in Trenton, N.J., was one of the first players recruited by McGuire when he began coaching at South Carolina in 1964. Harlicka was the leading scorer for the Gamecock varsity for three years, totaling 1,209 points.

Harlicka, a second team All-ACC choice in 1968, later became a "trivia question." He was the first round draft pick of the St. Louis Hawks, a franchise that was moved to Atlanta shortly thereafter. Harlicka then actually signed with Atlanta, making him the first player ever selected by the Atlanta Hawks.

Harlicka played a role in several of McGuire's great victories at South Carolina, including back to back wins on the road against nationally-ranked Duke and North Carolina teams.

HARLICKA: "My senior year we beat Duke at Durham, and when we arrived at the Columbia airport there were 5,000 fans there to greet us. Then several days later we went to Chapel Hill and defeated a North Carolina team that was ranked in the top five nationally.

"After the game we were celebrating in the dressing room and decided we should throw the coach in the shower. Well, we looked at each other and had some second thoughts. We weren't about to throw Coach McGuire in the shower.

"So we decided to do the next best thing and grabbed Donnie Walsh, Coach's top assistant, and threw him into the shower, clothes and all.

"When we got back to Columbia a crowd of about 10,000 people were there. They had to clear them from the runway so that the plane could land. Coach Walsh was one of the last people off the plane, and he was wearing a North Carolina shirt. After his unplanned shower at Chapel Hill that was the only dry shirt he could find."

HARLICKA LIGHTS UP

HARLICKA: "The story about the shower was an indication of what respect we had for Coach McGuire. And that respect--you might call it 'awe'–continued long after our playing careers were over.

"After I left the Atlanta Hawks I came back to Columbia and went to work for South Carolina National Bank. I had majored in banking and finance to prepare myself for life after basketball.

"One day my wife, Kathy, and I went over to Coach McGuire's home to go swimming. Well, I was out by the pool, and I lit up a cigarette. Then I walked inside to the den.

"Coach walked by and said to no one in particular, 'I thought I saw Skip light up a cigarette. But I know that's not the case.' And he just kept on walking.

"Here I was over 30 years old, but it was just like I was a college freshman, and I put that cigarette out in a hurry!

"That's the way it was with Coach McGuire. He was always your coach."

CHAPTER EIGHTEEN

PEOPLE OF NOTE

A VISIT FROM JAMES MICHENER

Author James Michener is famous for many accomplishments, but there was nothing in his credentials to indicate a strong interest in basketball. He had been awarded a Pulitzer Prize in 1948 for his *Tales of the South Pacific*, on which the super successful Rodgers and Hammerstein, "South Pacific," was based.

Three other successful Michener works were also made into motion pictures, including "Bridges at Toko-ri," "Sayonara," and "Hawaii."

As the age of 67 Michener could have rested on those laurels and lived happily ever after, but he launched headlong into a book that was completely out of character with the others, entitled, *Sports in America*.

When the subject of basketball came up, his advisors suggested that the first stop he should make was Columbia, S.C., home of Frank McGuire, who was still turning out winning basketball teams in his post-60 years.

MCGUIRE: "In November of 1973, I got a call from Michener, and he told me he was working on a book about sports and wanted to talk to me. He said he also wanted to attend a football game while he was here.

"He showed his diplomacy by telling me that everyone he talked to about this book said that, when it comes to basketball, the first person you want to talk to is Frank McGuire down in Columbia, South Carolina. I believe Michener, who was a native New Yorker, just like I was, made his home in Philadelphia at the time.

"We agreed on a time for him to come to Columbia, and he came down and spent about five days with use. It was a delightful experience for me, and he seemed to enjoy it also.

"One day I went out to the Coliseum floor, and there he was shooting baskets with Brian Winters. I understand that he even beat one of our managers in a game of "around the world." That's where you start shooting

from one corner and work your way to the opposite corner by hitting baskets to advance.

"Then I found out that he was no novice at basketball. He had played on the team at Swarthmore College in the mid 1920s.

"We had some long conversations, and visited around town. One day I decided to take him over to the administration building on the campus and introduce him to the president, Tom Jones. Although Jones was an engineer by trade, he was a well-rounded educator, and I knew that he would enjoy talking to someone of James Michener's stature.

"So, we went into Dr. Jones' office, and I told his secretary that I wanted to see him. She said that he had someone with him and couldn't be disturbed. I said, 'Tell him that I want him to meet my new assistant coach, and it won't take but a minute.'

"This went back and forth between Dr. Jones and his secretary, and, finally, he reluctantly agreed to come out for a few seconds. So, he rushes out the door, very impatiently, and I introduce the two men. 'Dr. Jones, I want you to meet James Michener.'

"The president made a very hurried response, something like, 'Glad to meet you,' then turned and hurried back toward his office.

"After several steps, he wheels around, looks at me, and says, 'Is there something wrong with my ears?' I said, 'No, this is James Michener!'

"He was really taken aback and was a little embarrassed over being so impatient to start with. But he recovered fast and was a most gracious host. He told him that he was reading *Hawaii* when they had their last child. He stayed and talked for two or three hours, and they both seemed to enjoy it thoroughly.

"Michener came out to our practices every afternoon while he was here, and later in the season he came to see us play in Madison Square Garden in New York and at the Palestra in Philadelphia.

"Several years later he was nice enough to come back to Columbia and participate in the program at a dinner that celebrated my induction into college basketball's Hall of Fame.

"James Michener and I have something very much in common, as far as our youth is concerned. As I mentioned earlier, a man named Ted Carroll had taken me under his wing and got me interested in basketball. He was a great influence in steering me in the right direction.

"Michener said that he probably would have become a juvenile delinquent had he not become involved in sports. He credited a man who worked with disadvantaged youth and in his spare time formed a basketball team. Michener played on the team and was very good. Good enough that he caught the attention of a high school coach, who became another strong influence on him.

"By helping Michener develop his athletic skills and his character, these two men enabled him to receive a basketball scholarship to Swarthmore College. Even in high school he had been an excellent student, and he obviously applied himself well at Swarthmore.

"Michener also told me that athletics were responsible for his making a complete recovery from a heart attack he suffered in the 1960s."

In his book, *Sports in America*, Michener said that most college coaches more than earn their salaries, observing, "Frank McGuire is worth a fortune to the University of South Carolina."

MARIO CUOMO DIDN'T CATCH ON

One would think that New York Governor Mario Cuomo was a born politician who always had the next election on his mind. And that has been his life for several decades, having been elected Lieutenant Governor under Hugh Cary in 1978, then winning the governorship in 1982.

However, as a freshman at St. John's University in 1950, he had completely different ideas about where his life was going. For one thing, he was an excellent athlete, envisioning himself as becoming the next Joe DiMaggio on the baseball diamond. Frank McGuire would play a role in the early development of Cuomo the athlete.

MCGUIRE: "In 1949 I was in my second year as both basketball and baseball coach at St. John's. This young Mario Cuomo had been a good athlete at St. John's prep, and I was looking forward to him trying out for the freshman basketball team. However, he broke his wrist--I don't remember how--and couldn't try out.

"His wrist had healed in the spring, and he came out for the baseball team and played in the outfield. Mario was a good outfielder and batted over .300. He was a very intense player, very determined--what you would call a 'take charge' guy. Sometimes his temper would be a problem, and he needed to work on that.

"In 1951 our catcher was hurt, and we didn't have a back-up. Mario was a good athlete, and I figured that he was the best person we had to take over the position behind the plate. I told him that I was going to try him there, and he didn't go for that at all. In fact, he said flatly that he wasn't going to be a catcher.

"Well, in those days, when your players came out of the student body, I always felt that if there were two very close friends trying out, that either both should make it or neither.

"Cuomo had a good friend named Joe Repice, who was also an outfielder, and I told Joe that his friend Mario had told me that he would quit the team before he would play catcher. I told him that I didn't want Mario to quit, and would he talk to him.

"Mario mentioned to Joe about my suggestion that Repice might be dropped, if he quit. So, they talked it over and agreed that both of them would be outfielders or nothing.

"On the other hand, I have always had a policy of being the coach or nothing. I have never let the players tell me how to run the team, and I wasn't going to allow that, even if it was just my third year on the college level. I'm sure I've made my share of mistakes in the profession, but never the one of not being in control of the team or the players.

"So, with that ultimatum from two players, I had to ask them to turn in their uniforms, and that was it. I believe Cuomo played on an amateur team, or somewhere, because when he was a senior Branch Richey signed him to a contract with the Pittsburgh Pirates organization, and he went down and played with Brunswick in the Class D Georgia-Florida League.

"Toward the end of his first season he was hit in the head by a pitched ball and sent to the hospital. That, for all purposes, ended his professional baseball career."

Cuomo went on to finish law school, even taught at St. John's School of Law, and practiced law prior to the beginning of his political career.

MCGUIRE: "I think it was around 1983 or 1984, when I was working for Madison Square Garden, that someone suggested that it would be nice for me to come back to a dinner at St. John's and present Governor Cuomo with the baseball letter that he didn't get from me in his student days. So, that's what happened, and we had a lot of fun there, talking about old times.

"When I presented Cuomo his letter, I said, "Mario, I never would have kicked you off the team if I had known you were going to become Governor of New York!"

And, of course, many times in his later life, Cuomo has found himself on the other end of that situation in which a choice has to be made as to who is in charge!

Frank Sinatra Takes a Picture

At one time Hoboken, New Jersey, an industrial town on the west bank of the Hudson River opposite New York City, was most famous for being the home of Hetty Green, who became the world's richest woman. She parlayed her father's $6 million estate into a $100 million fortune, living an austere life all the while.

In 1863, when city authorities tried to make her pay a two dollar dog tax, it was more than she could take, so she took her money and moved to New York City to spend the rest of her years.

Few New Jersians remember Hetty Green, but there aren't many who have not heard of Hoboken's now most famous native, Frank Sinatra. "The Voice," as he became known after achieving fame with Tommy Dorsey's orchestra and later in motion pictures and other activities, also had a Frank McGuire connection.

MCGUIRE: "I don't claim to be any great friend of Frank Sinatra, but I did make his acquaintance, and there was one case when he was involved in a basketball player that I was trying to recruit.

"I first met Sinatra while I was coaching the Philadelphia Warriors and made a trip to Los Angeles. I had a friend who knew the secretary of the Los Angeles Dodgers, and he made arrangements for me to have lunch with him and go to a baseball game.

"After lunch we went to the ball park, and Nat King Cole, who was one of the top singers of that time, was there to get his tickets. He knew that Frank Sinatra and Dean Martin were also coming to the game together. Cole asked where Sinatra and Martin were going to sit.

"I told him that I really liked Sinatra and Martin, and he said that he loved them too. But he said, 'I just don't want to sit near them. I came to watch the baseball game, and they'll be laughing and cutting up. If you sit near them, all you can do is listen to them.'

"That's where I met Sinatra, and I saw him other times over the years, mostly at things in New York.

"One of the top high school basketball prospects in 1976 was Jim Graziano, a 6-11 center from Farmingdale, N.Y. All the big basketball schools around the country were trying to recruit him. That included Nevada-Las Vegas.

"Las Vegas was Sinatra's base of operations then, because he was doing a lot of entertaining. He was a friend of Jerry Tarkanian, who was the Las Vegas coach, and he helped Tarkanian in trying to recruit Graziano. Of course, Sinatra had a lot of connections back in New York, and he felt that he could do some good.

"I believe Graziano might have narrowed his choice down to us and Las Vegas, but he ended up committing to come to South Carolina.

"There's a restaurant on 54th Street in New York--Weston's owned by Jimmy Weston, and Jimmy had a lot of pictures on the wall of people who came there. Some famous and some not so famous. My picture was one of them.

"Frank Sinatra usually went to Weston's when he came to New York, and he was there not too long after Graziano announced that he was going to South Carolina. He saw my picture on the wall, so he walked over and took it off. People who were there said that he gave it that familiar Sinatra smile and said, 'McGuire got Graziano, so I'll just take him with me. With that he walked out of the place with my picture under his arm.

"I never heard what he did with it!"

BILL COSBY SIGNS WITH MCGUIRE

MCGUIRE: "When I was coach of the Philadelphia Warriors in 1961-62, Guy Rodgers was what amounted to our point guard, because he was a great passer. He had also been a good scorer, but with Wilt Chamberlain on the team, it was more important that we have someone who could get the ball to Wilt.

"Rodgers was a 1958 graduate of Temple University in Philadelphia, and his college roommate was a young man named Bill Cosby. Cosby had played football and was an all-around good athlete, but was not on the Temple basketball team.

"Occasionally Cosby would come to our dressing room to see his friend Guy, but I didn't think much of it, because he was just another face in the crowd at that time. Anyhow, I saw him quite a bit.

"Some years later I was at a place up in the Catskills when this same Bill Cosby made his debut as a stand-up entertainer. He had a really funny act, but he was still just one of many young comics trying to make a move up the show business ladder. Obviously he made it to the top of the ladder and has become, not only a famous personality but also Temple University's best known basketball fan.

"I remember he once wore a Duke sweatshirt on his television show as a payoff for the Blue Devils beating the Owls in basketball.

"One encounter I had with Cosby took place after he was at the peak of his career took place in a restaurant in Greenwich Village.

JANE MCGUIRE "Some Friends wanted some Italian food, so we went to this restaurant back in Frank's old neighborhood--down on Houston Street. We were in there about 30 minutes, when the door opens and here stands two beautiful black women in drop dead minks down to the floor. Bill Cosby's wife was waiting for them in the back. We were about in the middle of the restaurant.

"Then, a few moments later, here comes Cosby loping across the room and making motions like he was dribbling a basketball. He gets to our table, stops, and then takes an imaginary hook shot. He looked at Frank and said, 'You didn't have the good sense to recruit me. And I can go to my left.'

"After Cosby went back to his table, our friend asks Frank if he would get Cosby's autograph for her. Frank said, 'I don't ask people for their autograph.'

"The waiter heard the conversation and went back and told Cosby, so he came over to the table and said, 'What do you want on this autograph?' She said, 'Make it to Paul and Roy and Jeaneanne.'

"Then, Frank added, 'And on the bottom put the Gettysburg Address!'"

AID TO GOVERNOR MCNAIR

When Frank McGuire became basketball coach at the University of South Carolina in 1964 Donald Russell was in his second year as governor, and Bob McNair was at the same stage of his term as lieutenant governor. Whoever is governor of the state serves as ex-officio chairman of the University's Board of Trustees.

That ex-officio position changed hands in April 1965 when South

Carolina's senior United States Senator Olid D. Johnston died. Russell resigned shortly thereafter so that he could be appointed by McNair, his successor in the governor's office, to fill the unexpired term of Johnston.

Two years later McNair began a full term as governor, having successfully run for the office in the 1966 general election. McNair had been a fine high school athlete in his native Allendale, S.C., and played some football and lettered in basketball (1942) while a student at USC. He earned his undergraduate and later law degrees from the school.

McNair had close connections in the University administration and on the Board of Trustees, not to mention the contacts that he had developed as a member of the state's House of Representatives and as lieutenant governor.

The president of the University, Tom Jones, had assumed his office in 1962, when McNair won his election to the lieutenant governorship. It was under the administrations of these two that Carolina Coliseum was built.

This was also the beginning of a close relationship between McNair and McGuire that endured throughout McGuire's life. McNair also learned early in his governorship that Frank McGuire was a valuable asset, not only as a basketball coach at Carolina but as salesman and promoter of the State of South Carolina.

MCNAIR: "One of the responsibilities of a governor, of course, is to play a leading role in bringing new industry into the state. Of course, we have a department for the purpose, but the governor has to be the front man.

"I found Frank to be a very valuable asset in that respect. Because he was a national sports figure and known by people all over the country, we would have him meet with prospects. He promoted the state on the basis of a transplanted New Yorker who found South Carolina an ideal place to live. Of course, he proved his sincerity by continuing to make this his home when he retired from coaching.

"When we went to places like New York to meet with prospects or to have dinner with a group of CEO's, for instance, we liked to take Frank along, because they usually knew about him and were impressed by what he had to say. I don't know that I could name a specific industry or business that located down here just because of Frank, but there is no doubt that he played an important role in the overall effort.

"I remember one major example of Frank's value to me as governor and to the state, and it had nothing to do with industrial development. I'm not sure of the exact dates involved, but this was in the late 1960s, while I was governor.

"We were informed that the International Longshoremen's Association was planning to call a strike at the Charleston shipyard. The rest of the port was non-union, and this made it a tempting target for the union movement that had found tough sledding against South Carolina's 'right to work' laws. In other words, under our state laws you didn't have to belong to a union to hold a job, even if that particular organization was unionized.

"The port of Charleston had just begun to realize its potential under a Ports Authority that had become more aggressive in promoting the port. For a strike to occur at that point would have several very damaging effects. Of course, it would have immediate impact on ships coming into Charleston, but just as critical was the fact that once you lost the shipping coming in that it was very difficult to get it back.

"When we attempted to contact the ILA to see what we could do to avert a strike, we found out that the president, Teddy Gleason, was in London. We were very anxious to head this thing off as fast as we could, and I had remembered that Frank McGuire was a friend of Gleason, so I called Frank and asked him if he thought that he could help us."

MCGUIRE: "Teddy Gleason was an old friend of mine. I had taught his son in high school, and at one point the young man wanted to drop out, and I talked him into staying. Later I helped get him into law school. Teddy appreciated that and became a lifelong friend. We saw each other on many occasions. He was a neighbor of mine in New York, and we both had houses at Greenwood Lake (NY).

"I talked to Teddy on the telephone, and he asked, 'How's that governor of yours down there?' I said, 'He's a nice guy--a friend of mine.'

"Then he said, 'They're gonna be in trouble down there when we strike.' So Teddy agreed to come down and talk. He brought his son, Tommy, that I had taught, and we went out to Sam Jones' place at Lake Murray and had a nice time together.

"Then we talked with Governor McNair, and the end result is that the strike of the Charleston shipyard was averted."

MCNAIR: "There is no question that, because of McGuire's influence in avoiding that strike, the State of South Carolina saved millions of dollars directly. There is no telling how much damage that averted in other respects.

"Another example of Frank's influence came after President Carter reacted to Russia's invasion of Afghanistan by placing an embargo against Russian goods entering American ports. It happened that there was a shipment of Russian chromium ore on a ship outside the port of Charleston. It was to be used by a plant in Charleston that processed the ore for use in the manufacture of aircraft.

"The ore was not on a Russian ship, but it still could not be unloaded, because of the embargo. It was very important that the chromium be received.

"This time, Frank, I and the head of the company that processed the ore in Charleston went to New York to meet with Teddy Gleason. We explained to Gleason the situation and how critical the chromium was to the national defense industry, and he understood. The end result was that he told us to go back to Columbia and to do nothing further. The ore was delivered, and that was the end of it.

"Those are tangible examples of the ways in which Frank McGuire was a valuable asset to our state."

A FAREWELL TO KENNY HORNE

Kenny Horne never dribbled a basketball, never executed a jump shot or controlled a rebound, but he was an enthusiastic follower of Frank McGuire's great teams of the 1970s. The young son of Bill and Frankie Ann Horne, who lived near Lancaster, S.C., loved a sport that he could never play. The reason he would never play it is that he was born with cerebral palsy, which robbed him of the chance to lead a normal boyhood.

Doctors said that Kenny would not likely reach the age of 20, and there was a real possibility that he would fall far short of that. The Hornes made the most of the time that Kenny was here on Earth, and following the Gamecocks became his prime interest.

On visits to Columbia they would roll Kenny's wheelchair into Carolina Coliseum to watch the Gamecocks practice. He owned several basketballs presented to him by the Carolina players, who welcomed him into their world. A card from McGuire was always part of his Christmas season.

This was not a young man who could ever do anything for McGuire or his basketball program, and he didn't come from a family of influence or financial means. There was nothing to gain materially or tactically from being attentive to young Kenny.

Inevitably, the end of Kenny's life arrived, although it was not as soon as the medical world had warned. He lived to the age of 21, but the miracle couldn't go beyond that.

Kenny's funeral was held at a small country church, where family and friends gathered to pay their last respects. On a day that was most difficult for everyone close to Kenny Horne, there was a presence that eased the pain and added to their faith in mankind.

Standing unobtrusively at the rear of the gathering was a well-dressed gentlemen who could have been at any number of more prestigious locations on that somber day.

It was Frank McGuire.

(Authors' Note: This story was derived from a column by Herman Helms, executive sport editor, in The State *newspaper on Christmas Day of 1983.)*

THE BUBBLY GROUP

When Frank McGuire arrived at South Carolina, not only did the basketball fortunes change, but there were many other improvements put in place by the Gamecock coach.

The mode of team travel changed dramatically. Prior to McGuire Carolina basketball trips were made by way of buses, vans, trains, and rarely on airplanes. McGuire felt that, if you couldn't travel by plane, it would be very difficult to recruit the caliber of player necessary to build a successful program.

This also meant that the team should enjoy first class accommodations on the road--something they hadn't experienced often in the past. For example, previously when the Gamecocks went to Durham to play Duke, they stayed in the living quarters behind Wallace Wade (football) Stadium. It featured cots and cold water for showers. All of this stopped when McGuire became the head coach in 1964.

Traveling with McGuire became fun for the team. For trips outside of South Carolina, the team traveled on chartered planes or flew commercially. They were quartered in excellent hotels that featured good food and service. The Gamecocks didn't travel alone for long.

As Carolina basketball success grew, many of the Gamecock fans began to follow them to games in other parts of the country. It wasn't uncommon to see Gamecock followers in such places as New York City, Philadelphia, Salt Lake City, San Francisco or New Orleans. For the longer trips larger planes were chartered, and there was room for more than just the official party.

However, there was seldom an empty seat, because the team was joined by enough fans to fill-up the 15 or 20 extra seats. This marked the beginning of what became known as the "Bubbly Group," comprised of mostly professional people who had the time and money to follow the Gamecocks on out-of-town trips.

Regardless of the outcome of the games, these fans had fun from the moment they left Columbia until they returned. The original 'Bubbly Group' included Dr. Charlie Crews, Dr. Waitus Tanner, Dr. Billy Gause, Dr. Bill Salter, Dr. Frank Martin, Dr. Thurmond Walker, Dick Long, Jack Morris, Joe Dunn, Leon Cooper, Peter Paul Lucas, Milt Evans, Mort Hymson and Jack Wingate.

The official party was made up of McGuire, his wife, assistant coaches, trainer Jim Price, sports information director Tom Price, the radio play-by-play crew of announcer Bob Fulton, color analyst John Terry and engineer Homer Fesperman. All of these traveled with the team during the 16 seasons in which McGuire was head coach.

The official party sat at the back of the plane, with the Bubbly Group in the middle and the team and coaches at the front.

Once a road game was over, and the group returned to the charter, it was party time for everyone except the players.

Win or lose, and it was usually win, the group in the back of the plane rarely discussed the outcome of the game. McGuire was a strong believer in leaving the game at the arena, although on a few occasions certain calls by officials that contributed to the loss were discussed!

The Bubbly Group and many other fans who followed the Gamecocks on the road contributed greatly to the team's success. Gamecock fans usually sat together and often made more noise than the home team's followers. McGuire never failed to thank them for their support, occasionally hosting a post-game party for added enjoyment.

When McGuire retired the Bubbly Group disbanded, but not for long. Members and some invited guests joined McGuire at a party at Dr. Crews' resort place at Lake Murray near Columbia. Everyone had such a good time that they decided that a group called "The McGuire Clan" would be formed and would meet several times a year.

Terry was the first president, followed by Judge Bubba Ness. A typical evening included a happy hour, steak supper and reminiscing about Carolina basketball under McGuire. Often members of the Carolina athletic staff were invited, along with guests from outside the Columbia area. One meeting was attended by Tommy Kearns, who played on McGuire's 1957 NCAA championship team at North Carolina.

The original members of the McGuire Clan included:

Dr. Charlie Crews, Dr. Pierre Laborde, Dr. Frank Harrison, Dr. Bill Salter, Dr. Waitus Tanner, Dr. Frank Martin, Mort Hymson, Sam Jones, Bunk Price, Peter Paul Lucas, Jim Cook, Leon Cooper, Joe Dunn, Milt Evans, Homer Fesperman, Bob Fulton, Ashby Gregg, Sr., Judge George Gregory, Tommy Gregory, Gene McKay, former Governor Bob McNair, Judge Bubba Ness, George Moore, W. J. Morgan, Jack Morris, Harry Parone, Bill Putnam, Alan Schafer, Lambert Schwarts, Cliff Terry, John Terry, Lou Vine, Furman Wingate and Jack Wingate.

McGuire continued to have a loyal following, and it wasn't unusual to have 100% attendance at McGuire Clan meetings. By having get-togethers these special fans were able to relive the memories of some of the most exciting moments in the history of Gamecock sports.

CHAPTER NINETEEN

FRANK MCGUIRE: THE FATHER

It was only proper that Frank McGuire met Patricia Johnson at a basketball related event. Frank was still a teenager and playing on a neighborhood basketball team, and post-game dances were as much of the routine as the games themselves. Pat was a big sports fan long before she met Frank, and that common interest definitely helped to break the ice.

Frank recalled that Pat was a great dancer, and she was the first girl to which he ever felt a strong attraction. That interest didn't wane while Frank was attending St. John's, but college students seldom got married before graduation, and that was not in the cards for Frank and Pat.

It wasn't until 1940, after McGuire had established himself as a high school coach, that he and Pat were wed. The marriage was blessed by three children, Patricia Jeanne, Frank, Jr., and Carol Ann. Pat lost a battle with cancer in September of 1967.

On June 3, 1972 Frank was married to Jane Henderson, who was at his side during the final decade of his storied career.

The story of Frank McGuire the family man is just as dramatic as that of Frank McGuire the coach. The first phase of that story is best told by Carol Ann, now Mrs. John Morgan, who lives in Irmo, a suburb of Columbia.

CAROL ANN: "If you asked me for a profile of my father, I've never really sat down and tried to sum it up. I think he was a superior father. He was a better father than he ever was a coach.

"He was very, very, funny--a good sense of humor. He didn't show that very often. He was the man at the birthday party with the rubber mask on. He was the mediator between people. He was the optimistic one. Didn't want to hear the bad news.

"He was well balanced. He revealed himself to us. What he showed you was nothing. That's what he had to do out there under the lights. He was very tender hearted. My mother was like that, too.

"He expected the maximum out of everyone. He couldn't tolerate pettiness. I think he was at peace with himself.

"I think he would like to have continued with coaching, although he could see that the change in basketball was not to his appetite. Like recruiting the type of ball players coming along. Of course, he didn't have the ACC any more, which made it tough. I think he was very happy with what he did.

"He was not a business man. Monetarily, I think he could have been extremely wealthy. He did well, but not as well as people thought. He gave a lot of it away. Money was never important to him. My father never took money for speaking anywhere. If they handed him a check, he was offended, and he would bring it here and say, 'Put it in Frankie's account.'

"He was just not a money-oriented person. Now I wish that he had been, and he could have been able to take care of himself better. They got along fine, though–Jane handled it well.

"I would like to have seen him do a book on his own.

"He didn't have any enemies. He either liked you and wanted to deal with you, or he had no opinion of you. He followed Malcolm Forbe's formula: Select your friends. If you can bring value into someone else's life, you're a friend. If they can bring value into your life, you want them there.

"If people couldn't bring value into our lives, they weren't in our home. If he could bring value into yours, he was there for you. He was loyal to a fault.

"I take after Dad in this respect--if there's trouble, I step into it. You're naive--you trust people too much. You're too easy to like people.

"My mother was more suspicious. She would lay back and watch. My father eventually caught onto that, and he became so cautious he squeaked when he walked.

"My mother could smell a phony a hundred miles away. She'd shake your hand and tell you exactly who you are. I think that's why men respected her--men who wouldn't ordinarily tolerate a female around them talking man's talk.

"My mother was a night person--didn't get up until ten o'clock in the morning. My father was up at daybreak. When Dad was coaching North Carolina we had this old DeSoto, and my father drove all the kids over to Durham to school. I went to the Immaculate Conception School in Durham, and father was the designated driver. It was my sister and I, and other kids he dropped off at their school. Then we took the bus back to Chapel Hill in the afternoon.

"Dad would get us up in the morning and give us Cheerios for breakfast. Then Dad would do my hair, while my sister would do her own. Dad knew how to braid my hair--like Star Wars.

"We had a great life on Oakwood Drive. My father had selected the house before my mother ever saw it. She and the rest of us were back in New

York while my father went down to sign as head coach of the University of North
Carolina.

"I will never forget his reason for selecting this particular home. It was
not that it had a two-car garage, or a large backyard, nor was it because it had
three bedrooms and a finished basement. His reason for selecting Number 11
Oakwood Drive, was because there was a black wrought iron witch flying her
tattered broom over the moon atop our chimmney, and it reminded my dad of
his little girl, Carol Ann!

"My mother was also born in New York City. Her father was Charles
Johnson, and her mother's maiden name was Mary Margaret Dooley. Her
father was a writer and a Christian Scientist--very much involved in that. Her
parents were also involved in the theater, and it was her mother that was responsible for getting my mother (Pat) a role in Mac Sennett's 'Our Gang' (later 'Little
Rascals') comedies.

"Sennett produced them in New York, and mother sometimes played the
part of Darla and other times would be another character in the comedies. It
was more for the theatrical experience than for money, but it was a great experience. Jackie Cooper and Spanky McFarland were both involved in the series, and
she got to know them well, of course. In fact, she heard from Jackie Cooper for a
long time.

"Years ago I would watch reruns of the 'Little Rascals' with Frankie, but I
couldn't bring myself to watch them now. I was in a store the other day, going
down the aisle and looked over and there she was on a paper bag. I said, 'That's
my mother. Somebody's making a helluva lot of money off this.

"Pat was a very good dancer and went into modeling after she outgrew
the 'Little Rascals.' I always understood that my mother and father met at the
21 Club in New York and didn't hit it off at first.

"Frank's family didn't accept Pat at first, because she was a Protestant.
No one made it to the kitchen unless they were accepted as family, and it took
Pat a long time to make it there. Outsiders sat in the dining room or foyer. I
understand that Buck Freeman didn't make it to the kitchen for 20 years!

"Pat was always very generous with Frank's family--always doing for them
and brought them gifts at Christmas. Of course neither of Frank's parents
were living when he married Pat. Frank always took care of his family and did
everything he could for them.

"When Dad was playing basketball his family didn't go to see him play.
They were very proud of what Dad was doing, but families just didn't do that
back then. It would have made Dad uncomfortable to have them there watching. I think he enjoyed the fact that his family wasn't in on that part of his
world.

"He still cherished the time with his family, but he wanted to spend that
on other things besides basketball. Even later on, time at home was time at
home. He never talked basketball.

"When my mother began to travel more with my father for out of town games, there was a tremendous concern for the care of our brother, Frankie. Ann Jennings, daughter of my father's sister Evelyn, moved away from her advertising job in New York, and moved to our home in Chapel Hill. Ann literally sacrificed her own life for ours.

"She took excellent care of Frankie and enabled my parents to travel on the road together. What a personal sacrifice she made. I do not believe we could have ever managed without her. She and Frankie had such a wonderful relationship based upon love and trust. To this day Frankie calls out her name, 'Amb,' and we realize at that moment he is remembering one of his favorite people. After my mother's death, which Ann helped us through, she moved to San Francisco to try and start a new life.

"Buck Freeman spent a lot of time in our home, but he and Dad never discussed basketball there. They would talk about it at the office, but not at home.

"When he would lose a game--say by one point--you'd feel so bad that they lost, and you'd go home feeling real low. Dad would come home with a big smile on his face, while we were looking like undertakers. Dad would say, 'Who died? What's your problem? It was a great game. Sorry we lost, but that's history.' He wouldn't talk about it.

"He was better after losses than he was after victories. He was the same way when my mother died. I didn't want to go see her. I had seen her suffer, and I was there when she died.

"Back in 1967 my father was away recruiting Tommy Riker, when my mother, who had been struggling with lung cancer, passed away. It was early on Thursday morning, September 21. Ann remained by my mother, while I ran to the doctor's house next door for help. Evidently the physician who was living there, called the coroner and a press release was immediately aired. My sister Patsy Jean was in her car taking her children to school in Sumter when the bulletin came over the radio. What an insensitive way for her to hear that her mother had died. It was totally unfair.

"In the meantime Ann had located my father over the phone, and they made arrangements for his return from New York. Dad instructed us not to remove Mother until he had arrived bringing Father Jerome Tierney with him.

"Ten hours later she was still in her bed where she died that morning, and my father walked into the room and knelt at her side. I had never seen before, nor have I ever seen since, such a desperate look on my father's face. This was a defeat he would have a hard time ever putting behind him.

"Then I had to take over the finances. My father had never written a check, because Mother handled all of that. He had no savvy whatsoever when it came to running a home, so he turned it over to me. I was just a kid, but Dad didn't have a clue as to what to do. He refuses to do anything like that. I've got my job--you've got yours.

"That's the way there were back then—the Irish. They went to work, came home, put the money on the table, and that was it.

"When Dad came home he and Mother were always dressed to the hilt. They had their happy hour. They danced before dinner, and we always left them alone. They had their 30 to 35 minutes. My mother never—never saw Dad in sneakers. Always in her high heels—impeccably dressed.

"We had a summer home in Greenwood Lake, New York, that my parents had purchased in 1950. It was truly a beautiful place, once owned by the Rockefellers. Each June when the school year ended, we would pack up our belongings in Chapel Hill and head north for the next three months.

"This German community tucked away in the mountains was a welcome escape from the heat down South. It also gave my parents a chance to see more of their families.

That house literally rocked on weekends! Friends and family members would leave the city on Friday night and take respite with us on Lakeshore Road. My father's sister Evelyn, an absolutely beautiful woman, and her wonderful husband Bill, took care of everything that needed to be done. Aunt Eve never batted an eye at the thought of cooking for 15 or 20 people at a time. They are at the top of my list of favorite people and there will never be anyone in my life like them again.

The village of Greenwood Lake was the melting pot for some very interesting characters who vacationed there. One of them was a man by the name of Salvadore Granelli, alias Solly Burns. Over dinner in his elaborate home, Solly made an offer to buy property for a basketball camp on the lake. In my father's usual gentlemanly fashion he refused the offer.

"The friendship lasted until the day my father was subpoenaed to testify before a Grand Jury. The FBI had photographs of the two men together, and someone wanted to know why.

"As wonderful as the Italian meals that we shared with Solly had been, they were not worth their inevitable danger. I guess not for Solly either, for a year later he was found in the trunk of his Cadillac with a dozen bullet holes in his body. It was obvious he had made some terrible mistake. Thank God we were only guilty of eating his pasta!

"Once when we were up at Greenwood Lake Dad took us girls into New York, and Mother stayed behind. Well, we stayed out until the wee hours, and when we got home there was Pat standing there with gloves on, purple stuff on her hair, and so forth. Dad says, 'Pat, we're home.'

"Mother had her hair brush. This beautiful woman looked like General Patton standing on the balcony. She was in her ankle socks—-not an attractive sight. Like something out of a tomb.

"She said, 'Where have you been with these girls until four o'clock in the morning?'

"Dad says, 'Well, we've been to Danny's. We've been here, and we've been there.

"Mother started coming down the stairs, and Dad was backing up all this time. 'Do you know how worried I was? You couldn't have called?'

"Dad always called, but this time he thought she wouldn't worry.

"Mother said, 'If you ever do anything like this again I'll kill you.' And she started chasing him with that hairbrush. We jumped into the bathroom and hid behind the shower curtain.

"It never happened again!

"My father really never had a chance to be a child. Both his parents were gone when he was very young, so he had to scrape for himself. That's what made him so determined--the responsibility he had back then at such a young age.

"He came from people who never discussed family business outside the family. Pat was converted to Catholicism, and usually, converted Catholics are the most devout.

"Dad didn't believe in telling off-color jokes in front of women. If someone started telling one, Dad would stop them and say, 'There are ladies present.'

"I've known my mother to prepare fish for dinner on Friday, and Dad would come home from basketball practice just starving. The house would smell of fish, and Dad would say, 'No, I'm not going to eat that.' We would wait until midnight, and out would come the meatballs. Mother made the best hamburgers you've ever tasted, so we'd starve until midnight and then have our meal!

"Mother's parents, Charles and Margaret Johnson, were in the cosmetics business. They had a complete line of cosmetics--lipstick, perfume, rouge, and so forth--and it was sold under the name of Charles of the Ritz. Then, along came the big depression, and they lost everything.

"The thing I liked best about my father was that he really wasn't interested in himself. He was most comfortable after the lights were out in the gym and all the people were gone. And Dad would come out of the locker room, and he would be talking to the guy who was cleaning the locker room--pushing the broom. And he spent more time talking to them than he did the press. He'd sit down and have a Coke with them.

"He enjoyed that more. Like talking to the guy who carried his bags at the airport. He was a godfather to all the little kids around the airport. He came from a very neat but humble home, and he liked that kind of people.

"Dad was very protective. We didn't get away with much. Once Dad took my cousin Margaret and me with him, and he told us to sit in the lobby of the hotel until he got back from a meeting. While we were sitting there Guy Rodgers and Wilt Chamberlain came down and sat there. They didn't know who we were--just two girls sitting in the lobby.

"They were talking to us, and my father got off the elevator and he came over where we were and said, 'Hey, you two clowns, that's my daughter, and that's my sister's daughter.' And they got very nervous!

"My sister Patsy Jeanne, who now lives in Corpus Christi, Texas, lost the father of her four children, Lieutenant Colonel Stephen F. (Butch) Johnson in April of 1980. He was killed while flying his F-16 over the Nevada desert.

"I will never forget Patsy's phone call. She sounded unusually calm, then she stated to me that Butch had been killed, and where can I find Daddy?

"Our father was with Jane teaching a clinic in Spain. The Red Cross assisted in locating them, and they left immediately for Texas.

"My father truly loved Steve, everybody did. He was a terrific person to be around and quite a success story. It was not only traumatic for my father to see his daughter's husband buried, but that he was buried on his grandson William's 21st birthday and one week prior to Patsy's. My sister Pat has not had an easy time of it; we are so proud of how she and her children have continued to grow and do well.

"I am now married a second time, to John Morgan, and we are very happy together. John's father, Lloyd, worked as a superintendent for Cannon Mills for 42 years, and his mother, Mildred , served as a vice-president for Citizen's Savings and Loan in Concord, N.C.

"I thank God every day that after 13 years of their union, they finally had John. He's an extraordinary man who stepped into a very difficult situation. It was not because of the existing children, nor that it was Frank McGuire's family.

"It would be made almost unbearable by the conditions surrounding Patrick's health. Patrick adored John from the first time they met, as did Michael. In the pursuing years Patrick would be diagnosed with an unknown degenerative disease that would rob him of a normal life and place him motionless in a hospital bed. Had it not been for my husband's physical strength, enduring patience and genuine love, we would have never been able to keep Patrick at home. When we lost Patrick (in 1992), I thought our lives together would end, but because of God's help and Michael's determination to keep us together we have grown stronger in our marriage.

"Michael has been an absolute treasure to us. Not only has be been an excellent student academically, but he is equally gifted in the arts. Michael has spent years entertaining his brother at home while other children were out playing in the streets.

"At the present time, Michael has begun his second year at one of the most outstanding art schools in the world, the Savannah College of Art and Design. He will acquire his degree in Computer Art and Video and has hopes of attending film school. The president of the college, Richard Rowan, and his wife Paula have been close friends to our family. In fact, it was Richard who dressed Dad for his funeral.

"As I look at my brother Frankie, who at birth was stricken with cerebral palsy, I cannot help but think of how it affected my father, a man who surrounded himself with the finest of athletes. When Frankie was born, the doctors said he would never see his 13th birthday but on June 29, 1995, he blew out candles on his 44th birthday cake.

"I believe that he has lived this long because of the way he has been loved and cared for. My father recognized the very fine line between pushing too far and acceptance of his limitations. In order to make Frankie more independent, he now spends his week at Midlands Center in Columbia. He continues to come home weekends with John, me and Michael, and helps light up the space Patrick vacated. Frankie will always be 'Daddy's Boy,' and he knows it.

"Years ago, when someone questioned Frankie's disability, my father said, 'We treated him as what he is....a blessing. We thank God that he gave him to us to take care of.

"I learned a valuable lesson I never dreamed I would have to repeat with my own son, Patrick. My father's legacy in this instance was one of parenthood. He taught me to love my children no matter what condition they came in and never ever to abandon them.

"To so many my father exemplified what the perfect friend should be. He did not believe in character assassination nor idle gossip. The sky was the limit for those he held dear. He never promised what he could not deliver, nor did he expect in return anything for a favor rendered. He once said to me that a true friend is a person who will step in front of a bullet for you.

"My father never met a stranger! You could be the president of a major airline or the gentleman carrying his bags, he treated each with respect and dignity. He valued people, he reflected on where they came from, and he never forgot how well people treated him. This was his legacy of friendship, something we can all learn from.

"Strength of character seems to evolve with the number of adversities and personal challenges we meet in our lives. Even though our family has had our share, we dare not question why. My father taught us to call upon God's help, face the problem and move ahead.

"He was not an escapist and did not respect those who were. He was a man devoted to his church and the clergy. In the late afternoon, when everyone else was heading home in the five-o'clock traffic, one would often find him in the Green Street chapel, St. Thomas More's, praying his rosary. Dad demonstrated his faith to his family, players, fellow coaches and friends. This was his legacy of Christianity. I can thank my mortal father for teaching me that I cannot serve two worlds and gain entrance to Heaven.

"It can be said that even though his legacy to the public is one as a basketball icon, for his family we will continue to remember him as a most honorable man. We are the ones who are blessed."

CHAPTER TWENTY

FRANK MCGUIRE: THE HUSBAND

It wouldn't have been unusual for Jane McGuire to spend Sunday morning, June 4, 1972 , at the registration desk of her husband's basketball camp at the University of South Carolina. Someone had to greet and register the young boys who gathered there to learn from one of the game's great coaches. It wouldn't have been unusual, except that this was Jane's honeymoon.

Less than 24 hours earlier she had been Jane Henderson. That was before her marriage to Frank McGuire on Saturday morning in the Catholic Church at the University. A basketball camp was not a romantic place to spend a honeymoon, but it was a practical way for Jane to begin her indoctrination as the wife of a basketball coach.

Reflecting on her 22 1/2 years of marriage to McGuire, Jane was resigned to such situations as part of her role. It goes with the territory. There were a number of adjustments to make, as she made the transition from fiancee to member of a family.

JANE MCGUIRE: "Frank loved his basketball camp, so there I was registering little people on my honeymoon. We had spent Saturday night in my apartment, but on Sunday night we went out to his house.

"I showed Frankie (McGuire's son) my ring. He was 18 years old then, and we were alone together. He looked at my hand with the ring and said, 'Jane, mommy?'

"I said, 'Yes, I'm going to be your mommy, but I'm not going to take your mommy's place. But I love you.'

"Frank's grandson, Patrick, who was about three and a half at the time, came back to the bedroom and got into the bed with me. He was a loving child. While we were sitting there Frank came in, looked at us and said, 'Patrick, this is my girl. Now you'll have to find your own!'

"Being married to someone as famous as Frank had many pluses, and few, if any, minuses. It never really bothered me that he got most of the attention. I enjoyed it. I'm not a jealous person.

"I have had women literally throw themselves at Frank with me standing there. But I knew that he was going home with the girl who came with him. He was very strict about marriage, which came somewhat from his Catholic upbringing.

"One thing that I learned when we first started dating was that it was very hard to have dinner with Frank, because he was so popular. Now, my mother taught me that when people were talking to you, you put down your fork and didn't eat. People would come over to talk to Frank and ask for autographs and so forth, so I would put down my fork and wait for them to leave.

"After about the third time this happened, Frank said, 'Jane, if they're going to be rude enough to stand there forever, go ahead and be rude enough to eat.' Of course HE never did that.

"I really didn't know much about Frank when I met him in the latter part of 1968. I had seen only one of his games, and that was the first game in the Coliseum (vs. Auburn) in November of that year. I met him at a dinner that Alan Schafer, who owns South of the Border (a motel and shopping complex near Dillon, South Carolina) was having for his employees in Columbia.

"I had a date for the dinner, but Frank didn't. We were sitting across the table from each other, and he kept cutting his eyes around at me--flirting. And I kept saying, 'I'll get the coach a drink, and he would laugh.

"Frank had a kind of magnetism that drew both men and women to him. However, after that evening I didn't think much about it. Then, that Christmas, Alan sent some towels and things from his shop for Frank. And he left the package at my apartment for Frank to pick up or for me to deliver.

"I called Ginger (Ridgon, McGuire's secretary) and told her that I wanted to deliver a package. She told me, 'No, Coach McGuire wants to pick it up.' And the package stayed there and stayed there.

"At the time, Frank's office was in a trailer behind the administration building on Pendleton Street, because the offices in the Coliseum hadn't been completed. The old field house had burned down, so the basketball team had practiced in the old ROTC building at the corner of Pendleton and Pickens. This was just across the street from Senate Plaza, where I was living. So, I always knew when he was in the office.

"One day Frank called and said he was coming to pick up his package. He came by, and we talked awhile. Then he asked me if I'd like to go out to dinner one night. So he took me out to dinner.

"When I first started dating Frank I didn't know a lot about him, because he didn't talk about himself that much. I had to learn from other people.

"For example, once he took me out to the Columbia Shrine Club for a dance. The Harry James orchestra was playing, and that's where I met some of Frank's good friends. John and Cliff Terry. Sam Jones. W.J. Morgan. W.J. got a huge kick out of the fact that I didn't know that Frank had won a national championship. He thought that was the most wonderful joke on Frank.

"After Frank and I started dating I moved to Hampton House where

Becky Shirley and I had an apartment, and Emily Wheeler had a place at the other end of the hall. And I must say that my interest in basketball had increased quite a bit!

"One day Emily and I were at Richland Mall, and it started snowing. South Carolina was playing N.C. State at Raleigh that night, and Emily and I decided to drive to Raleigh in the snow.

"The Carolina team was staying at the College Motel, I believe, so we went there. I had to have a reason to go by Frank's room, so I got a couple of aspirin and went to the door. He came to the door, and I held out my hand with the aspirin and said, 'I heard you had a headache, so I brought you some aspirin.'

"This was one of several times that I went to games when snow was on the ground, so Frank started calling me 'the Snow Witch!'

"It was also a snowy night the first time I met Lou Vine, a veterinarian in Chapel Hill who had become a very close friend of Frank when he was coaching at North Carolina. We were playing North Carolina in the North-South doubleheader in Charlotte. On the way to the game, Lou said, "I know we've just met, but I must tell you that Frank is going to get beaten tonight. So be prepared.'

"I said, 'No, he's not. We're not going to get beat.'

"Lou said, 'I don't think you understand how strong these teams are.'

"I said, 'Frank is not going to get beat.' And that's the night that John Roche just wore 'em out.' (South Carolina won 68-66).

"Going into 'my second season' (1969-70), I must have felt that I was becoming an authority on basketball, because Frank asked me, 'How many games can we lose?'

"I said, 'Three,' and he told me that was cutting it pretty short. I started to say we'd just lose one, but the final count was three. We lost the first home game by one point to Tennessee (55-54), and Davidson beat us (68-62) in the Coliseum.

"Our only other loss was in the finals of the ACC tournament at Charlotte, after John Roche sprained his ankle against Wake Forest in the semifinals. (N.C. State beat the Gamecocks, 42-39, in two overtimes.) I cried my eyes out, and Frank gave me some good advice. He didn't like cry babies, no matter how tough the going got.

"Win or lose, or regardless of what happened, Frank would never talk about basketball after a game. He'd let you talk about it--wind down on your own--but he always said that if he came home and he was down that Frankie would feel it. As far as Frankie was concerned, Daddy won. After the Wake Forest game everybody was dejected, but Frankie said, 'Daddy won!'

"One of the highlights of that season was my receiving an engagement ring from Frank on Christmas Day. Out of the blue one night he said, 'Let's get married. Then he gave me the ring for Christmas, and that was the beginning of a 2 1/2-year engagement. Irishmen love long engagements.

"One of the nicest things about Frank is that he had great respect for women, and he didn't' allow anyone else not to have great respect for them. He wouldn't use profanity--wouldn't even wear a hat around them and always held the door.

"He made women feel like they were special. He could walk into a room and make every woman in that room feel like she was a queen. Something that you're born with. He was very close to his mother and his sister Evelyn. Evelyn had fought Frank's battles for him when he was a frail boy. That was her little brother, and nobody was going to harm him.

"The McGuire family was very private, and before you were accepted into it, you first had to make it back to the kitchen of their home! If they didn't let you sit on the kitchen bench, you could not get engaged. His sister, Veronica (the oldest) gave her approval--I met her first--so I made the bench.

"Frank could have married many a wealthy woman. I know two who had millions. He dated some of them--that was before Jane--and he got a lot of letters. But he cared nothing about money.

"The first time I met Dean Smith he was with Lou Vine. Dean came in, and Lou introduced me and said, 'This is Jane Henderson--she's dating Frank.'

"Dean said, 'Do you want me to put in a good word for you?'

"I said, 'No, I don't need anyone to put in a good word for me.' I was pretty cocky at that age. Too many years younger than Frank, most people thought.

"However, after so long a time--over two years--I got upset, because things just kept going on and on. Daddy thought I was never gonna get married.

"One morning at six o'clock I went to his house. To one of the back doors. Frank said, 'What's the matter?'

"I told him, 'Take this ring--either pee or get off the pot!' I had had it up to here, and I left.

"I was working at Georgia Pacific at the time, and he called me at work that morning. He asked me if I would go to lunch with him. I told him that I had other plans.

"Later he called me back and said, 'If John Foard (Columbia Attorney) is in my office at noon with a marriage license, can you meet me for lunch?' John brought the paperwork to Frank's office, we filled it out, and Tommy Riker drove around the block while I went into the courthouse and got the license.

"I went to Five Points and bought my wedding dress--pink, with a shawl to go over my head. We didn't tell anybody what we were doing, and we didn't invite anyone to the ceremony, because if you do that, you're going to leave out a lot of people. We didn't even have our families there.

"We were to be married in the Catholic chapel at the University, and, because I was Baptist, we needed to get dispensation from the Vatican (Pope Paul VI). We requested it through Bishop Omnikofer and asked him how long it would take. He said it would take a long time.

"It came the next week, and in the Bishop's letter to me, he wrote, 'Dear Miss Henderson, you must have the strongest prayers of anybody I know.'

The only people at the wedding--it was in the old chapel on Pickens Street--were Ginger Rigdon, Father Jerry Tierney, who performed the ceremony, Father Reginald Ready and Mr. and Mrs. Charles Poole. Father Tierney had remarried Frank and Pat on their 25th anniversary. Mrs. Poole played the organ at the chapel.

"Joe Petty (sports director at WIS-TV) heard that we were getting married, so he came and took pictures, but he sat outside during the ceremony. That night Frank's daughter, Carol Ann, had dinner for the wedding party.

"The next morning I was officially the coach's wife, as I registered little people for Frank's basketball camp.

"Frank always got along well with my family. My father, Slim Henderson, was sheriff of Newberry County, and he also had a farm. Daddy was originally from Texas, but my mother, Azilee, was born in Newberry. I attended high school in Newberry and went to Newberry College.

"Frank was anything but a country boy, but he liked to go to the farm with my father. Frank didn't like to hunt, but he would go along with Slim. He had never been around farm animals, and this reminds me of a funny thing that happened.

"One day Daddy had Frank out there trying to call the cows, and you should have heard it! Whoooooo cow! They had never been called in a New York accent. Daddy thought that was a hoot!

"On another occasion Daddy's bull got loose. A registered Brahma bull. There were four young guys running after him, and they got him cornered in the field somewhere.

"So Daddy gets behind the wheel of Frank's Cadillac, and they go driving across the field. Now, Frank didn't want you to do anything to his Cadillac. You could have eaten out of the trunk or off the floor. He had it washed and vacuumed twice a week.

"So Daddy stops the car near where the bull was, and Frank gets out. Then the bull started running straight toward Frank. As the bull got close Frank jumped flat-footed off the ground and landed on the hood of the car. If that had been a basketball court, he could have slam-dunked the ball!

"Frank pulled himself together and calmly said, 'That bull could have killed me.'

"Frank was not a country boy, but he loved country food. Particularly my mother's cooking. At the farm we always had big meals on Sunday, and Frank loved that.

"Although he went to a lot of fancy restaurants in New York and elsewhere, he liked plain foods. He loved pork chops, and he loved ham. Any way you cooked them. He ate most anything, but it if was something he especially liked, he called it a 'trump dish.'

He loved tomato catsup on anything. I think he would have eaten it on ice cream. And he loved peanut brittle. Becky's mother, Ruby, must have made four tons of peanut brittle for him.

"Frank never was a cook, but he told me that, when he was a boy, he would come home from school and make fried potato sandwiches. That was another 'trump dish.'

"Although he had to eat out a lot during his career, Frank really preferred to eat at home, or in privacy. When we were on trips we would have meals sent to our room much of the time. He just wasn't much of a sightseer. Had it not been for other wives on trips I would have traveled all over the United States and wouldn't have seen a thing.

"Frank never had much of a weight problem. He took good care of himself. However, once I went on Weight Watchers, and I put us both on a diet and was very strict about it. Frank started calling me, 'The Warden.' He'd have lunch with Mort Hymson (owner of Velvetex, a silk screen printing company), and I made them tuna fish every day. They would eat at Mort's house. Mort didn't need to be on a diet, so one day he said, 'Mugsy, you've got to stop eating this tuna fish. Every cat in the City of Columbia is following you around!'

"Privately, Frank was a completely different person. He was fun. Always laughing and joking and cutting up. He didn't talk basketball when he was away from the game. He was just funny. Could crack you up.

"Even when he was very ill, he didn't lose his sense of humor. Like the last function he went to--to receive an award from the NABC (National Association of Basketball Coaches) coaches in Charlotte. He got the award, along with a couple of others.

"When it came Frank's time to speak--this was typical--when he made a speech something would always happen to make people laugh. He was in a wheel chair, and they got him up on the podium and handed him the mike.

"He said, 'I want you to know that I wouldn't be here, it if were not for my wife, Jane. Because she got me dressed in a suit, and I hope its an Oxford.'

"Dean Smith said, 'I felt it, Coach, and it is. I even looked at the label.'

"Then Frank went on, 'I hope she's going to bury me in one.' And I did.

"Then he thanked everyone in Charlotte for all they had done through the years. He had played the first game in the old Charlotte Coliseum when he was at North Carolina. He went on and on, and they kept trying to give him the trophy.

"Finally, he looked at Billy Packer (TV analyst and former Wake Forest star) and said, 'Listen, do you know why they're trying to give me this trophy? They're trying to shut me up. So, I'll give them this microphone back.'

"As for Frank's like of Oxford suits, this was indicative of his pride in his appearance. (McGuire was once listed among the ten best dressed men in America by a national magazine.) However, he didn't spend as much money on clothes as it might have seemed.

"He had a nephew, Raymond Reher, who was in the clothing business on the West Coast, and he would get suits for Frank at a big discount. And he had a lot of things given to him. Such as the cashmere coats that Jeff Hunt would give him every Saint Patrick's Day.

"When our house burned it dawned on me that Frank had about 250 sets of underwear, believe it or not!

"He liked things that money could buy, but he cared nothing about money itself. He never signed a check, unless he had to. And he never wrote a check. I handled all the bills. And when Pat died, Ginger or Jack Wingate (Columbia accountant) handled his business.

"He never made speeches for money, and if it was given to him, he would give it away. He loved to give things away."

The house fire that Jane referred to occurred on December 16, 1987, when fire gutted the McGuire home in the Whitehall section of Columbia. The home had been built soon after McGuire became basketball coach at USC.

McGuire said, as firefighters poured water on the smoldering ashes, "All we escaped with were the clothes on our backs, and I had my Hall of Fame ring in my pocket. We're lucky to be here. I was running for my life."

Lost in the fire was most of McGuire's collection of memorabilia. The origin of the fire was believed to be a gas leak that was ignited when Jane plugged in the Christmas tree around 5 p.m. The four-bedroom house was a total loss, along with trophies, awards, photographs and scrapbooks gathered during McGuire's 40-plus years in coaching.

JANE MCGUIRE: "After the fire we moved into this condominium. (A multi-story building at the west end of the Congaree River bridge.) We both wanted to rebuild the home in Whitehall, but we were insured for a certain amount of money. Not nearly as much as we should have had for what was in there. But we didn't know any better. And every quote we got to rebuild would have put us in hock.

"Frank said, 'Jane, I don't have to prove anything to anybody.' Although he loved the house and the pool, which had a special ledge around it for Frankie, he just couldn't see going into a huge debt, when there was just the two of us.

"As it turned out, it was the best thing for me, in view of what happened to Frank a few years later. With his illness, I couldn't have taken care of him and the home. It was much better in our condominium."

Shortly after the fire Herman Helms, Sports Editor of *The State* newspaper, led a drive to replace as much of the McGuire memorabilia as possible. The response was widespread, and the items collected were presented to the McGuires at a testimonial dinner.

JANE MCGUIRE: "With all the bad breaks in his life, it was a wonder that Frank wasn't bitter. But he never was.

"His father died when he was three, his only son had cerebral palsy, his wife died of cancer, his son-in-law was killed, our house burned down, and then, the stroke. (McGuire's son-in-law, husband of his oldest daughter, Patsy, was killed in the crash of a fighter plane during training near Las Vegas in March of 1981.)

"And he had to retire from doing what his whole life was based on--coaching--sooner than he wanted to.

"It eased the pain of his retirement from coaching when he took the job of bringing basketball back to Madison Square Garden. It gave him something to do that he enjoyed, it wasn't full time, and there was not a lot of pressure in it.

"They gave Frank a salary of only $25,000, but they also provided him an apartment and gave him an unlimited expense account for entertainment, which was worth more than money. Sonny Werblein, President of the Garden, was great to work for.

"One day Frank said to someone in Sonny's presence, 'I work for Sonny.'

"Sonny said, 'No, Frank, we work together.'

"Frank's apartment was right next door to Jimmy Weston's restaurant, so he saw a lot of old friends there. He held court, you might say.

"Frank was able to attract some games and tournaments to the Garden, including the Big East Championship Tournament.

"Frank's best friend, Jack LaRocca, who works for the International Longshoremen of America, lives in New York. Frank used to say, 'The definition of a friend is a guy who would put himself between you and the bullet. Jack would do that for me, and I would do it for him.'

"Going back and forth between Columbia and New York, got old after awhile, and Frank wasn't able to see Frankie as often. His relationship with Frankie was something to watch. He took him everywhere he could, and he helped him with everything when he was at home.

"Frank really felt that Frankie was a blessing, rather than a burden. He learned a lot of patience because of Frankie, and he tried to treat him as normally as possible. And he wanted other people to react normally to Frankie being there.

"Frankie has been at Midland Rehabilitation Center for a number of years. It's a gorgeous place and looks like a college campus. When Frankie first went there the road wasn't paved, but Frank helped them to get the County to pave it.

"Doctors said that he is better off with people in his circumstances and could cope with everyday life on a level with boys and girls like he is. Then he can be the 'big cheese.'

"One day in a meeting they told Frank that Frankie didn't know the difference between a baseball and an airplane. Frank said, 'Now, you've picked the two subjects in the world that I know he understands the difference between. Because he's watched baseball in big league parks all his life--Yogi Berra loved him--and he probably knows it better than you do. And he loves to fly on airplanes and has been flying since he was a child. So, you'll have to find another comparison, because that one doesn't fit him.'

"Frankie has been out there 19 years but has always come home on weekends and still does.

"Frank never tried to hide Frankie. Every Carolina fan could see him stop by Frankie's seat behind the Carolina bench before every home game and hug and kiss Frankie. At out of town games, at the end of the post game radio show, Frank would always say, 'Good night, Frankie.'

"When Frank stopped coaching, we stopped taking Frankie to the games, because he wouldn't understand why Daddy wasn't coaching.

"It was enough to tear your heart out, when Frank was close to dying, and Frankie would hardly recognize the man he saw in the wheel chair. He would say, 'Daddy's boy.' Then he would turn and look at Frank's portrait on the wall and say, 'Hello, Daddy.'

"We didn't take Frankie to the funeral, and he didn't go to his mother's funeral, because of what the repercussions might be. How do you explain such things to him?

"Frankie is now 44 years old, although his life expectancy is supposed to be about 25. He's about six feet, two inches tall even when he's not standing up straight. He's a very handsome man, with beautiful blue eyes, and he's strong as he can be.

"Frank found out how strong when he lost patience with Frankie for the only time in his life. Frankie grabbed him and threw him all the way across the room. It was amazing.

"His relationship with Frankie was an enlargement of his compassion for people in general. He felt very deeply about other people's problems, particularly those who were close to him. He was a very sentimental person, too. Used to send me roses a lot and always gave me candy on Valentine's Day. We had Christmas every day at our house, he used to say.

"I remember many times his sending cards or mementos to people in the hospital that he didn't even know. Especially children.

"We would have 'happy hour' everyday when he came home. And I would get dressed for it. He was very organized, even in routine things we did. He made things special.

"Perhaps most coaches are superstitious, but Frank had to be at the top of the list. He would never let you hand him salt--you had to put it down and let him pick it up. He wouldn't change seats during an event and certainly not during a basketball game.

"He would never have his hair cut on the day of a game, and he considered brown to be his lucky color. His lucky number was three. He would kiss me three times when he left to go somewhere.

"His sisters had a statue of Saint Anthony, a patron saint of the Catholic Church, and that statue played a role in his superstitions. For instance, when Frank's team was on the road, and they were listening to the game at home, they would bring out Saint Anthony. And if we lost they put him in the john. When Frank called home he would ask, 'Is Saint Anthony in the john?'

"Frank was taking a medicine for his arthritis, and he was supposed to take it with food. But sometimes he'd get in a hurry to go to practice, and take it without food.

"One day, it was about the 1975 season, Frank told Ben Jobe (USC assistant coach) that he had to go home, because he wasn't feeling well.

"He lay down on the sofa, and we called the doctor (Dr. Walter Roberts), who said it sounded like Frank had the flu and to give him aspirin and hot tea. Which I did. But I insisted that the doctor come out to see Frank, and he did.

"Well, Frank went into the bathroom and didn't come out for a long time, so I went to see why he didn't come back. There he was lying face down in enough blood as if four people had been murdered! I went tearing out and got Walter. When he came in there he turned as white as this piece of paper and just went to pieces himself. Frank had a bleeding ulcer.

"We got an ambulance there, put Frank on a stretcher and started out the front door. Even in his weakened condition, Frank raised up and said, 'Wait a minute. I came in the back door. I have to go out the back door.'

"And, so, they turned around and took him out the door that he came in. That was one of his superstitions. He always left through the same door through which he arrived.

"There were expressions that Frank used on many occasions, and I can still hear him saying them. One was, when he wanted you to keep quiet–'Socks, nix and the billygoat.' I never quite understood why, but that meant to shut up.

"When we were out somewhere in a restaurant or in a crowd, if he said, 'That guy over there is riding the Erie,' that meant that he was listening to us. Like the Erie Railroad.

"One of his favorites was, 'Play Mickey the Dunce and you'll learn more that way.' That meant listen to what other people are saying and act like you don't know anything about it, and you'll learn more.

"Basketball fans were in such awe of Frank that they couldn't think of him as a human being. But he was--very much so. He was the same with people in all walks of life. He came from a background where people fought their way up. In the neighborhood where Frank grew up you were either a policeman, a priest or a gangster.

"As a husband, he liked to do certain tasks around the house. He didn't like to cook, but he loved to wash dishes. I guess that when he was washing dishes he didn't have to listen to any of our small talk after we had dinner. We always had a crowd.

"He liked to sweep, and, although he liked to work in the yard at our beach place, he didn't work in the yard at home. I was the 'yard man' at home. But we had good help, and we worked well together.

"Frank loved music, particularly the old big band music, and he used to listen to a station out of Cincinnati until the wee hours, because that's what they played, and he didn't sleep much. He always said, 'Sleep is for the dead.'

"Frank didn't bear grudges, and he was very forgiving. It meant a lot to him that Eddie Cameron came to him right before he got sick. *(Cameron was athletic director at Duke University and was instrumental in an ACC ruling in 1966 that declared All-America prep star Mike Grosso ineligible to play at South Carolina.)*

"Eddie apologized to Frank and told him that Duke was going to get out of the ACC, if he didn't do something about Grosso. He said he really never looked into it. I wish Frank were here to tell you verbatim what Eddie said.

"Frank was a very religious person and devoted to the church. There was no question of whether or not you were going to church. You were going. When he went somewhere the first thing he did was find where the church was—before you unpacked the clothes.

"The hardest thing he ever experienced was to be a coach one day and not be a coach the next day. But he had great spiritual strength. His faith in God had everything to do with him. He didn't talk about it, but he lived it. You could see it.

"This faith saw him through all the hard times. So he never second guessed himself. He had no regrets. No 'what ifs.'

"Now, this again shows a combination of his spiritual side and his humorous side. About four days before he died he was lying there with his eyes closed and said to me, 'I see Annie' *(Frank's mother)*.

"I said, 'Your Mommy Annie? How is she?'

"'She's fine,' he said.

"'And I saw Azzie,' (that's what he called my mother.) 'How is she?' I asked. He answered, 'She's fine, too.'

"Then I said, 'Well, how about Slim *(Jane's father)*?

"Frank managed a trace of a smile and said, 'Oh no. He's not here! I think he's behind the 'Slim Tree!'

"Frank was not only loyal to God and the church, but to human beings, as well. Loyalty was one of his strongest qualities. People always knew where he stood. He was the same today as he was yesterday. He was loyal to you, and he expected you to be loyal to him, but don't cross him, or you were dead meat.

"Even when he knew you were wrong, he would support you, but expected you to explain it to him.

"Sometimes people would 'use' Frank to do things, such as open a door for them. However, he didn't mind that, because he wanted to help people, if he could. As long as they weren't doing something wrong or taking unfair advantage of someone.

"Frank was sick for over two years, but he was more fun sick than most people are well. Thank the Lord he could still talk. He was a very good patient.

"Yes, I'll admit that sometimes I'd stop and think, 'Why me?' But I would do it all again tomorrow. I don't remember him sick anymore. I remember him as bigger than life. The way I want to remember him. I could remember him the other way, but I don't.

"And that's a blessing from God."

THE FINAL CHAPTER
BORN A MAN--DIED A COACH

People from all walks of life began gathering at St. Peter's Catholic Church early on the morning of Thursday, October 13, 1994. They were there to pay their last respects to Frank McGuire, who had touched their lives in one way or another—as basketball coach, associate or friend.

McGuire's life had come to an end on October 11 at his sixth-story condominium besides the Congaree River overlooking downtown Columbia and Carolina Coliseum. For the better part of two years McGuire had survived the damaging effects of a stroke that had rendered him dependent on his wife, Jane, and others for most of the routine activities of life.

Those who gathered at Dunbar Funeral Home on the evening of October 12 to extend sympathy to the McGuire family and exchange memories about the Hall of Fame coach included many basketball luminaries. There were Dean Smith, whom McGuire brought to North Carolina as an assistant; former St. John's and New York Nets coach Lou Carnesecca, who played on McGuire's St. John's baseball team; Ben Carnevale, a close friend and former coach at North Carolina and Navy; many former players under McGuire; and friends and associates from far and wide.

They talked mostly of how McGuire had been a positive influence in their lives and helped them toward success in life, as well as basketball.

As the 11:00 A.M. service began, St. Peter's was filled to overflowing. Dr. Richard Conant of the USC School of Music introduced the service by singing Schubert's "Ave Maria," followed by the congregational hymn, "How Great Thou Art."

The Most Reverend David B. Thompson, Bishop of Charleston was the celebrant, setting the tone of his eulogy by observing that "Frank McGuire has once again made the finals."

In his eulogy Bishop Thompson, who had met McGuire only once, did a masterful job of reminding the congregation of some of the coach's most prominent qualities.

BISHOP THOMPSON: "Unknown to most of you, there is a very human reason of appropriateness for my celebrating Frank McGuire's funeral Mass. I met and talked to Coach McGuire only once. It was five years ago at the Epicurean Restaurant in Columbia. Dining with several other priests, I was approached by our waiter: 'Bishop, Coach McGuire would like to meet the bishop.' A thrilling moment for me.

"I arose, and the Coach and I met at half court. He was so friendly, warm, respectful, gracious toward me. We spoke of his many accomplishments and just a few of mine. Then the Coach looked at my bishop's ring. With his captivating smile, the very breadth of his handsome face, Coach McGuire showed me his ring of 1957, the NCAA ring, the National Championship ring. (Actually, his Hall of Fame ring.)

"'Bishop, I have a ring, too.'

"Frank, I know, and you have to be very proud of it. I'm coaching in my court; you coached in yours. And, Frank, you are the Bishop of Basketball.' And I meant it.

"How obvious it is that Coach McGuire was a bishop, and 'overseer' of basketball. Just read the stories and glories of him in the newspapers and watch or listen to the other media. I thank these public communicators for their positive and wonderful presentation of the great good Frank McGuire did in his life here on Earth. Thank you, for not interring his goodness in his bones.

"We are in church. Frank worshipped here often; brought his players here. He taught them how to block out; in the first row where he assembled them, they blocked out the rest of the congregation. Frank McGuire was thoroughly Catholic, and he would want me to proclaim that here today. So I will. I'll do this in Frank's style. I wear distinctive garb; didn't the Coach? He wore French cuffs; I'll pull on mine. I wear no tie, but I can tug on the bishop's pectoral cross, as if it were Frank's tie.

"Our first reading today, from the Book of Wisdom, speaks of the just man, the man whose soul was pleasing to the Lord. While not perfect in his life, Coach McGuire was certainly known as the Credible Catholic, so diligently and loyally did he strive to practice his Catholic Christian faith. He was not only a strong, front-running basketball coach, Frank was a professed Catholic, always out front with his respect and love for his religion and his Church. He was admired for this; and, by the practice of his faith, Frank McGuire preached the gospel of nobility to many in an oftentimes ignoble world.

"For many, Frank McGuire could be described as the Coliseum Christian, not only because he inspired the erection of the Carolina Coliseum and filled it to capacity and defeated lions, tigers and gators, but because of the way he coached and taught his players to play the game of basketball. He made his players responsible, accountable to him and their teammates. He had them pray to God for help, teaching them dependence upon their creator. 'No one lives as his own master.' And while many players blessed themselves before attempting foul shots, the Coliseum Coach was realistic enough to say his own prayer: 'Lord, I hope he can shoot.'

"The last two years did not present the best of times to Frank McGuire. He did not enjoy good health; his stroke robbed him of his normal strength and abilities. It was in these days Coach McGuire patiently awaited his time to accept the Lord's gospel invitation: 'Come to me, all of you who are weary and find life burdensome, and I will refresh you.' This past Tuesday, Frank felt the divine embrace, became the Caressed Christian he lived to be, entered God's Hall of Fame.

"For a believer like Frank McGuire, for a competitor and achiever like this illustrious, noble basketball coach, death was his final opponent. Today we celebrate his glorious victory over death, thanking God for giving us this star of His creation.

"Well done, Coach McGuire; you have run the game of life; victory, glory, rest, peace."

Also participating in the service were former players, Bobby Cremins and George Felton, who read passages from The Bible. Cremins is head basketball coach at Georgia Tech, and Felton, who had been head coach at South Carolina, was an assistant coach at St. John's, where McGuire had begun his college coaching career.

McGuire was survived by his wife, Jane; son Frankie; daughters Carol Ann Morgan of Columbia and Patricia Jeanne Ventling of Corpus Christi, Texas; two sisters, Cecelia McGuire and Evelyn Jennings, both of Laurence, N.Y.; six grandchildren and one great-grandchild.

One day during McGuire's final year of coaching, the 1979-80 season, assistant coach Danny Monk asked McGuire, "If you could put anything you wanted to on your tombstone, what would your epitaph be?"

McGuire thought for a moment, then answered, "Born a man, died a coach."

This is the inscription on the gravestone that marks Frank McGuire's final resting place in the St. Peter's Cemetery.

FRANK MCGUIRE, NOVEMBER 8, 1913--OCTOBER 11, 1994

BORN A MAN, DIED A COACH

APPENDIX

COACHING RECORDS

NATIONAL RANKINGS

POST-SEASON TOURNAMENTS

COACHING HIGHLIGHTS

THE PLAYERS

FRANK MCGUIRE'S COACHING RECORD

McGuire's Record at St. Xavier High School
11 Years–Won 126, Lost 39–76.4%

St. John's University

Year	Won	Lost
1948	12	11
1949	16	9
1950	24	5
1951	26	5
1952	25	5
Totals	103	35

5 Years

University of North Carolina

Year	Won	Lost
1953	17	10
1954	11	10
1955	10	11
1956	18	5
1957*	32	0
1958	19	7
1959	20	5
1960	18	6
1961	19	4
Totals	164	58

9 Years

*Won NCAA Championship

Philadelphia Warriors (NBA)

Year	Won	Lost
1962	49	31

University of South Carolina

Year	Won	Lost
1965	6	17
1966	11	13
1967	16	7
1968	15	7
1969	21	7
1970	25	3
1971	23	6
1972	24	5
1973	22	7
1974	22	5
1975	19	9
1976	18	9
1977	14	12
1978	16	12
1979	15	12
1980	16	11
Total	283	142

16 Years

OVERALL COACHING RECORD

	Years	Won	Lost	Pct.
St. Xavier High School	11	126	39	.764
St. John University	5	103	35	.746
University of North Carolina	9	164	58	.739
Philadelphia Warriors	1	49	31	.613
University of South Carolina	16	283	142	.666
Totals	42	725	305	.704

NATIONAL RANKINGS IN FINAL POLLS

Year	School	Associated Press (AP)	United Press International (UPI)
1950	St. John's	9th	No UP Poll
1951	St. John's	9th	9th
1952	St. John's	10th	9th
1956	North Carolina	13th	11th
1957	North Carolina	1st	1st
1958	North Carolina	13th	12th
1959	North Carolina	9th	6th
1960	North Carolina	– – –	14th
1961	North Carolina	5th	6th
1969	South Carolina	13th	20th
1970	South Carolina	6th	6th
1971	South Carolina	6th	6th
1972	South Carolina	6th	5th
1973	South Carolina	– – –	16th
1974	South Carolina	19th	16th
Total Final National Rankings			15

NCAA AND NATIONAL INVITATIONAL TOURNAMENT APPEARANCES

Year	School	Tournament
1949	St. John's	NIT
1950	St. John's	NIT
1951	St. John's	NCAA & NIT
1952	St. John's	NCAA & NIT
1957	North Carolina	NCAA
1959	North Carolina	NCAA
1969	South Carolina	NIT
1971	South Carolina	NCAA
1972	South Carolina	NCAA
1973	South Carolina	NCAA
1974	South Carolina	NCAA
1975	South Carolina	NIT
1978	South Carolina	NIT
Total Post-Season Tournaments		15

McGuire's Coaching Highlights

Selected NATIONAL COACH OF THE YEAR at three different schools:
    -St. John's
    -North Carolina
    -South Carolina

Only coach in NCAA history to win more than 100 games at three different schools:
    -St. Johns 103
    -North Carolina 164
    -South Carolina 252

Only coach to win ATLANTIC COAST CONFERENCE CHAMPION-SHIP at two different schools:
    -North Carolina, 1957
    -South Carolina, 1971

Named to the NAISMITH BASKETBALL HALL OF FAME, 1976

Named to the COMMISSION ON PRESIDENTIAL SCHOLARS BY PRESIDENT JIMMY CARTER, 1978

Received the FIRST ANNUAL GROSSINGER'S ACHIEVEMENT AWARD for contributions to basketball--1978 (Grossinger, NY)

HONARARY DEGREE--Doctor of Humane Letters--Belmont Abbey (NC) College, 1958

ST. JOHN'S SPORTS HALL OF FAME--Charter member, 1984

FRANK MCGUIRE ARENA in Carolina Coliseum was named in his honor, 1977

THE PLAYERS

ST. JOHN'S UNIVERSITY
(Players who lettered under Frank McGuire at St. John's University, 1948-1952)

Barreras, Joseph 48, 49, 50
Buckley, Dan 48, 49
Calabrese, Gerry 48, 49, 50
Coyle, Jim 52
Dalton, Jack 48, 49, 50
Davis, Jim 52
Dombrosky, Ray 49, 50, 51
Duckett, Dick 52
Dunn, Don 51, 52
Fannon, Pete 50
Geoghan, Walter 48
Giancontieri, Frank 51, 52
Griffin, Gerry 48, 49
Harvey, William 48
Jakobson, Larry 48
Kalabrese, G. 48
Macgilvray, Ron 50, 51, 52

McGuire, Al 49, 50, 51
McGuire, Dick 48, 49
McMahon, Jack 50, 51, 52
McMorrow, Jim 52
Midwinter, Ray 48
Mulzoff, Frank 49, 50, 51
Noonan, Don 49, 50, 51
O'Shea, Tom 50, 51
Oldham, Archie 48, 49
Redding, Ed 48, 49, 50
Sagona, Philip 52
Tolan, Thomas 48, 49
Walker, Solly 52
Walsh, Jim 52
Wassmer, David 49, 50, 51
Weston, "Shadow" 48
Zawoluk, Robert 50, 51, 52

UNIVERSITY OF NORTH CAROLINA
(Players who lettered under Frank McGuire at the University of North Carolina, 1953-1961)

Brennan, Pete 56, 57, 58
Brown, Larry 61
Brown, Lou 59, 60
Carter, Jippy 53
Clancy, Gene 53
Conlon, Martin 61
Crotty, John 58, 59, 60
Cunningham, Bob 56, 57, 58
Donohue, Hugh 59, 60
Goodwin, Frank 55
Greene, Hilliard 55, 56
Grimaldi, Vince 53
Henderson, Willis 55
Helland, Gehrmann 57, 59

Hudock, Jim 60, 61
Jones, Harry 61
Kearns, Tommy 56, 57, 58
Kepley, Dick 58, 59, 61
Kocornik, Dick 54
Krause, Dieter 61
Larese, York 59, 60, 61
Lifson, Al 53, 54, 55
Likins, Paul 53, 54, 55
McCabe, Jerry 54, 55, 56
Moe, Doug 59, 60, 61
Phillips, Bob 53
Poole, Grey 58, 59, 60
Quigg, Joe 56, 57

UNIVERSITY OF NORTH CAROLINA
*(Players who lettered under Frank McGuire at the
University of North Carolina, 1953-1961)*

Radovich, Tony 54, 55, 57

Rosemond, Ken 56, 57

Rosenbluth, Lenny 55, 56, 57

Salz, Harvey 58, 59, 60

Schwarz, Ernie 53

Searcy, Roy 56, 57, 58

Shaffer, Lee 58, 59, 60

Stanley, Ray 58, 59, 60

Sutton, Ed 55

Taylor, Cooper 52, 54

Vayda, Jerry 53, 54, 55, 56

Wallace, Jack 52, 52, 53

Winstead, Skippy 53, 54

Young, Bob 55, 56, 57

UNIVERSITY OF SOUTH CAROLINA
(Players who lettered under Frank McGuire at the University of South Carolina, 1965-1980)

Atkins, Henry 80
Augustus, Golie 75, 76, 77, 78
Aydlett, Rick 70, 71, 72
Burkholder, Lynwood 65, 66, 67
Carnevale, Corkey 68, 69, 70
Carver, Bob 70, 71, 72
Clements, Jim 73, 74
Connaughton, Mark 77, 78, 79, 80
Cremins, Bobby 68, 69, 70
Cox, Tommy 73, 74
Darmody, Kevin 80, 81, 82, 83
Davis, Nate 74, 75, 76, 77
Derrick, Scott 80
DiRugeria, Eddie 76
Doyle, Mike 77, 78, 79, 80
Dunleavy, Kevin 78, 79, 80
Dunleavy, Mike 73, 74, 75, 76
English, Alex 73, 74, 75, 76
Farrell, Charlie 65, 66
Farell, Tom 67
Felter, Bob 67
Felton, George 74, 75
Fox, Jim 65
Fredrick, Zam 78, 79, 80
Gause, Bill 76, 77
Gilloon, Jack 75, 76, 77, 78
Gorgrant, Bob 66, 67
Gorsage, John 63, 64, 65
Graziano, Jimmy 77, 78, 79, 80
Gregor, Gary 67, 68
Greiner, Mark 73, 74, 75, 76
Grevey, Bryan 76, 77
Grimes, Billy 70, 72
Harlicka, Skip 66, 67, 68
Harty, Steve 78, 79
Hordges, Cedrick 79, 80

Joyce, Kevin 71, 72, 73
Kickey, Skip 66, 67, 68
Klitenic, Stu 74, 75, 76, 77
Lovelace, Earl 65, 66, 67
Manning, Casey 71, 72, 73
Martin, Hank 68, 69
Mathias, Bob 73, 74, 75, 76
Mousa, Rick 72, 73, 74
Owens, Tom 69, 70, 71
Peterson, Ed 72
Powell, Dennis 69, 70, 71
Powell, Eddie 68
Powell, Jimmy 70, 71, 72
Reynolds, Kenny 77, 78, 79, 80
Ribock, John 69, 70, 71
Riker, Tom 70, 71, 72
Roche, John 69, 70, 71
Salvadori, Al 65, 66, 67
Schroeder, John 65, 66
Schwartz, Michael 80
Sherwood, Chuck 74, 75, 76, 77
Spencer, Gene 68, 69, 70
Standard, Frank 66, 67, 68
Strickland, Jim 79, 80
Terry, Tommy 68, 69, 70
Thompson, Jack 66, 67, 68
Traylor, Danny 71, 72, 73
Truitt, Billy 75, 75
Twayman, Jay 79
Vacca, Charlie 68, 69
Walsh, Billy 69
Walsh, Jimmy 73, 74, 75
Wejnert, Rich 78
Wimbush, Tom 79, 80
Winters, Brian 72, 73, 74
Womack, Larry 66, 67

INDEX

Walker, Solly 34, 38-42, 221
Walker, Dr. Thurmond 192
Wallace, Grady 51, 81, 111
Wallace, Jack 45, 222
Walsh, Bill 94, 99, 223
Walsh, Donnie 58, 62, 67, 83, 128, 158, 178, 181
Walsh, Jim 33, 221
Wertz, Arthur 129
West, Jerry 66
Weston, Jimmy 186

Wheeler, Emily 204
Wingate, Furman 193
Wingate, Jack 192, 193, 208
Winters, Brian 99, 113, 115, 116, 119, 120, 134, 136, 151, 168, 223
Wooden, John 21, 111, 114
Woolpert, Phil 52
Yarbrough, Bill 82
Young, Dick 36
Zawoluk, Bob 26, 27, 30, 32, 36, 37, 136, 140, 221